GOD:

FACT OR FICTION?

Brendan Roberts

REVEALING THE RELATIONSHIP

BETWEEN SCIENCE, RELIGION

AND THE ORIGIN OF LIFE

KIWI GRAPHIX PUBLISHING, AUCKLAND, NEW ZEALAND

Published by Kiwi Graphix
9 Elm Place
Tikipunga
Whangarei
New Zealand

Cover design © 2003 Critical Mass Studios (d.gianotti@xtra.co.nz)
Unless noted Scripture is from The New Jerusalem Bible: Pocket Edition

ISBN 0-473-09786-9

Imprimatur: Patrick Dunn DD
                  Bishop of Auckland
                  New Zealand
                  26 August 2003

Nihil Obstat: Rev Msgr Vincent Hunt

DEDICATION

This book is dedicated to those who are genuinely searching for the truth. Whether you be searching through science or through religion, may this book help you on your quest.

I would also like to dedicate this book to those who have believed in me, and supported me in my years as a writer. You have persevered with me through the tough times. Thank you.

Also I am deeply grateful for those who have assisted me with this book: James Rodgers and Monsignor Hunt for your assistance with some philosophical aspects; and Chris Miller for tips relating to biochemistry. You have supported me with such generous attitudes, and I'm very grateful.

For those faithful readers who have bought copies of my books, and stuck with me on this process spanning several years, I am grateful.

Last of all, but most importantly, I dedicate this book to the First Cause, the Creator, without whom, not only would I not be here, but I never would have dreamt of being an author.

AMDG

CONTENTS

INTRODUCTION 1

PART *1* - SCIENCE
CATACLYSMIC BANG 5
Expansion of the Universe 5
Background Radiation 6
Big Crunch 7
Big Bang Vs Naturalism 9
Eternal Universe? 11
Origin of the Universe 11
Who created God? 12
DO OUR ORIGINS REVEAL A CREATOR? 14
Micro and Macro Evolution 14
Natural Selection 15
Darwin Questions Natural Selection? 19
Darwin's Failed Theory 21
The Origin of Life 22
Darwin's dedication 23
Do Animals Have Souls? 25
Darwin's Religious Beliefs 26
Natural Selection and a Creator 27
PROBABILITY OF LIFE BY CHANCE 30
The Watchmaker Model 30
Life By Chance? 31
Materialism 33
Suspect Motives 35
Intent 36
DID HUMANS EVOLVE FROM APES? 40
The Soul 41
What Was The Earliest Human Ancestor? 43
Factors Causing Extinction 47
INTELLIGENT DESIGN 49
Contingency, Specification and Irreducible Complexity 49
Cosmological Argument 53
Problems of Evolution Without Design 54
Creationists 55
UNLOCKING THE CHEMISTRY OF LIFE 60
The Cell 60
The Irreducible Complexity of the Cell 63
Information Bearing DNA 64
Sequence Complexity of DNA 65
Human Genes Vs Monkey Genes 68

Proteins – 3D Structure 68
Protein Folding 72
Shaky Chemical Evolution Theory 75
Mascot of Intelligent Design – Flagellum 75
CLUTCHING AT STRAWS 82
Pre-biotic Cocktail Experimental Flaws 84
Monkeying Around 86
Controlled Experiments 87
Evidence Against Macro-Evolution 89
UNCOVERING TRANSITIONAL SPECIES? 94
Evidence of Transitional Species 95
Prehistoric Fish Found Alive 98
THE WONDER OF THE UNIVERSE 101
Intricacies of the Big Bang 102
Age of the Universe and the Earth 103
Anthropic Principles 105
Planets and Guardians 110
Mankind comes from dust 112
Man's Advancement 113
EVIDENCE UNCOVERED BY THE SANDS OF TIME 117
Problems Facing Archaeology 117
Biblical People and Places Confirmed 118
King David 123
Crucifixion Confirmed 125
New Testament Evidence 126

PART 2 - RELIGION
TRUTH: OBJECTIVE OR SUBJECTIVE? 132
Objective Truth 132
Moral Truth 133
Free Will 136
Relativism 137
Skepticism 138
Experience 139
The Ontological Argument 140
Does Truth Reflect a Creator? 141
Scripture That Attests to Truth 142
ON THE WINGS OF FAITH AND REASON 145
Faith 145
Faith and Reason 147
Causation 148
Quest for Meaning 150
Revelation 151
Mysteries 155

EVIL: DOES IT EXIST? 158
Moral Evil 158
Suffering and Evil 159
Natural Evil 162
THE PHILOSOPHY OF GOD'S EXISTENCE 165
St. Thomas Aquinas' 5 Ways 166
Pascal's Wager 171
Experience 172
MIRACLES TRANSCENDING NATURE 178
Macro-Evolution – A new religion? 178
Free-Will 179
What is a miracle? 180
Miracles investigated painstakingly by the Church 181
The Greatest Miracle 182
DOES SECULAR EVIDENCE CONFIRM JESUS'
EXISTENCE? 202
Jewish Historian 204
Roman Historians 205
Evidence Re Pontius Pilate 206
Apostolic/Church Fathers 208
Evidence re the death of Jesus 209
SCRIPTURAL EVIDENCE 212
Authors of the Gospels 212
Authenticity of the Gospels 214
Son of Man 215
Earliest Writings of the New Testament 218
Falsifying Facts in the Gospels? 220
Old Testament Prophecies of the Messiah 223
Evidence re the Resurrection of Jesus 230
Hallucinations 232
PERSONAL GOD 236
Power of God 236
Who Caused God? 237
The Incarnation 243
The Mediator of God 245
Know Yourself 248
Heart burning with love 253
Prayer 254
Answer to Prayer 257
IS GOD DEAD? 261
CONCLUSION 264
AUTHOR'S NOTE 268
INDEX 269

INTRODUCTION

Is God Dead? Did God ever exist? Or is the concept just a figure of mankind's imagination?

These crucial questions have posed themselves to humans since the awakening of human consciousness. In *God: Fact or Fiction?* I explore such diverse subjects as science; micro and macro-evolution – hence Natural Selection, speciation and variation; and God. Do they coexist? Are they diametrically opposed? Are any of them obsolete? Is religion just a crutch for the weak to grasp hold of, while the intellectuals don't need to believe in God?

Through *God: Fact or Fiction?* you will draw your own conclusions as to whether God exists as I reveal the relationship between science, religion and the origin of life. Many think that never the twain should meet, but actually you should discover quite a harmony by the time you reach the end of this book.

This is an opportunity to discover where the majority of the evidence resides as science has exploded exponentially in the last century. It has uncovered wonderful truths about our world and the universe during the 20th Century while simultaneously developing areas of knowledge which make many tremble.

In the process of writing this book, I have felt myself drawn towards utilizing philosophy more and more. Therefore you will find elements of it within Part 1 and much more in Part 2. I'm sure you will appreciate that this has been included to such a degree. It has proved to be such an important part of the evidence towards the existence of a Creator. Here it is important to note that the evidence I'm using throughout the book should be taken in its entirety. Like the example of a court case utilized in this book, it's important to look at the big picture, and use all the evidence to prove beyond reasonable doubt that a Creator exists.

Part 1

Often it is perceived that science has been at loggerheads with religion. The Enlightenment provided the opportunity for the attack on religion and as a result there was a backlash from the days when science and a belief in a Creator/Designer were intertwined. As a result science seemed to throw God out the door, followed with a swift kick. Science has explained a lot of the unknown which formerly was attributed to God's direct intervention and control. In effect, as science discovered the natural laws and processes there was a swing from one extreme to the next – assign everything to God, then assign nothing to God. But worse, science seemed to say, "There is no God!" But as you will read in this book, there is a swing away from the extreme view of "There is no God!" What is this view? You will soon discover the relationship between science, religion and the origin of life.

Maybe the subject of science brings back fond memories, or maybe it makes you sweat. We are drawn back to those experiments with the Bunsen Burners and trying to blow up the lab, or worse for those squeamish types who had to endure the dissection of frogs in the science of biology.

In the first section of *God: Fact or Fiction* we will delve into the very beginning of the universe; the intricacies of evolution; the question whether a Creator or God exists; the possibilities for the random occurrence of life; and the explanation of Intelligent Design. Furthermore we will explore such diverse aspects of science such as:

- the universe and the relationship of space, time, matter and energy with its inception. The wonderful and awe inspiring facts of our universe including: it's size and composition; what science has revealed about the distance of certain planets from us; the delicate fine-tuning that was needed for the origin of life – now these are fascinating!; and we delve into whether the universe could in fact be expanding eternally?
- the theory of Intelligent Design with irreducible complexity (explained in detail).
- the wonder of the human cell, proteins and different aspects of biochemistry. Prepare to be astounded by the information-rich capacity of DNA.
- Paleontology and whether the fossil record has the evidence for macro-evolution.
- the stunning secular evidence to the actual existence of Jesus, and historical figures revealed in Sacred Scripture.
- the fascinating discoveries made through archaeology which substantiate different parts of Sacred Scripture.

The labyrinth-type complexity within nature will engross and astound you, bringing you deeper into the amazing intricacies and inherent order residing there.

Moreover, you will traverse the theory of man not only evolving from the ape kingdom, but having an ancestry even dating back to amphibians and bacteria. As a consequence we naturally ask, "Does this theory exclude God? You will ponder the apparent answers of the feasibility of life happening by chance, without a Creator. Furthermore, you will learn what mathematicians have deduced in relation to the mathematical possibility of life evolving by chance. Plus the revelation of whether macro-evolution and God are compatible will be discussed. Within the subjects of Astronomy and Biochemistry I seek to open a wonderful world of intricate order, design and details that will astound you.

Part 2

The second section looks at such diverse subjects encompassing religion such as:

- truth being subjective or objective
- whether evil exists
- can we prove the existence of God?
- historical evidence that supports places, events or people revealed in Sacred Scripture – includes sources taken from extra-biblical historical records
- aspects that distinguish us from the animal kingdom?
- if there is a God, what is this God like? Has God revealed himself? Do we reflect images of such a God?
- what is a miracle? Do they still happen?
- do we need Faith, Reason, Revelation and Experience?

There are many different perceptions of the word religion and what it entails. But simply religion is the practice of one's belief in a Creator. Though sadly the concept is now being widened to a belief in anything, which astonishingly includes Jedi being a class of religion on the New Zealand Census papers.

Therefore you can discover how both religion and science can help you ponder on the likelihood of the existence of God and whether such a God can or does intervene in the world today.

Throughout this book when talking about the Bible, I use the term Sacred Scripture, as this reveals a deeper meaning to such an inspiring book, which is in fact the best selling book ever.

Within *God: Fact or Fiction?* I use humour and wit to bring relief to what some parts may be heavy and somewhat challenging subjects. Plus, it's so much part of me that I couldn't omit this part of my personality.

Writing is developing into a career for me. Therefore I have another five or so concepts of books I would like to write, so please do drop me a line so that I can keep you up-to-date with what is on the publication line. Furthermore I really value feedback. If you found this book as inspiring as stated by Dr. Michael Behe on the back cover, or you thought I should include, or change some aspect, then please don't hesitate to send me an email at brendanr@ihug.co.nz or mekiwi_@hotmail.com or write to the address you'll find in the author's note at the back of *God: Fact or Fiction?*

The research undertaken to write this book has been exciting and fascinating. Hopefully, you will be able to capture the brilliance and wonder of some of the enthralling discoveries that I have researched. Like me, you may have been ill-informed concerning some of these discoveries, but once you reach the end of this book, it is my desire that you will be equipped to set out on your journey to undertake your own research, and that the door to many wonderful aspects of the relationship of nature, science and religion, will be opened to you. Enjoy!

CHAPTER 1

CATACLYSMIC BANG

A brilliant burst of light flashes through the darkness. Black metamorphoses into a resplendent surreal glowing light. But there is nothing to be seen in the light or around it; the stillness is as haunting as a deserted island. Then a thunderous noise shatters the silence; a gigantic explosion rips through the solace, and rolling clouds of matter explode through the now expanding universe, followed by billions of additional explosions. If you were a witness of such an event, you would be filled with awe and maybe a touch of fear. The sound would be deafening as you observe the very universe exploding into being. With this sudden beginning the laws of nature have been set in motion, and wait to be discovered. But if you knew what was coming you would be engulfed with a burning enthusiasm, and an electrifying and somewhat agonizing anticipation.

But now a period of millions of years passes; fast-forwarded in time the universe continues to take shape, transforming before your eyes. The cosmic dust whirls around within the newly formed space, dazzling and mesmerizing as it forms into clumps, and then planets. The planet earth morphs from a barren landscape, to a world with the vast sea of blueness; brown and green colours canvas the planet; you are in awe as you gaze from your vantage point above. But then you are taken on a journey down to earth, still in this fast-forward motion. Now you marvel as life roams the earth; with prehistoric beasts, such as dinosaurs, roaming the land, and after perhaps millions of years, birds, and the vast animal kingdom begins to appear with tigers, bears, mammoths, elephants, etc; and then humans. You would be observing the dawn of life!

This illustration of the nucleus, or heart of life is referred to as the Big Bang. What a rather insignificant name to give such an incredible explosion; the gigantic bang, or the cataclysmic bang would be more fitting.

Expansion of the Universe

In California, during the year 1929, Edwin Hubble gazed at the universe through the humble version of the telescope. In his observations

Hubble discovered that whatever direction he explored, the galaxies of the universe are moving away from us. He also discovered that the farther the galaxies are from us, the faster they are moving away. In other words the universe is in fact expanding.

But this revelation wasn't new to science. It had its birth with Einstein's formulation of the theory of relativity. In 1922 Alexander Friedmann, the Russian mathematician, used Einstein's theory to explain that the universe must be expanding or contracting, but can't be static. As a result Theoreticians concluded that if the universe is expanding then it was once smaller, and that all the matter and energy in the universe used to be concentrated only in the one place. From that place, which was an infinitely small point, exploded into being the origin of the universe with the force of an atomic-like explosion; and so formed all the matter that became the stars, planets, rocks, and living organisms of the universe.

The question we are faced with, the quest for life, which captivates, and galvanizes mankind, concerns the origin of life: how did this Big Bang occur? Was it by chance? Or was there a cause, a designer of this Big Bang and the subsequent formation of life? This question has even haunted mankind as some have spent a lifetime proving there was no God, and consequently on their deathbed had doubts about their disbelief, and tortured themselves because they couldn't make the final step to reach out to God for help, as if their pride was the final hurdle to overcome.

Background Radiation

Two Physicist's Ralph Alpher and Robert Herman, helped form the Big Bang Theory. They also formulated the belief that if the Big Bang happened it could be scientifically confirmed. In 1948 Alpher and Herman calculated that if the universe started by such an explosion, then a residue of the incredible heat created should still exist. This heat would in fact be a cosmic radiation that would be pervading the entire universe.

> Because we have a good idea of how much helium was 'made' from hydrogen when the Universe was young, and because we know a good deal about the nuclear reactions and the conditions required to allow this kind of fusion, by 1950 it was possible to get a rough idea of what happened to the Universe as it expanded away from the initial singularity. [1]

The radiation residue permeating the universe was weak but could be easily detected with simple radio telescopes at microwave frequencies. Therefore in 1964 the Russian Scientist, Yakov Zeldovich and his associates, ID Novikov and AG Doroshkevich proposed that the existence of the radiation might be tested by radio astronomy, a radio telescope.

At Bell Laboratories, Holmdel, New Jersey, two astronomers, Arno Penzias and Robert Wilson were using a radio telescope, a horn antenna. Though they were unaware of the work of the Russians, they were agitated because a perplexing static that they could not explain or eradicate, was obstructing their work using the horn antenna. Strangely, the sound did not vary, no matter what direction they aimed the antenna, or what time of day or season it was. The sound did not change in relation to the antenna's position, or that of the earth, the solar system, or the entire galaxy (the Milky Way). In fact, the sound appeared to be coming from the entire universe.[2]

The unevenness of the sound coming from every direction was vivid evidence that it indeed permeated the entire universe. However it was too even; the background radiation was apparently the same emanating from every direction.

The solution to this quandary came when a satellite was launched in 1989. It was capable of detecting unevenness in the cosmic background radiation. Therefore it was named, the "Cosmic Background Explorer". The mission to detect the background radiation was such a success that the satellite detected the ripples (variations), in the temperature of the background radiation (light, radio and other electromagnetic waves). This success led George Smoot, the leader of the mission, to exclaim, **"If you're religious, it's like looking at God."**[3]

Big Crunch

Scientists have deduced two possibilities regarding the future of the universe. The first, that the universe will expand forever. The other includes a component which is much scarier and would change the universe as we know it.

The Big Crunch Theory expounds that the universe will expand to a certain distance due to the consumption of available energy. Depending on whether there is enough matter, eventually gravity will pull harder and overcome the expansion; hence the expansion of the universe will slow to a halt. As a result the universe will collapse faster and faster under the incredible contraction until it is squashed into another explosion, another Big Bang. Then maybe it will expand again, and thus the Big Bang, Big Crunch cycle would be repeated forever. The scientist, Carl Sagan is a trumpeter of such a theory, believing in its eternal process. He likens it to an accordion opening and closing.[4]

Astronomers conducted tests to ascertain whether there was enough matter in the universe for the Big Crunch, and the results have been startling:

> After four year's work, a six-man team of British, Australian and Chinese astronomers concluded that the mean density of matter in the Universe is only 14% of that required for the Universe to collapse back on itself.[5]

Their conclusion was that the Big Crunch theory was flawed. Harold Slusher, author, painstakingly illustrates another defect and the effect that the theory has on evolutionist astronomers:

> We can calculate the amount of gravity that must be present to keep the galaxies together. Knowing the amount of gravity in turn allows us to calculate the amount of mass it would take to hold the clusters together. The result has surprised and astonished evolutionist astronomers. In the Coma Cluster the mass is too small to counterbalance the velocity dispersion by a factor of seven. In other words, for every 7 kilograms of mass necessary to hold the cluster together, only one kilogram can be accounted for. This is not a trivial matter. *There is only fourteen percent of the matter in the cluster to stay together. Astronomers have looked "high and low" for this "missing mass", but it is nowhere to be found.* Things get worse in this search when clusters other than the Coma Cluster are studied; from two to ten times the needed mass is "missing" for many. For the Virgo Cluster, it turns out that there should be fifty times more mass present than is observed. Ninety-eight percent of the mass expected is not found.[5]

Why can only one seventh of the amount of matter required to hold the universe together be detected? This incredible discrepancy is leaving evolutionist astronomers baffled.

Is there matter in existence that cannot be detected or calculated? And if there is such an undetected matter is God the Creator of it?

How Now Shall We Live by Charles Colson and Nancy Pearcey, refutes such a theory as the Big Crunch and the notion that the universe could have been in existence forever. He uses entropy to refute Sagan:

Sagan's speculation runs up against the basic laws of physics: Even an oscillating universe would use up the available energy in each cycle, and it would eventually run down. The second law of thermodynamics, the law of decay, shoots down any notion of an eternal universe. (The energy described here is energy available for work, not total energy.)[7]

Big Bang Expansion Rate

Stephen Davis, Professor of Philosophy and Religion, reveals the fine tuning needed for there even to have been a Big Bang and the formation of stars and galaxies:

Galaxies (and thus stars, and thus planets) would have been impossible had the expansion rate and the total mass of the universe not been finely tuned to each other. Too rapid a rate of expansion relative to the total mass would have overpowered the gravitational attraction of the various bits of matter to each other, and no gases could have been formed, let alone the galaxies that the gases later became. Too slow a rate of expansion relative to the total mass would have caused too much gravitational attraction, and the universe would have collapsed back into itself billions of years ago. The expansion rate lies perilously close to the borderline between recollapse into a crunch and total dispersal of all matter.[8]

Philosopher of Science, J.P Moreland explains acutely the fine-tuning needed. He says, "A reduction by one part in a million million would have led to collapse before the temperature could fall below ten thousand degrees. An early increase by one part in a million would have prevented the growth of galaxies, stars, and planets."[9]

Big Bang Vs Naturalism

The reality of the Big Bang theory, "deals a near fatal blow to naturalistic philosophy"[10] Those who followed naturalist philosophy believed that an unbroken cause and effect could be traced back forever. However, their theory was extinguished by the Big Bang theory. Resistance has swept through the naturalist community of scientists; the physicist Arthur Eddington summed up what many of his colleagues felt, that the idea of a beginning is philosophically "repugnant".[11]

A definite beginning is repugnant to those who have hatred against a Creator. It forces them to face the philosophical, and religious question: what existed before the Big Bang?

They are faced with the fact that the Big Bang happened from an infinitely small point. It is the smallest point in physics, 10^{-43}. From this infinitely small point the universe came into being, and continues to expand. What is scintilating about this theory is that this infinitely small point is equivalent to nothing. Therefore the Big Bang happened from nothing. From this point, the universe was given its birth, in conjuction with space, time, matter and energy.[12] As there must be a first cause of an event then whatever caused this space, time, matter and energy must have been outside these components. Therefore this points either to a Creator, and therefore God, or to a spaceman in the 21st dimension. Scientists hold more to the likelihood of a Creator being the cause. This concept of creation from nothing, fits hand-in-glove-like, to the Christian doctrine *Ex Nihilo*, in which material and spiritual things are produced by God from nothing. Therefore with the Big Bang God creates from nothing.

Some philosophers and scientists who try to disprove God, insist that if God exists then the beginning of the universe shows that God is just a first cause that started things off, and has left the world to self-exist. There you go, a windup creation.

However as you will discover in this book, this is partly true. God has created the world to self-exist but only after creating the foundational nature (birds, animals and humans, plants, etc) and the laws of nature (e.g. gravity, and the workings of the human cell and DNA), but God also enables the universe to continue existing; He created nature itself – time, space, matter and energy, but He can and does intervene in the Universe. I will elaborate on this throughout *God: Fact or Fiction?* – especially in the chapters *On the Wings of Faith and Reason* and *Miracles Transcending Time*.

St. Augustine of Hippo was born in Tagaste in North Africa in AD 354 to well to do parents. After a rather wild adolescence and a child out of wedlock, he was a 'marked man' as his Mum ardently prayed for his conversion. In AD 387 he was baptised by St. Ambrose; In AD. 391 he was ordained a priest; and three years later he was consecrated the Bishop of Hippo. He became one of the greatest figures in the history of Christian spirituality, leaving behind his legacy, his autobiographical *Confessions*. He elaborates upon the concept of the origin of time:

Time does not exist without some movement and transition … Then assuredly the world was made not in time, but simultaneously with time. For that which is made in time is made both after and before some time – after that which is past, before that which is future.[13]

Eternal Universe?

The Big Bang theory and the fact that the universe is continuing to expand are exhilarating revelations. It does not disprove a Creator or a Designer of the universe, but in fact quite the opposite; and the fact that the universe is expanding proves that it had to begin somehow – we are told it was from a single point, an infinitely small point, the Big Bang. There is more evidence pointing towards the likelihood of a Creator than disproving God from this theory.

I have entitled this chapter, "Cataclysmic Bang" because it should be defined more expansively than a Big Bang. It seems more appropriate as cataclysmic means a "sudden, violent change." This description is much broader than stating it is big; maybe "Super Cataclysmic Explosion" would be even more fitting.

With this cataclysmic explosion we are left with a few basic questions which will be covered throughout this book: What? How? Whom? Why? When?; What was there before?; How did it happen? Who or what caused it? Why did it happen? When did it happen?

Origin of the Universe

The expansion of the universe happened from the infinitely small point/space – the origin of space, time, matter and energy. Therefore whatever caused the Big Bang from what can be classified as nothing, could not be constricted by these components. In fact, whatever caused it had to be outside of time, space, matter and energy.

Australian Physicist, and famous author, Paul Davies relates the concept to time:

The infinite density of matter and the infinite squashing of space also mark a boundary to time. The reason is that time as well as space is stretched by gravity…The conditions at the Big Bang imply an infinite distortion of time, so that the very concept of time (and space) cannot be extended back beyond the Big Bang. The conclusion that seems to force itself upon us is that the Big Bang was the ultimate beginning of all physical things: space, time, matter and energy. It is evidently meaningless to ask (as many people do) what happened before the Big Bang, or what caused the explosion to occur. There *was* no before.[14]

While it is meaningless to ask what happened before the Big Bang, it is not meaningless to ask: What made it happen? Or, what caused it?

Whatever caused it had to be outside space, time, matter and energy. The logical conclusion is that it was either a spaceman, or a Creator.

It points to a loving God who didn't create the universe and then forget about it. Instead he created the world and has intervened in history, like a loving parent, in order to ensure we don't wander too far. This concept is also elaborated upon later.

Who created God?

The most common question in response to the claim that God created the cosmos is, "So who created God?"

While the answer can be as simple as "No one created God as he wasn't bound by time, space, matter or energy", there needs to be an elaboration. St. Athanasius, a recognized theologian of the Early Church (also known as an Early Church Father), writing against the Arian heresy that the Word (God made flesh/human, Jesus) was only a creature and not divine, explains that creatures make objects out of already existing substances, for if the Word was a creature then how, "is he able to frame things that are nothing into being?[15]

Throughout this book, I will cover the concept of Contingent Beings and a Necessary Being (see *The Philosophy of God's Existence* chapter). But for now it will suffice to explain that God is not bound by time, space, matter or energy. Therefore if He created it out of nothing and with so much power, then it is very possible that He could exist forever.

So if no one created God, and God created the universe, then God has existed forever, and it is most likely he still exists. If he still exists, then what are we doing? Are we trying to seek the truth? Are we spending time in getting to know the Creator?

Summary

We have explored such concepts as the Big Bang; the fascinating rate of expansion of the universe; and that most scientists believe the Big Bang reveals a Creator outside of space, time, matter and energy.

In fact it confirms Sacred Scripture's *Ex Nihilo* (creation from nothing). This theory haunts some and abdicates others. Without the Creator's intervention the universe will continue expanding, possibly forever (unless some matter is detected which could cause the universe to stop expanding). It's fascinating exploring the likelihood that no one created God. While some die-hards would be thrilled if God had been killed, I would like to share my conviction as you will read throughout this book, that the Creator of the universe is in fact very much alive, and has an active interest in His creation. But the big question is: Now that such a theory reveals a Creator, do other areas of science reflect a Creator? You will discover this answer as we explore further.

Chapter 1 – Bibliography

1. R A Alpher, RC Herman, "Evolution of the Universe," *Nature* 162, 1948, 774
2. RH Dicke, PJE Peebles, PG Roll and DT Wilkinson, "Cosmic Black-Body Radiation", *Astrophysical Journal* 142 (1965) p 414-419; AA Penzias, RW Wilson, "A Measurement of Excess Antenna Temperature at 4080 mc/s," *Astrophysical Journal 142* (1965), p 419-421.
3. For Smoot's description of the research, see George Smoot and Keay Davidson, *Wrinkles in Time* (New York; Morrow, 1993
4. Carl Sagan, *Cosmos,* New York: Random, 1980, 259.
5. *The Australian* newspaper. Nov 11, 1983
6. Harold Slusher, *Age of the Cosmos,* San Diego, California, Institute for Creation Research, 1980, 12
7. Colson & Pearcey, *Now How Shall We Live*, Illinois, Tyndale House Publishers Inc, 1999, 60
8. Stephen T. Davis, God, *Reason & Theistic Proofs*, WMB Eerdmans Publishing Company, Grand Rapids, Michigan, 1997,108
9. J.P Moreland, *Scaling the Secular City: A Defense of Christianity*, Grand Rapids, Michigan: Baker Book House, 1987) 52-3
10. Colson & Pearcey, *Now How Shall We Live*, Illinois, Tyndale House Publishers Inc, 1999, 59
11. Arthur Eddington, as quoted in Hugh Ross, "Astronomical Evidences for a Personal, Transcendent God," in *The Creation Hypothesis,* ed. J P Moreland (Downers Grove, Ill: InterVarsity Press, 1994), 145-46.
12. Stephen Hawking & Roger Penrose, "The Singularities of Gravitational Collapse and Cosmology" *Proceedings of the Royal Society of London*, Series A, 314 (1970): 529-48
13. Augustine: De Civitate Dei XI:6
14. Paul Davies, Weidenfeld & Nicolson, *The Last Three Minutes*, London, 1994, 24
15. Athanasius: Contra Arianos II: 21, 22: c.f. II:27, 31. 57ff

CHAPTER 2

DO OUR ORIGINS REVEAL EVOLUTION?

Imagine life evolving from the first organisms; lightning zaps protein molecules in a pool deserted by the tide, and then over billions of years life evolves from the first protein molecules, to the formation of bacteria, fish, amphibians, mammals and eventually humans; this is the theory of macro-evolution. But macro-evolution implies this happens purely by luck, that is, by a random occurrence. Though Darwin believed Natural Selection chooses what organisms to modify, the first protein molecules that evolved would have had to have happened as the result of a random occurrence, that is, by luck. Darwin's theory even says that Natural Selection must have something in which to improve upon by slight modification. Once we look at the Biochemistry chapter, *Unlocking the Chemistry of Life*, it will be striking how improbable such a situation could arise. But before you flick through to that chapter, let's look at the theory of evolution.

The Collins Pocket Dictionary describes evolution as:[1]

1. a) the development of a species, organism, etc. from its original to its present state
    b) a theory that all species of plants and animals developed from earlier forms
2. an unfolding; process of development
3. a movement that is part of a series

Micro and Macro Evolution

From this definition the evolution theory can be split into two definitions: micro and macro-evolution. Micro evolution is the hypothesis that change has occurred within a species as a result of adaptation to the environment (refer to point 2. above). This could be due to climatic change or a fight for survival due to predators. Subsequently, macro evolution is the theory that life has appeared without a Creator, and that all species of plants and animals evolved from their ancestors – hence from different species (refer to point 1(b) above).

Charles Darwin

We will cover two major questions in this chapter: What is the origin of the theory of evolution? What questions don't evolution answer? Firstly, let's explore the origin of the theory of evolution. Its contributors existed before Darwin, but I will focus mainly upon him and his successors. Charles Darwin was born in February 1809 in Shrewsbury, England. Darwin asserts that he wrote his first notebook of facts concerning the origin of species in July 1837 when he was 28 years old. What inspired him to do so was his observation of the relationships between living and extinct species during his five-year voyage around the world on HMS Beagle. The mission of the crew was to chart poorly known areas of the South American coastline, but Darwin spent most of his time on shore, studying, and collecting thousands of specimens of fossils, living plants, and animals.

While Darwin was studying flora and fauna in South America, the pinnacle of his observations were the slight variations among species, especially variations found amidst the remote Galapagos Islands. On each new island he discovered species living in isolation from neighboring islands and amidst similar environmental conditions. The main species he studied were the land and marine iguana. The latter he observed basking on the rocks like sunbathers at the beach.

At first he was puzzled about the nature of selection as he relates, "how selection could be applied to organisms in a state of nature remained for some time a mystery to me"[2]

Natural Selection

Darwin's relief came six years later, in October, 1838, when reading the famous *Essay on Population* by the Rev. Thomas Malthus. Through this essay he was able to assimilate the intense struggle for existence of living things, compared to the speed at which the food supply increased. Thus Darwin adopted the foundation of his theory:

> Being well-prepared to appreciate the struggle for existence which everywhere goes on, from long-continued observation of the habits of animals and plants, it at once struck me that under these circumstances favorable variations would tend to be preserved and unfavorable ones to be destroyed. The result of this would be the formation of new species. Here, then, I had at last got a theory by which to work.[3]

Darwin's theory of evolution encompassed *Natural Selection.* He viewed Natural Selection as rejecting variations in organisms and species and accepting what was good. But how could nature, which has no mind, work on such a principle?

Darwin's theory of Natural Selection encompassed several ideas, which are divided into the following categories:

- Random variations
- Struggle for survival
- Survival of the fittest

Darwin describes his belief in Natural Selection, especially utilizing the idea of random variations:

> Species have been modified, during a long course of descent, ...chiefly through the natural succession of successive, slight, favorable variations, aided in an important manner by the inherited effects of the use and disuse of parts; and in an unimportant manner, that is in relation to adaptive structures, whether past or present, by the direct action of external conditions, and by variations which seem to us in our ignorance to arise spontaneously. It appears that I formerly underrated the frequency and value of these latter forms of variation, as leading to permanent modifications of structure independently of Natural Selection.[4]

One major flaw of evolution, is whether there is intermediate proof of evolution whereby a species has changed into another species. This proof should be inherent in the fossil discoveries. Darwin says:

> We see nothing of these slow changes in progress, until the hand of time has marked the lapse of ages, and then so imperfect is our view into long-past geological ages, that we see that only the forms of life are now different from what they formerly were.[5]

Millions of fossils have been discovered since Darwin's era. Has any proof been discovered? You will read the answer later as I reveal the overwhelming result of whether there are intermediaries in the fossil record.

Darwin was a genius, modifying the theory of evolution to the extent that there were few flaws. One example of this brilliance is that there could only be positive variations that would survive:

In order that any great modification should be effected in a species, a variety when once formed must again, perhaps after a long interval of time, present individual differences of the same favorable nature as before; and these must be again preserved, and so onwards step by step. Seeing that individual differences of the same kind perpetually recur, this can hardly be considered an unwarrantable assumption.[6]

Evolution and Time

While Darwin uses time as a factor of evolution he does not rely solely upon it. He explains the relationship:

The mere lapse of time by itself does nothing, either for or against Natural Selection. It has been erroneously asserted that the element of time has been assumed by me to play an all-important part in modifying species as if all the forms of life were necessarily undergoing change through some innate law. Lapse of time is only so far important, that it gives a better chance of beneficial variations arising, and of their being selected, accumulated and fixed.[7]

Darwin was so brilliant and cunning. He sought to throw the burden of proof on his "opponents to 'demonstrate' that something could not possibly have happened – which is essentially impossible to do in science".[8]

But this theory stretches beyond the logical. How can there only be favorable variations? Why can't a species have both favorable and unfavorable variations and yet survive its cousins/predecessors? Darwin's theory states that it is due to an intense struggle – the survival of the fittest. If there are only favorable variations, then this constitutes an order beyond logic; and such an order would point to a designer. Such a theory paves the way for his ardent followers to doctor computer programs to only accept positive variations/mutations. Michael Behe, Professor of Biochemistry at Lehigh University, and author of *Darwin's Black Box*, says, "Generally a single mutation can, at best, make only a small change in a creature."[9] He points out that some changes seem big, such as legs growing out of the head of a lab fruit fly, in place of its antennas. But this change though hideous, just moves the legs from one place to another. Once again Darwin's cunning shines through. Though he may not have been out to deceive people with his theory of macro-evolution, I believe his safeguards such as positive mutations, set up the scene for his critics and supporters to doctor many of their experiments. As you will read in the chapter on "Clutching at Straws" these experiments emerge into the bizarre and absurd categories.

Michael Denton, an Australian molecular biologist and author, reveals the limits that "further change" or Natural Selection can reach:

> There was also the disturbing point, which Darwin was well aware of and had tried rather unconvincingly to dismiss at the end of Chapter Two of the *Origin*, that while breeding experiments and the domestication of animals had revealed that many species were capable of a considerable degree of change, they also revealed distinct limits in nearly every case beyond which no further change could ever be produced.[10]

This severely contradicts Darwin's claim of an almost infinite level of change.

Transitional Species Evidence

Denton reveals that out of the millions of living species known to biology, only a handful are considered to be in any way intermediate between other species. Obviously this is not sufficient evidence when Darwin claimed there should be numerous intermediary species. Denton uses the example of the lungfish to state the evidence that the lungfish does not fit into such a category. He says that:

> In the case of the lungfish, its fish characteristics such as gills and its intestinal spiral valve are one hundred percent typical of the condition found in many ordinary fish, while its heart and the way the blood is returned to the heart from the lungs is similar to the situation found in most terrestrial vertebrates. In other words, although the lungfish betrays a bewildering mixture of fish and amphibian character traits, the individual characteristics themselves are not in any realistic sense transitional between the two types.[11]

Harvard paleontologist Stephen Jay Gould reveals that modern text books are misleading:

> The extreme rarity of transitional forms in the fossil record persists as the trade secret of paleontology. The evolutionary trees that

adorn our textbooks have data only at the tips and nodes of their branches; the rest is inference, however reasonable, not the evidence of fossils.[12]

As a result of the theory of macro-evolution we are faced with several questions: If we could travel back in time would we see animals slowly evolving into new species? How did life evolve? What about the sexual organs on these species? Did they gradually appear or was it a sudden occurrence? Darwin says that Natural Selection occurs only slowly. Several animals within a species would have had to evolve these organs and within a relatively short period of time. Is there such evidence for transitional species fossils? How did animals first reproduce? If they couldn't reproduce, then how could they survive as a species? Why is reproduction now the only method that animals or humans have for subsequent generations survival?

Other questions that confront us are: Why are male species different? For example, the male frigate bird inflates his bright red chest into a large balloon to attract the female, and the female lacks a red chest; Why do the majority of species have to reproduce in order to survive? There are very few hermaphrodite animals, but these species still need a mate to reproduce e.g. snails; If all species evolved from one organism, why do specific species have to mate with their own species e.g. birds? Why can't they mate with the animal they have evolved from? Now it is obviously repugnant to think us humans would mate with an ape isn't it? Though there are evolutionists who say that this is completely OK, and that we don't need morals, however we know that morality alone overrules bestiality. This will become clearer after reading the Chapter, *Truth: Subjective or Objective?*

Darwin Questions Natural Selection?

Darwin was nonplused about *Natural Selection* in relation to the multitude of lower forms, the reason why they still exist and why some forms were more highly developed than others. In the *Origin of Species* Darwin says:

Why have not the more highly developed forms everywhere supplanted and exterminated the lower? Lamarck, who believed in an innate tendency towards perfection in all organic beings, seems to have felt this difficulty so strongly that he was led to suppose that new and simple forms are continually being produced by spontaneous generation. Science has not as yet proved the truth of this belief, whatever the future may reveal.[13]

Once again Darwin's cunning comes to the fore. His answer is:

On our theory the continued existence of lowly organisms offers no difficulty; for Natural Selection or the survival of the fittest does not necessarily include progressive development - it only takes advantage of such variations as arise and are beneficial to each creature.[14]

When analyzing these statements we can point to the fact that not all forms of species are supplanted or exterminated. Utilizing the theory of evolution and Natural Selection, if this were the case, if the bacteria evolved into fish, the fish into amphibians, the amphibians into mammals, the mammals into apes, and the apes into humans, then life sure would be boring; the result would be that every lower species would be supplanted or exterminated. But it is a fact that there are thousands of species of bacteria, fish, animals, and hundreds of species of humans, which all exist today. This variation reflects design and the possibility for a Creator to cause such variation.

Darwin's contradiction

As mentioned previously, Darwin's theories were not perfect, though some macro-evolutionists seem to believe so. I have highlighted a contradiction concerning Natural Selection, and below is another example from Darwin's writing:

Natural Selection will never produce in a being any structure more injurious than beneficial to that being. If a balance be struck between good and evil caused by each part, each will be found on the whole advantageous. Under changing conditions of life, if any part comes to be injurious it will be modified; or if it be not so, the being will become extinct as myriads have become extinct.[15]

Darwin is saying that it is impossible for Natural Selection to ever produce any structure that is more injurious than beneficial to that being. And he covers his tracks by saying any negative mutations will cause the being to become extinct. But his statement is rather contradictory. It seems Darwin's cunning was not without limits.

Human Origins

12 years after Darwin wrote *The Origin of Species* he explored the concept of human origins in *The Descent of Man (1871).* Ian Barbour explains:

> He tried to show how all human characteristics might be accounted for in terms of the gradual modification of anthropoid ancestors by the process of Natural Selection. The close resemblance of humans and gorillas in anatomical structure had already been widely noted; Darwin indicated how upright posture, larger brain size, and other distinctive changes might have been produced. He insisted that human moral and mental faculties differ in degree rather than in kind from the capacities of animals, among which there are rudimentary forms of feeling and communication. Human existence, hitherto considered sacrosanct, was thus brought within the sphere of natural law and was analyzed in the same categories applied to other forms of life.[16]

How can morality be compared between an animal and a human? Do animals have any sense of morality? For the answer see the later chapters, *Truth: Subjective or Objective?* and *Faith and Reason.*

Darwin's Failed Theory

Darwin is treated like a prophet by some, or even worse, as infallible. Though he was neither a prophet, nor infallible there is some truth in his theories. However, first let us dwell on one of his theories that failed.

Darwin included in his beliefs what French naturalist, Jean Baptiste Lamarck expounded; that the best explanation for fossils and for the diversity of life is that organisms evolve. However, Lamarck is also well known for proposing how species evolve; by using or not using its body parts, an individual tends to develop certain characteristics, which it passes onto successive generations. His example, is one, which some still profess to, that is, the giraffe acquired its long neck because its ancestors stretched higher and higher into the trees to reach the leaves, and that over time successive generations developed longer necks. *Biology: Concepts and Connections*, a pro-evolution resource book touts this view as erroneous and states:

> This mistaken idea, known as the inheritance of acquired characteristics, obscures the important fact that Lamarck helped

set the stage for Darwin by strongly advocating evolution and by proposing that species evolve as a result of interactions with their environment.[17]

The same book provides an illustration of what they term "an imaginary ancestral iguana population" to show how Natural Selection works:

> Following Darwin's lead, we now start to look at the connection between variation and Natural Selection. The figure here is an idealized model summarizing the effect of Natural Selection on inherited variation in successive populations. The top row represents an imaginary ancestral iguana population living on a small island. The population is varied with most individuals having nonwebbed feet and a rounded tail, and two having webbed feet and a flattened tail...Over the generations, individuals with webbed feet and flattened tails leave proportionally more offspring. Natural selection has eliminated most of the individuals with nonwebbed feet and rounded tails.[18]

This is clearly only a hypothesis. It would have been more beneficial to use a clear example of fact as an illustration. It is strange that they only claim what could have happened, and not used an example such as from the Galapagos Islands, if it really happened. Could it not swing around later on with the opposite happening, a disease affecting those with the webbed feet, and then those with the nonwebbed feet becoming "naturally selected".

The Origin of Life

After Darwin published the *Origin of Species* many began to dwell on the problem that Darwin had failed to address; while he had covered how life could have gradually grown more complex over time from one or a few simple forms, he did not explain how life came to be in the first place.

Now humanity is faced with various definitions of evolution: it is a fully naturalistic, process without purpose which by Natural Selection and mutation has produced all living things without a Creator; or simply, that organisms have changed over time; and finally that God could work through evolution. However focusing on the naturalistic evolution, for the first amino acid to have formed it would have done so, merely by chance. Darwin's Natural Selection theory could only work on living things; there had to be something guiding the first formation of an amino acid and so it couldn't be Natural Selection.

While it seems obvious that if there is no Creator, then all life has purely come into existence by chance or luck, evolutionists tend to differ by saying that Natural Selection has 'selected' or directed something to happen. But for the first amino acid to form would in effect be by chance. Darwin's Natural Selection theory works only on living things. In *Man Science and God* by John Morton, the author, surprisingly as a Christian supports even macro evolution. This is what he reveals about the concept of chance and Natural Selection:

> An important question that arises is, whether there are situations in which such small indeterminate events can play a part in the lives of organisms. This has been claimed to happen in the mutation of genes, and in the firing of nerve cells initiating specific pieces of behavior. These activities, in essence, may both spring from chance phenomena at the level of individual particles. But the result as we see it will be very far from chance. An event that offers advantage will be 'selected'.[19]

Darwin's dedication

Darwin is to be admired for the incredible amount of time he dedicated on research; for 20 years he meticulously collected facts to support his theory. He manifested wonderful dedication, and yet simultaneously it appeared to consume him as he testifies to losing his love of music, "My soul is too dried up to appreciate it as in the old days." If we let something consume us as much, to the point of neglecting what is important, then other things fade into oblivion.

What is a Soul?

OK, so Darwin recognized he had a soul, but what is a soul? A soul enables us to communicate with God, enabling God to 'hear' our prayers, and for us at times to 'hear' God or God's will.

In most dictionaries you will find the word, soul. The Collins Pocket English Dictionary defines soul as:[20]

> The part of one's being that is thought of as the center of feeling, thinking, will, etc., apart from the body
> The moral or emotional nature of man

Spiritual or emotional warmth, force, etc.
Vital or essential part, quality, etc.
The central or leading figure.
Embodiment; personification
A person [a town of 1,000 souls]

While obviously the Collins Pocket Dictionary takes several definitions of the soul, it is the person that controls the will, rather than the soul per se. Moreover, the soul gives us the ability to reason between right and wrong, which includes our moral nature – that is why animals do not have the concept of morality.

But if we look for a religious definition, we find the Pocket Catholic Dictionary great in explaining the soul:

> The spiritual immortal part in human beings that animates their body. Though a substance in itself, the soul is naturally ordained toward a body; separated, it is an "incomplete" substance. The soul has no parts, it is therefore simple, but it is not without accidents. The faculties are its proper accidents. Every experience adds to its accidental form. It is individually created for each person by God and infused into the body at the time of human insemination. It is moreover created in respect to the body it will inform, so that the substance of bodily features and of mental characteristics insofar as they depend on organic functions is safeguarded. As a simple and spiritual substance, the soul cannot die. Yet it is not the total human nature, since a human person is composed of body animated by the soul. [21]

One major difference given by this explanation is that the soul is immortal or imperishable, and each soul is individually created by God. Furthermore, the soul and the body are meant to be together; in the definition of the spirit the same dictionary explains:

> That which is positively immaterial. It is pure spirit if it has no dependence on matter either for its existence or for any of its activities. God is uncreated pure Spirit; the angels are created pure spirits. The human soul is more properly called spiritual. Although it can exist independent of the body, it nevertheless in this life depends extrinsically on the body for its operations, and in the life to come retains a natural affinity for the body, with which after the resurrection it will be reunited for all eternity. [22]

Therefore our body and soul will be resurrected and reunited upon our death. As Jesus conquered death in the Resurrection, we too will conquer death! We will be reunited with our bodies. The resurrection of the body seriously refutes the idea of reincarnation, which I will cover in more depth, in my next book.

> Someone may ask: How are dead people raised, and what sort of body do they have when they come? How foolish! What you sow must die before it is given new life; and what you sow is not the body that is to be, but only a bare grain, of wheat I dare say, or some other kind; it is God who gives it the sort of body that he has chosen for it, and for each kind of seed its own kind of body
> Not all flesh is the same flesh: there is human flesh, animals have another kind of flesh...Then there are heavenly bodies and earthly bodies; the heavenly have a splendour of their own, and the earthly a different splendour.
> 1 Corinthians 15:35-40

Therefore, upon our death, and following our judgment we will be given a glorified body.

Do Animals Have Souls?

The definition of the soul in the Pocket Catholic Dictionary reveals that Philosophy tells us that plants and animals do have souls; they operate as "sensitive and vegetative principles of life."[23] But, unlike the human soul, these souls are perishable. So I'm sorry to say, you won't see your favorite tree or animal running around in heaven.

Darwin Rejected The Supernatural

In *Religion and Science*, Ian G Barbour reveals that Darwin in fact did not believe in the supernatural:

> Darwin rejected miracles, revelation and special creation, and he objected on moral grounds to the idea of hell. He said that suffering in nature, which he had seen so frequently, was inconsistent with the notion of a beneficent God. He argued that detailed providential design would have resulted in perfect adaptation, but he saw evidence only of differential adaptation, which was all that was required for Natural Selection to be effective.[24]

Therefore Darwin believed that if there was a beneficent or loving God then design would have resulted in perfect adaptation, which lends one to think that everything should be perfect, including you. Perfect God, and therefore perfect creation. Imagine that, if we were perfect, we would be walking on water, as we are reminded within the gospels when Jesus walked on water.

Darwin's Religious Beliefs

Three years before Darwin died, he testified to his religious beliefs as agnostic:

> "In my most extreme fluctuations I have never been an Atheist in the sense of denying the existence of God. I think that generally (and more and more as I grow older), but not always, that an Agnostic would be the more correct description.[25]

Agnosticism is the belief that either "knowledge or certitude about ultimates is impossible"[26] or "one who cannot know whether there is anything beyond material phenomena"[27]. Therefore someone who is agnostic is not certain whether there is a God. It also brings to mind how they could believe in gravity, since gravity could be considered beyond material phenomena.

It's very revealing to delve into what beliefs Darwin once had, and thus see what central beliefs he discarded.

> The old argument from design in *Nature*, as given by Paley, which formerly seemed so conclusive, fails now that the law of Natural Selection has been discovered... There seems to be no more design in the variability of organic beings, and in the action of Natural Selection than in the course which the wind blows... At the present day the most usual argument for the existence of an intelligent God is drawn from the deep inward convictions and feelings which are experienced by most persons... Formerly I was led by such feelings...to the firm conviction of the existence of God and the immortality of the soul...I well remember my conviction that there is more in man than the mere breath of the body. But now the grandest scenes would not cause any such conviction and feelings to rise in my mind. Another source of conviction in the existence of God...follows from the extreme difficulty, or rather impossibility,

of conceiving this immense and wonderful universe, including man and his capacity for looking backwards and far into futurity, as the result of blind chance or necessity...This conclusion...has gradually, with many fluctuations, become weaker...I, for one, must be content to remain an Agnostic.[28]

Natural Selection and a Creator

Does Natural Selection exclude a Creator? I see no reason why Natural Selection would nullify such a being. It may explain how species adapt to a new environment, and even the possibility of it transforming into another species, but this does not rule out a Creator, as a Creator could put in place the mechanisms or laws for this to happen. So it is perfectly possible for the species to be programmed to adapt to their environment; and with climatic change or an attack from predators that species could adapt in order to survive. God could have devised such a law as Natural Selection. Though I believe it is possible, this isn't the issue. The issue at stake is macro evolution, especially when it denies the existence of a Creator. I believe that macro-evolution is only possible with a Creator. Could God cause a species to evolve – of course if that was His desire. God would be perfectly capable of creating millions of species, or a few with the ability to evolve. What concerns me mostly is that macro-evolution implies that there is no God, and no designer. However as you explore more of *God: Fact or Fiction?* the evidence should speak for itself – you will uncover such amazing aspects of creation that point so strongly to design, and thus a designer.

The Catholic Pocket Dictionary in defining evolution, sums up what the Christian attitude should be, especially towards an atheistic view of macro evolution:

> The theory that something was or is in a state of necessary development. Materialistic evolution assumes the eternal existence of uncreated matter and then explains the emergence of all living creatures, of plants, animals, and human beings, both body and soul, through a natural evolutionary process. This is contrary to Christian revelation. Theistic [involves God] is compatible with Christianity provided it postulates the special divine providence as regards the human body and the separate creation of each human soul.[29]

Therefore the fact whether the evolution theory is real is not a big deal, but when it excludes the existence of God or that God created an imperishable soul in each of us, then this is contrary to Christianity.

Summary

There are many flaws of macro-evolution, while micro-evolution is sound. Darwin covered his butt by ensuring there was no escape clause to his theory – Natural Selection only selects positive mutations. But in doing so he gives Natural Selection mindlike qualities of purpose or intent. Therefore there is some mind at work behind the theory of Natural Selection. Additionally that mind has to be powerful to work upon positive mutations only. Could Darwin have been so close to rediscovering His Creator, but was held back by some distrust, or pride?

The variation within and transcending the species reveals more of a creative mind, hence a Creator, than it does pure luck. But does luck or chance hold any firmness within science? Do any scientists hold to the luck being integral to the origin of the universe, and the origin of life? The following Chapter answers these questions.

Chapter 2 – Bibliography

1. Collins Pocket English Dictionary, London, 1986, 295
2. *Life and Letters of Charles Darwin,* Francis Darwin ed., New York: D. Appleton, 1887, i:83
3. Ibid, i:68
4. *The Origin of Species by Charles Darwin: A Variorum Text,* ed. Morse Peckham (Philadelphia: Univ. of Pennsylvania Press, 1959), 747-48
5. *Charles Darwin,* Abridged by Richard Melbourne, *The Illustrated Origin of Species* Oxford University Press, Melbourne, Australia, 1979
6. Ibid, 77-78
7. Ibid, 85
8. Michael J Behe, William A Dembski, Stephen C Meyer, *Science and Evidence for Design in the Universe*, Ignatius Press, San Francisco, 2000, 25
9. Michael Behe, *Darwin's Black Box*, Simon & Schuster, New York, 1996, 40
10. Michael Denton, *A Theory In Crisis*, Checy Chase: Adler & Adler Publishers Inc. 1986, 64
11. Ibid, 109
12. Stephen Jay Gould, "Evolution's Erratic Pace" in *Natural History,* May 1977, 14
13. *Charles Darwin,* Abridged by Richard Melbourne, *The Illustrated Origin of Species* Oxford University Press, Melbourne, Australia, 1979, *91-92*
14. Ibid, 92
15. Ibid, 120

16. Ian G Barbour, Religion & Science, SCM Press, 1998, 53
17. Biology: concepts and connections
18. Biology: concepts and connections, pg 270
19. John Morton, Man Science and God, Collins, Auckland, New Zealand, 1972, 19
20. Collins Pocket English Dictionary, London, 1986, 802
21. John A Hardon, S.J, *Pocket Catholic Dictionary*, Image Books, (Doubleday), New York, 1985, 413
22. Ibid, 414
23. Ibid, 413
24. Ian G Barbour, Religion & Science, SCM Press, 1998, 58
25. *Life and Letters of Charles Darwin,* Francis Darwin ed., New York: D. Appleton, 1887), i:68)
26. John A Hardon, S.J, *Pocket Catholic Dictionary*, Image Books, (Doubleday), New York, 1985, 12
27. Collins Pocket English Dictionary, London, 1986, 16
28. Life and Letters, I, 309-12) (A N Field, *The Evolution Hoax Exposed,* 1971 first published as *Why Colleges Bread Communists* in 1941, p 62
29. John A Hardon, S.J, *Pocket Catholic Dictionary*, Image Books, (Doubleday), New York, 1985, 136

CHAPTER 3

PROBABILITY OF LIFE BY CHANCE

The Watchmaker Model

Darwin would have studied William Paley's book *Natural Theology* in which his famous analogy relates how a lone figure on a deserted island stumbles across a watch. On careful observation it is quickly determined that the watch is obviously designed, and therefore there is a designer who created it; the parts are clearly integrated, an example of a single purpose. As a result this analogy was lauded by Christians and deplored by macro-evolutionists.

The Doctrine Commission of the Church of England (Episcopalian) criticizes the watchmaker model, and proposes two new models:

> The first is that of *the artist and the work of art.* The artist's vision changes and is reformulated as the work proceeds. Moreover, the medium (the sculptor's wood or stone, for instance) always imposes constraints on the artist. God has similarly chosen a medium that imposes inescapable constraints; God exercises a limited control and redeems imperfections rather than preventing them.[1]

This analogy is good to help explain why everything isn't perfect now, saying "God redeems imperfections." But it also raises many questions. Who is to say to God what the imperfections are? Are we imperfect if we aren't Einstein, a swimsuit model, top of our class, or the best at our sports field? Are we imperfect if we have one arm? I believe there are imperfections as a result of the Fall of mankind and the presence of evil as you will read in later chapters. But what we term to be imperfect does not necessarily mean God sees you as imperfect.

The analogy seems rather strange when you consider the Commission states that the artist's vision changes and is reformulated as work proceeds. I think God is much bigger than that. God's vision would only change as the result of man's disobedience and yet his overall plan would remain the same – God's kingdom on earth. But take the image of the artist, God would know what He is going to create before

He starts. Therefore this is a limited analogy. But to support the analogy, God has chosen a medium with constraints – the constraints of giving humans free will.

Life By Chance?

I was in an evolution related chatroom on the internet where the young people were adamant that chance isn't a theory supported by evolutionists as pertaining to our origin. But after some research it is abundantly clear, that this is what evolutionists cling to when defending their theory. However, it may be one part of the theory that is not expounded at our schools.

French biologist Jacques Monod in his book *Chance and Necessity* refers to chance when claiming that religion has been defeated by evolution, "The ancient covenant is in pieces: man at last knows that he is alone in the unfeeling immensity of the universe, out of which he has emerged only by chance."[2]

Notorious writer and Australian Physicist, Paul Davies says, "So whilst complying with the laws of nature, the actual route to life must have owed much to chance and circumstance – or contingency, as philosophers call it."[3]

Davies writes eloquently regarding the DNA and chance. However the chapter, *Unlocking the Chemistry of Life* will reveal how absurd the idea is. He writes:

> Inside each and every one of us lies a message. It is inscribed in an ancient code, its beginnings lost in the mists of time. Decrypted, the message contains instructions on how to make a human being. Nobody wrote the message; nobody invented the code. They came into existence spontaneously. Their designer was Mother Nature herself, working only within the scope of her immaculate laws and capitalizing on the vagaries of chance. The message isn't written in ink or type, but in atoms, strung together in an elaborately arranged sequence to form DNA, short for deoxyribonucleic acid. It is the most extraordinary molecule on Earth.[4]

Biologist Stephen Jay Gould claims we are the by-product of chance, "We are glorious accidents of an unpredictable process with no drive to complexity, not the expected results of evolutionary principles that yearn to produce a creature capable of understanding the mode of its own necessary construction."[5]

However you will read in the chapter, *Unlocking the Chemistry of Life* whether increased complexity is evidence for design or purpose in our universe.

When macro-evolutionists claim that life happened by chance, they exclude the possibility of a Creator. Colson and Pearcey explain how the theory of chance is being refuted:

> But the computer revolution put an end to any chance theory of life's origin. Beginning in the 1960s, mathematicians began writing computer programs to simulate every process under the sun, and they cast their calculating eyes on evolution itself. Hunched over their high-speed computers, they simulated the trial-and-error processes of neo-Darwinian evolution over the equivalent of billions of years. The outcome was jolting: The computers showed that the probability of evolution by chance processes is essentially zero, no matter how long the time scale.[6]

Mathematicians claim that, statistically, any odds beyond 1 in 10^{50} have a zero probability of ever happening.[7]

The famous astronomer, Sir Fred Hoyle relates the possibility that life happened by chance, to lining up 10^{50} blind people, giving each one a scrambled Rubik's Cube, and finding that they all solve the cube at the same moment.[8]

Moreover Hoyle makes a startling claim, that Darwin's theory of evolution should be buried:

> The likelihood of the formation of life from inanimate matter is one to a number with 40,000 noughts after it…It is big enough to bury Darwin and the whole theory of evolution. There was no primeval soup, neither on this planet nor on any other, and if the beginnings of life were not random, they must therefore have been the product of purposeful intelligence.[9]

De Duve uses a great analogy regarding the possibility of life happening by chance. In Bridge, the card game, each of four players is dealt 13 cards from a deck with hearts, diamonds, spades and clubs. The odds of any player receiving all thirteen spades is an astonishing one in 635 billion. De Duve then compares this analogy with the impressiveness of life.[10]

> We are dealt thirteen spades not once but thousands of times in succession! This is utterly impossible, unless the deck is doctored.

What this doctoring implies with respect to the assembly of the first cell is that most of the steps involved must have had a *very high likelihood of taking place under the prevailing conditions.* Make them even moderately improbable and the process must abort, however many times it is initiated, because of the very number of steps involved.[11]

De Duve is stating that the probability of life happening by chance is virtually impossible. The process includes a number of steps, and like any recipe, the steps must be in sequence, or else it is doomed to failure. The Bridge analogy is pertinent; just imagine playing Bridge and being able to get thirteen spades thousands of times in a row! It just defies logic.

Therefore following de Duve's logic the universe must be "pregnant with life";[12] The process which life used to come into being must be natural and something must have caused the universe to be pregnant.

Materialism

The philosophy of materialism permeates the theory of macro evolution when it excludes God's involvement. The more we delve into the materialistic philosophy the more we are reminded of some evil characters of history, and consequently of some still existing.

Materialism is the philosophy that everything can be explained by matter. While naturalism is something based on natural desires or instinct. Dr. Neil Broom, Biochemist at the University of Auckland, and author, elaborates on how these two philosophies have influenced science and society:

The philosophy of materialism or naturalism very largely dominates the modern, scientific understanding of the natural world. This conceptual model has profoundly influenced the way we view ourselves as human beings within nature...Scientific materialism views humanity as a mere artifact, a fluke biological by-product of the vast, impersonal flow of a wholly natural set of processes. We are 'caused' by the cosmos, not the reason for it. Modern man is finally not anything unique or special.[13]

As you read in the previous chapter in the section entitled, *Human Origins,* Darwin brought how people view humans down to the same level as animals, saying both had different levels of morality. Once again we see this view echoed through the philosophies of materialism and naturalism.

Herbert Simon, computer theorist, psychologist and Nobel prize-winner also supports the notion of man losing his uniqueness:

> The definition of man's uniqueness has always formed the kernel of his cosmological and ethical systems. With Copernicus and Galileo, he ceased to be the species located at the center of the universe, attended by sun and stars. With Darwin, he ceased to be the species created and specially endowed by God with soul and reason. With Freud, he ceased to be the species whose behavior was–potentially–governable by rational mind. As we begin to produce mechanisms that think and learn, he has ceased to be the species uniquely capable of complex, intelligent manipulation of his environment. What the computer and the progress in artificial intelligence challenge is an ethic that rests on man's apartness from the rest of nature.[14]

Though this article was written by Herbert Simon back in 1977, we all know that computers are generally much smarter than humans. Plus they won't answer you back. LOL! ("lol!" is computer speak for laughing). But seriously, we also know that computers have been designed and created by man. So without man there wouldn't be any computers. Just as man is designed and created by God, so without God we would not exist.

Computers do not destroy man's uniqueness, and man's wonderful creativity. They may interfere at times, but they also enhance and contribute to man's creativity too (just look at the cover of this book which was created on the computer). Also from the above article by Herbert Simon it seems rather absurd to think of a computer as a species – a computer can not breathe, nor think for itself. A computer is not a being, does not have a personality, and unlike humans, it can't freely choose between right and wrong, good and evil, (reason) and does not have a soul, not even a perishable one.

The reason begs to be asked, "But how can an animal reason between right and wrong, good and evil?" The animal does not have a sense of morality, and since morality is intrinsically linked with reasoning between good and evil, then the animal is not moral. I will cover this more indepth in the chapters, *Truth: Subjective or Objective?* and *Faith and Reason.*

We actually are still the species located at the center of the universe. Anybody who has studied physics and astronomy are well aware that an analogy that can be used is that space is like circles that are drawn on a balloon. If you were standing on any of the circles when the balloon was inflated it would be as if you were at the center of the universe.

Suspect Motives

One of the most outspoken statements of the philosophical motivation of some of those who follow Darwinism comes from Harvard geneticist Richard Lewontin. In an article in which he argues for the superiority of science over religion, Lewontin admits, "in the struggle between science and the supernatural," we "take the side of science." The answer to why Lewontin and obviously other Darwinists take this side is quite revealing: "Because we have a prior commitment to materialism." Unfortunately, because of their commitment they have to deny there is a God.

This type of bias by Darwinists permeates Chapter 4, *Clutching at Straws*, as I reveal some of the bizarre theories of macro-evolution.

Nobel Laureate, Jacques Monod gives another classic example of materialism. One which is filled with a rather morbid, and dreary philosophy:

> Man must at last wake out of his millenary dream; and in doing so, wake to his total solitude, his fundamental isolation. Now does he at last realize that, like a gypsy, he lives on the boundary of an alien world. A world that is deaf to music, just as indifferent to his hopes as it is to his suffering or to his crimes… The ancient covenant is in pieces; man knows at last that he is alone in the universe's unfeeling immensity, out of which he emerged only by chance.[10]

Darwin & Morality

Darwin showed inconsistency in some of his theories. He believed in a "higher morality", which encouraged respect and love towards all people, including the weak and disadvantaged. But simultaneously he thought such a morality would lessen the competitive struggle and therefore undermine what he believed to be the source of his progress.

This higher morality was implied in some passages of his writing as he said that anything humans do is an expression of Natural Selection. Therefore if progress is a result of the process, then no human decision can hinder it.

The culmination of this philosophy of materialism bears its ugly fruit as a result of Darwin placing humans and animals on the same moral plain. It seems to have an eerie ring about it, one that brings to mind images of the holocaust and World War II as Hitler invaded and raped so many countries, and treated humans as worthless and expendable.

Darwin warned that future progress would be hindered by sentimental policies that protect weaker individuals. Hence, he set the stage for Hitler to seek the elimination of the sick, maimed, lower classes or races, or anyone who got in his way. This conjures up images of the 20th and 21st Century with the amounts of wars, abortions (the most defenseless humans in our world), and also what is now trying to take a foothold in Western countries, euthanasia. Euthanasia has opened up the door for the handicapped and elderly to end their lives, or in some cases for someone to end it for them. In Holland people are making living wills, stating that they do not want to be euthanised (killed) if they get sick.

The best summary of materialism comes from philosopher, William Barret:

> The success of the physical sciences leads to the attitude of scientific materialism, according to which the mind becomes, in one way or another, merely the passive plaything of material forces. The offspring turns against its parent. We forget we should have learned from Kant: that the imprint of the mind is everywhere in the body of this science, and without the founding power of mind it would not exist.[16]

Intent

Some scientists, who trumpet Darwinism and macro-evolution, declare that all species including at the level of microbiology, have an intention to excel – hence Natural Selection. But how can a micro-organism have any intent in which to improve itself? The distinguished evolutionary biologist, Theodosius Dobzhansky warned:

> I would like to plead with you, simply, please realize you cannot use the words "Natural Selection" loosely. Prebiological Natural Selection is a contradiction in terms.[17]

Richard Dawkins (now, I had to refrain myself from making any joke about his surname) explains deliberateness within evolution in relation to the eye by using the metaphor of climbing a mountain, "Going upwards means mutating, one small step at a time, and only accepting mutations that improve optical performance." [18]

But Dawkins statement oozes with purpose. Sylvia Baker does a brilliant job of refuting Dawkins:

All the specialized and complex cells that make up our eyes are supposed to have evolved because of advantageous mutations in some more simple cells that were there before. But what use is a hole in the front of the eye to allow light to pass through if there are no cells at the back of the eye to receive the light? What use is a lens forming an image if there is no nervous system having evolved before there was an eye to give it information?[19]

If there is purpose it's there because it has been programmed – hence there is a programmer. Attributes of purpose/intent can only be related to the mind, and of course mere organisms do not have such a thing. It is a weak metaphor to attribute something resulting from the mind to merely an organism. In addition, to accept only positive mutations is also short sighted! What a narrow focus that position is. Yet to only accept positive mutations is reminiscent of Darwin – it is his legacy. In the following, written by Darwin, you will find many references that can only be attributed to the mind:

> It may be said that Natural Selection is daily and hourly scrutinizing, throughout the world, every variation, even the slightest; rejecting that which is bad, preserving and adding up all that is good; silently and insensibly working, whenever and wherever opportunity offers, at the improvement of each organic being in relation to its organic and inorganic conditions of life.[20]

The question begs to be asked; where does Natural Selection's intention come from? It is also extremely bizarre to relate something as intentional or deliberate when chance is so central to the theory of macro-evolution. Therefore intentionality leads more to a designer and it does not go hand-in-hand with chance: Michael Polanyi elaborates:

> The fact is, therefore, that every living organism is a meaningful organization of meaningless matter and that it is highly probable that these meaningful organizations should all have occurred entirely by chance. Moreover, looking at the general direction the evolutionary development of living organisms has taken, one must in all fairness admit that this direction has been toward more meaningful organizations, more meaningful both in their own structure and in terms of the meanings they are able to achieve. From microscopic one-celled plants, able to do very little more than to provide for their own sustenance and to reproduce, to minute animals, sensitive as individuals to their surroundings and

able to learn very rudimentary sustaining habits, to more complex animals, able to do many more things, to the higher mammals, and finally to man, who is able to achieve so many things that he frequently supposes himself to be a god able to achieve all things – this evolutionary history is a panorama of meaningful achievements of almost breathtaking proportions.[21]

When evolutionists utilise an example of a computer to suggest that man is not unique anymore, it is wise to consider the questions, "Who designed the computer?" and "Who created the computer?" Thus man retains his place as capable of complex, intelligent manipulation of his environment. Man remains creative and the steward of creation. It begs to ask the question; "how many people would class a computer or artificial intelligence as a "species"? God created man with the complimentary roles of ruler and steward of creation. With regards to Intelligent Design we can adapt the previous questions to: "Who created the universe? Who created humans?"

Summary

Though many macro-evolutionists believe that life happened by chance, the overwhelming evidence is that mathematically the probability of life happening by chance is virtually nil. The philosophy of materialism states that we are caused by the cosmos, and thus are not unique or special. Darwin fuelled materialism by placing mankind on the same moral plain as animals. Natural Selection oozes with mindlike qualities such as intent or purpose. Therefore the question must be faced: *What mind is actually behind this intent of Natural Selection?* Could it in fact be God? Design, chance, materialism and intent do not all go together. While design and intent are compatible, chance and materialism are perfect for each other. But though chance has been claimed to be feasible, the evidence shows it has a shaky foothold. In fact design and intent have more in common, leading us towards a designer and thus God.

Though materialists may claim that man doesn't have an immortal soul or reason endowed by God, you will discover the truth as you continue your journey through the subjects of science and religion. Man is not isolated, as you will discover that a Creator has left clues for us to learn more about Him and His very nature.

Chapter 3 – Bibliography

1. Doctrine Commission of the General Synod of the Church of England, *We Believe in God,* London: Church Publishing House, 1987, Chap 9
2. Jacques Monod, *Chance and Necessity* (trans. A Wainhouse, Collins, London 1972), p167
3. Paul Davies, *The Fifth Miracle: The Search for the Origin of Life,* Penguin Books, New York, 1998, 5
4. Ibid, 15
5. Stephen Jay Gould, *Life's Granduer,* Jonathon Cape, London, 1996, 216
6. Charles Colson and Nancy Pearcey, *How Now Shall We Live* Tyndale House Publishers, Inc, Wheaton, Illinois, 1999, 73 [refers to Stanley L Miller, *From the Primitive Atmosphere to the Prebiotic Soup to the Pre-RNA World* (Washington D.C: National Aeronautics and Space Administration (NASA), 1996]
7. See I.L Cohen, *Darwin Was Wrong – A Study in Probabilities,* Greenvale, NY: New Research Publications, Inc., 1984 , 205: See also Emil Borel, *Elements of the Theory of Probability,* New Jersey: Prentice-Hall, 1965, 57.
8. Fred Hoyle, *The Intelligent Universe* (New York: Holt, Rinehart, and Winston, 1983), 11)
9. "Hoyle on Evolution," *Nature,* 294, No. 5837 (Nov. 12, 1981), 148
10. de Duve, C, *Vital dust: The origin and evolution of life on earth.* New York: Basic Books, 1995a, 8:
11. Ibid, 9
12. ed. William Dembski, *Mere Creation: Science, Faith and Intelligent Design* (with contributions by Michael Behe, David Berlinski, Philip Johnson, Hugh Ross, etc), InterVarsity Press, Downers Grove, IL, 1998, 395
13. Neil Broom, *How Blind is the Watchmaker?* Theism or atheism: should science decide?, Ashgate Publishing, Brookfield, Vermont, 1998, 33
14. H. Simon, 'What computers mean for man and society', *Science,* Vol. 195, 1977, 1186-1191
15. Jacque Monod, *Chance and Necessity,* Fontana, 1974, 160
16. W. Barrett, *Death of the Soul,* Oxford University Press 1987, 75
17. T. Dobzhansky, The Origins of Prebiological Systems and of Their Molecular Matrices. Ed. S W Fox, Academic Press, New York, 1965, 310
18. A pessimistic estimate of the time required for an eye to evolve'. *Proceedings of the Royal Society of London,* B 1994, Vol. 256, 151
19. Sylvia Baker, *Bone of Contention* (Evangelical Press, 1981), 17
20. Charles Darwin, *On The Origin of Species.* Facsimile of the first (1859) edition, Harvard University Press, 1966, 84
21. M. Polanyi and H Prosch, *Meaning,* Chicago University Press, 1975, 172

CHAPTER 4

DID HUMANS EVOLVE FROM APES?

Humans alone can reason (knowingly choose between right and wrong, good and evil); we are the only creatures to be in such awe of creation, and that seek to travel not only over the oceans, the skies, but also our galaxy; and only we are moral beings. While animals work by instinct. John Morton illustrates the instinctual actions of animals:

> A parent bird will feed nestlings only on sight of their open bright yellow mouths. A male robin is stimulated to fight at certain seasons by his antagonist's red breast. A mere tuft of red feathers on a wire will release fighting, but a perfect robin without the red will not. Instincts then are stereotyped and not well adaptable to unusual situations. The responses may look foolish and inept if the conditions change. A herring-gull shows a strong territorial attachment to the nest, but if the clutch of eggs be removed it will show no concern about these, even if they are visible a few feet in front of it...A hen looking for a lost chick reacts to its cheeping call only. Muffle this sound under a glass bowl and, though the chick's distress is perfectly visible, the mother will not notice it. [1]

These examples clearly show a built-in instinct. But man also has instinctual reactions, for example, a delicious dessert is left on the table, our instinct is to devour it. However we have the ability to control our instincts. Often before we act we think of the consequences the action will bring to ourselves or others; sadly some people have a conscience which has been watered down or almost ceases to exist. Though we want to devour the mouth watering dessert, we can reason whether to eat it. This could be due to it belonging to someone else – we were told not to eat it; it's been sitting there for days, or because we are on a diet. Therefore we may salivate with the desire to eat it, especially if it is fresh, but we can reason whether to eat it or not.

Animals do not have this reason, they will only hesitate if they are commanded not to, for example a dog may hesitate if commanded to stop, or you kick the cat – it will surely take notice. They do not think, "it's been out of the fridge for days so I won't eat it" – but they may not eat it if it smells really bad. They don't think, "that's my masters dinner" – have you ever had an animal (and I don't mean your roommate, lol) eat your dinner before you had the chance to enjoy it? That is pure instinct. And damn annoying!

The differences between humans and apes are broader than instinct, and include man's prolonged childhood, which results in an extended learning period as John Morton reveals:

> In a rhesus monkey, by comparison, infant dependency lasts for one year, as against eight in man. In ourselves sexual maturity is delayed to the thirteenth or fourteenth year as compared with the fourth in the monkey.[2]

The Soul

As you read in the previous chapter, Humans are the only creatures with an immortal soul. If we evolved from apes then not only did we evolve from instinct to reason, but an ape would have had to give birth to a human. The question we are faced with is: Could God still have caused this? The Catholic Church has stated the following on the subject:

> The materialistic view of evolution, according to which man as to his whole being, both body and soul, developed mechanically from the animal kingdom, is to be rejected. The soul of the first man was created immediately by God out of nothing. As regards the body, its immediate formation from inorganic stuff by God cannot be maintained with certainty. Fundamentally, the possibility exists that God breathed the spiritual soul into an organic stuff, that is, into an originally animal body. In fact, noteworthy, even if not absolutely decisive paleontological and biological grounds seem to point to a genetic connection between the human body and the highest forms of the animal kingdom.[3]

Pope Pius XII released an Encyclical[4], "Humani Generis" in 1950, in which he covers the question of the origin of the human body being open to free research by natural scientists and theologians:

> He insists on the careful weighing of the pros and cons of the grounds for its origination from an already living material, and warns the faithful against the assumption that discoveries up to

the present determine and prove the origin of the human body from an organic stuff, and points out that in this question, the need for the greatest reserve and care emerges from the sources of Revelation.[5]

Fundamentals of Catholic Dogma continues by showing the line of reasoning from another angle:

According to the immediate, literal sense, God created the body of the first man immediately out of inorganic material ("from the slime of the earth") and vivified it by breathing into it a spiritual soul. The idea that the spiritual soul was created in an animal body is foreign to the letter of Holy Writ [Sacred Scripture] and to the Fathers [The Early Leaders of the Catholic Church – up to about 800 AD]. The question of the descent of the human body from the animal kingdom first appeared under the influence of the modern theory of evolution. The Biblical text does not exclude this theory.[6]

Therefore the Church is stating that though the theory that the spiritual soul was created in an animal body isn't in Sacred Scripture, Sacred Scripture doesn't exclude it. Therefore it's possible that God created man by putting an imperishable soul into an animal (from the earth), such as an ape. Also it is possible that God created man and gave him a soul. We are warned that the evidence is not conclusive that we have evolved from "organic stuff", apes. I don't believe it is really a big deal how God did it, but it is very important to remember and believe that God created man and also gave him an imperishable soul.

If the woman was taken from Adam's rib, which is abhorrent to some women (lol!), then is it not possible that God used another one of his creation, which He loved (He saw all of it as being good), to form a human? You could say man is the perfection of the ape – superior yes, in intelligence and creativity, to name just a couple of attributes.

Yes though it is possible, I don't think God did it that way. As you will read in the *Unlocking the Chemistry of Life* chapter the difference between chimps and humans is DNA, millions of nucleotides long. However the real key here is, God was involved in the process, and gave man an eternal soul.

However we are faced with several questions in relation to the theory of humans evolving from the ape kingdom. These include: Did all apes give birth to humans? Or did several? If it was all apes then we are faced with the question that also relates to Natural Selection, why are there still apes in existence? Obviously humans are the enhanced variation, so the apes should have died out as humans were "naturally selected." If it was only one ape that gave birth to a human, then when its offspring mated he/she would have had to mate with an ape (bestiality), or the offspring would have had to mate with his/her brother/sister (incest). It is important to realize that if there was no Creator then bestiality or incest would not mean anything, as there would be no morality if we happened by mere random action.

What Was The Earliest Human Ancestor?

The question posed by mankind whether there was a human ancestor of another species, has now transformed to: Did humans have an ancestor of another species? In *Sudden Origins*, we are told about the search:

> In late 1993, a team of paleonthropologists, whose members came from Japan, Ethiopia, and the United States, discovered the oldest fossil remains of a potential human ancestor – almost 4.5 million years old. These fossils were even older than the famous specimen nicknamed Lucy, which had been referred to as the species *Australopithecus afarensis*. For more than fifteen years, this species had held the exalted position of being the earliest human ancestor. The new fossils were found along the Awash River in the northern part of Ethiopia.
>
> The specimens – the bits and pieces – that actually formed the basis of this new, most ancient of potential human ancestors were not very spectacular as far as fossil finds go. There were only fragments of arm bones and skulls and, literally, a handful of isolated teeth, representing different individuals of various ages.[7]

It is surprising that we are given illustrations of what are claimed to be our ancestors, when no one had a camera back in the days when the particular species roamed the earth. The question must be asked: Is it possible that these ancestors could be part of another species and not related to man?

When you study the articles of new fossil finds, often you'll read what one expert claims to be an ancestor of a human, and yet another expert argues that the specimen is not an ancestor but another species.

In addition it must also be noted that there have been distinguished and historical finds that have claimed that humans evolved from the ape kingdom, but they have been proved to be elaborate hoaxes. The evidence presented to us is often dubious at best. Let's take a look at a couple examples where we are told that our ancestor's remains have been recovered, but are not told what else has been discovered at the same site. This tends to be like fossil scrabble, except that this is no game. Java man, otherwise known as *Pithecanthropus erectus*, or Trinil man, was discovered in 1894 by Dr. Eugene Dubois. He discovered the following:

- Skull-cap of chimpanzee type with no forehead and beetling brows
- Two molar teeth
- A diseased thigh-bone of human type

A N Field in *The Evolution Hoax Exposed* states that:

> Whoever owned the Java thigh-bone very obviously stood upright, which no ape does. As for the two teeth, they are generally described as ape-like but unusual. Combine the fragments, and the result is a creature standing erect, with chimpanzee brows and no forehead, a human thigh, and with face, feet, body and arms left to be sketched in according to fancy.[8]

Field reveals that many more animal fossil remains were uncovered from the same site:

> In his Berlin address on his discoveries, Dr. Dubois stated that "associated with these bones" he had found fossil remains of Stegodon (an extinct elephant) and of a small deer, and "further away" remains of buffalo, antelope, ox, pig, rhinoceros, and hyena. Sir Arthur Keith in his *Antiquity of Man* says that altogether Dr. Dubois removed from this spot in the bed of the Bangawan River between 1891 and 1894 fossils of twenty-seven different kinds of mammals. A German expedition under Madame Selenka also spent two years from 1906 making much more extensive explorations in the same spot and unearthed an immense quantity of miscellaneous fossils, but got no traces of monkey-men.[9]

In 1938 Dr. Dubois himself recants his conviction of the fossil remains belonging to our ancestor. He "announced that after prolonged study of anthropological textbooks, of the *Pithecanthropus* bones, and "*of other material from the same provenance in his possession, for the most part not previously published,"* he was of the opinion that "we are here concerned with a gigantic gibbon."[10]

The second example we will focus on is Piltdown man, otherwise known as *Eoanthropus,* or *Dawn Man.* This fossil was discovered in 1913 near the bottom of a small gravel pit, four feet deep, about eight miles north of Lewes in England. Field tells us about the discovery:

> Piltdown man consists of nine small fragments of skull-bone, and rather less than half of a chimpanzee-like jaw bone. There was not much of him altogether, and he was discovered in sections over a considerable period of years by Mr. Charles Dawson, solicitor of Lewes, an amateur fossil-hunter.[11]

Piltdown Man was exposed as a hoax; it was "found to be a portion of a human cranium combined with a piece of the lower jaw of an orangutan. The bones were stained with chemicals to give the appearance of great age, and the orangutan teeth were filed to resemble human wear and match the human teeth in the upper jaw."[12] Remarkably, the fraud was not uncovered for 40 years, during which it had been trumped as proof of human evolution.

Isn't it interesting that minimal remains were uncovered at each of these sites, and that especially Java Man was a site which consisted of a 'supermarket' of fossil remains pertaining to many different creatures? When we take into consideration the discovery of Peking man in 1929, we realise how absurd the claims are when it is claimed that only seven thigh-bones of Peking man had been discovered. Field describes these fossil bones:

> Mostly incomplete shafts , and according to the descriptive matter they lacked the human characteristics of the Java thigh-bone... it may be noted that along with Peking man there were also found in the cave floor remains of over fifty types of mammals, as well as fossil frogs, snakes, turtles and birds.[13]

The remarkable evidence pertaining to these cases was presented by evolutionist, Professor H Woollard, professor of anatomy at University College, London. He submitted an article to a respected scientific quarterly review, *Science Progress* and it was published in the July edition, 1938. Professor Woollard says there can not be absolute certainty that the fossil remains of Java Man came from the same individual. In addition due to later fossil discoveries in relation to Piltdown Man he rejects the jaw as not being connected with the skull fragments. Field reveals the teeth of the article (pun intended, lol), that Professor Woollard:

> remarks that Java Man, Peking Man, and Neanderthal Man form a series rising in cranial capacity, and are regarded by palaeontologists as forming a sequence in the emergence of man from the lower animals. He adds: "The difficulty in feeling content with this view arises because in sharp contrast with these fossil types others have been discovered which are in no way different from modern man, and which are as old, or even older, than those just described...obviously people living contemporaneously cannot be ancestors to one another.[14]

So where are humans supposed to have evolved? From which part of the ape kingdom did they evolve? Jeffrey Schwartz in Sudden Origins, claims that Orangutans are "like humans":

> Humans, *Homo sapiens*, are the only living species of what we now know had once been a very species-diverse evolutionary group. The three living great apes – the orangutan of Southeast Asia and the two African apes, the chimpanzee and the gorilla – are also the only surviving species of their individual evolutionary group. Unfortunately we have not yet recovered any fossils that appear to be specifically related to either of the African apes, but we do have a good fossil record of numerous potential orangutan relatives. Orangutans are like humans. They are the sole surviving species of what had once been a very diverse evolutionary group of species. When you put the whole picture together, you get a very unreal situation in nature – unreal when compared with virtually any other group of related organisms. Even though the three living great apes are more closely related to us than to any of the other living primates, and one or two of these great apes are probably our closest living relatives, the actual, *closest* relatives of *H. sapiens*, and of each great ape, as well, are now extinct.[15]

The statement is hypothetical as it states humans were once a species-diverse evolutionary group. It has not been proven conclusively that we have actually evolved from apes.

The claim is our closest relative, with its specific species, is now extinct. The question remains: Why did Natural Selection allow the orangutan, the chimpanzee, and the gorilla to survive, while other ape-like animals have become extinct, if man is the better variation?

Fingerprints

Why do humans have the unique trait of each individual having his/her own unique fingerprints. There is no advantage for Natural Selection or evolution to produce this trait in us.

The science of fingerprinting "acknowledges three premises: fingerprints are formed well before birth, the patterns remain the same throughout life, and every human being is a unique creature."[16] It is the location of the forks, swirls, bifurcations, endings and other details that make it a mathematical impossibility to have identical fingerprints between individuals. It's remarkable that even identical twins from one split egg, have their own unique fingerprints. Harold Cummins and Charles Midlo in *Finger Prints, Palms and Soles* explain that the probability can be likened to throwing 25 coins and each one of them landing heads-up on a previously designated square on the square – a probability of 1/50 to the power of 25. You can try it if you want, lol.

Not only are fingerprints and DNA used for identification, but now the eye can be scanned to identify you. Therefore your eye and fingers are unique – you are unique.

Factors Causing Extinction

As with the theory of macro-evolution, an evolving species would have to contend with several factors which could determine their extinction; Such possible factors include predators, parasites, infectious diseases, competition for food, and the climate in a particular area.

Though it was possible, personally I do not believe that God made humans from apes. There are two many questions that remain unanswered. The questions will most probably not be answered, until heaven.

Summary

We humans are the only ones that can reason between right and wrong, good and evil. You don't see an animal such as a dog hesitate in a rescue situation in, seemingly having second thoughts about rescuing someone. The evidence that we evolved from the ape kingdom is at least flimsy, as there have been elaborate hoaxes exposed; and the biological jigsaw often happens as a result of more than one species discovered at a site. In the face of this, we humans are so unique; we have our own unique fingerprints (you will also read about genetic fingerprints in *Unlocking the Chemistry of Life* chapter), we can think abstractly, marvel at creation, explore not only our world, but our galaxy, and we are highly creative beings. We indeed have come a long way in relation to adapting to our environment than any other species.

Chapter 4 – Bibliography

1. John Morton, Man Science and God, Collins, Auckland, 1972, 30
2. Ibid, 33-34
3. Dr. Ludwig Ott, Fundamentals of Catholic Dogma, TAN Books and Publishers, Illinois, 1974, 94-95
4. An Encyclical is a papal document that covers such matters pertaining to the general welfare of the Church. Though in the past it was written mainly for the Bishops of the Church, the recent Popes have included the whole Church. Encyclicals often contain pronouncements on faith and morals that are *de facto* infallible because they express ordinary teaching of the Church. (See Pocket Catholic Dictionary)
5. Dr. Ludwig Ott, Fundamentals of Catholic Dogma, TAN Books and Publishers, Illinois, 1974, 94-95
6. Ibid, 95
7. Jeffrey Schwartz, *Sudden Origins*, Chichester, Wiley, New York, 1999, 14
8. ibid, 34
9. ibid
10. ibid, 36
11. ibid
12. Gerard Keane, *Creation Rediscovered*, Evolution and The Importance of The Origins Debate, Tan Publishers, 1999, 306
13. A N Field, The Evolution Hoax Exposed, 1971 first published as Why Colleges Bread Communists in 1941, 38
14. ibid, 39
15. Jeffrey Schwartz, *Sudden Origins*, Chichester, Wiley, New York, 1999, 18-19
17. Gerard Keane, *Creation Rediscovered*, Evolution and The Importance of The Origins Debate, Tan Publishers, 1999, 32

CHAPTER 5

INTELLIGENT DESIGN

Now that we have explored the theory of evolution and Natural Selection, we can delve into the theory of Intelligent Design.

Over the following chapters we will traverse the wonders of the universe through studying the sciences of paleontology (fossils), astronomy, genetics, biochemistry, philosophy and religion.

In setting the scene to this chapter a quote from Isaac Newton is perfect. He queries:

> Whence is it that nature does nothing vain; and whence arises all that order and beauty which we see in the world? How come the bodies of animals to be contrived with so much art, and for what ends were their several parts? Was the eye contrived without skill in optics? Does it not appear from phenomena that there is a being incorporeal, living, intelligent?[1]

Contingency, Complexity, Specification and Irreducible Complexity

The Intelligent Design theory is based on contingency, complexity, specification and irreducible complexity. *Science and Evidence for Design in the Universe*, a collection of essays, co-authored by William Dembski, Michael Behe and Stephen Meyer explains the first three concepts:

> Contingency, by which we mean that an event was one of several possibilities, ensures that the object is not the result of an automatic and hence intelligent process. Complexity ensures that the object is not so simple that it can readily be explained by chance. Finally, specification ensures that the object exhibits the type of pattern characteristic of intelligence.[2]

There are various methods that are used every day to identify if intelligence is at work. For example, police try to distinguish whether someone died of natural causes, or whether there was some other intelligence involved that congtributed to their death – such as poison being in the blood, or someone else's fingerprints being on the bottle of pills. In addition there may have been forced entry into the living quarters. The whole pattern may show some other intelligence was involved.

Specificity can lead us to deduce Intelligent Design. Steven Meyer states the relationship between specificity and information:

> As it turns out, the joint criteria of complexity and specification (or "specified complexity") are equivalent or "isomorphic" with the term "information content", as it is often used. Thus, Dembski's work suggests that "high information content" indicates the activity of an intelligent agent. [3]

Furthermore Meyer explains that specified complexity inherently relates to an intelligent mind, "Indeed experience affirms that specified complexity or information content not only routinely arises but always arises from the activity of intelligent minds. When a computer user traces the information on a screen back to its source, he invariably comes to a mind – a software engineer or programmer".[4]

Moreover, Meyer refers to anything that has high information content or a code must have been designed: "Our experientially based knowledge of information confirms that systems with large amounts of specified complexity or information content (especially codes and languages) always originate from an intelligent source – that is, from mental or personal agents."[5] Additionally Meyers tells us that the "letters in a section of meaningful text" and "the parts in a working engine represent a highly improbable and functionally specified configuration." This is going to be very important to remember, especially when you read that the chapter on *Unlocking the Chemistry of Life* reveals whether DNA contains an awesome information content which reflects an intelligent agent.

Mathematician and author William Dembski states that, "Events that are both highly complex and specified (that is, that match an independently given pattern) indicate design."[6] Though he does not equate coincidences with design, "It is simply not the case that unusual and striking coincidences automatically yield design."[7]

Irreducible complexity means that something is machine-like in its operation and complexity, and if it lacks one of its components, the system will cease to function. Then as we read below, it points to Intelligent Design and thus an Intelligent Designer. Michael Behe explains the concept of irreducible complexity in the book with several contributors, entitled *Mere Creation*:

> An irreducibly complex system is one that requires several closely matched parts in order to function and where removal of one of the components effectively causes the system to cease functioning.[8]

The classic example of an irreducibly complex system is a mousetrap. If you remove any of the parts such as the board, or the cheese, or spring, the system will cease to function. However the macro-evolutionist speculates that an irreducibly complex system has come together through an indirect route; maybe the mousetrap began as driftwood, was changed into an apple crate and then somehow ended up as a mousetrap without any intervention by man. Michael Behe elaborates on this concept of design:

> Design is evident when a number of separate, interacting components are ordered in such a way as to accomplish a function beyond the individual components. The greater the specificity of the interacting components required to produce the function, the greater is our confidence in the conclusion of design.[9]

Behe gives a wonderful analogy of the concept of irreducible complexity using the analogy of the Bugs Bunny show. In one episode the mischievous and loud-mouthed rooster, Foghorn Leghorn bugged the hell out of the young chicken he was babysitting. Behe recalls the young chick scribbling equations on a piece of paper (ahuh! He revealed he would be exacting his revenge in a precisely scientific manner). Then Foghorn was sauntering along, minding his own business (behaving himself for once), when he stumbled across a dollar bill laying on the ground. Impressed with his stroke of luck, he picks up the dollar note. But unknown to the poor sucker, he has set off a chain reaction of events; The dollar was tied by a string to a stick that was propped against a ball. So when the dollar note was pulled, the attached string pulled down the stick, and the ball began rolling away, cascading off a cliff, crashing onto the raised end of a seesaw which hurtled a rock through the air. Attached to the projectile was a piece of sandpaper which struck a match projecting out of the cliff, and lit the fuse to a cannon.

Foghorn was rather perplexed at the deafening boom of the canon, but was still unaware that this was a master plan in action. On the downward trajectory the cannonball flirted with the rim of a funnel, touched-down, and hypnotically rolled around the edge before falling through the funnel. Upon emerging out the other end the cannon ball triggered a lever that started a circular saw. The startled Foghorn observed the saw cutting through a rope holding a telephone pole in its place. But he was like a transfixed possum caught in the headlights of an approaching car. As it registered in his brain that he was in extreme danger, his demise appeared to happen in slow motion as he saw his life flashing before his eyes; the pole smashed the poor fellow mercilessly into the ground.[10]

As we reflect on the recent crop circles in Great Britain which were widely reported throughout the world as an unusual phenomenon, and possibly alien, we see a great example of deducing Intelligent Design. We can now categorically say that it was the Intelligent Design of humans. These huge geometric patterns which appeared in wheat fields caused rumors to run riot. But a couple of shrewd and innovative men admitted responsibility and to everyone's surprise their equipment consisted merely of a very large version of a stylus and string. The men worked tirelessly and cunningly at night – therefore it was difficult to be observed in action.

You have probably often heard that science studies natural causes, and if we try to introduce God into the situation then we are blamed for invoking supernatural causes, or alternatively we are called a religious nut. William Dembski in *Mere Creation* reveals this is the wrong contrast – the proper contrast is between undirected natural causes and intelligent causes:

> Intelligent causes can do things that undirected natural causes cannot. Undirected natural causes can throw scrabble pieces on a board but cannot arrange the pieces to form meaningful words or sentences. To obtain a meaningful arrangement requires an intelligent cause.[11]

Therefore intelligence is needed for complex, meaningful systems e.g. the mousetrap. I shall reveal more systems that are the results of intelligent causes in the chapters, *The Wonder of the Universe* and *Unlocking the Chemistry of Life*. In the former chapter you can discover whether there is an intelligent cause behind our universe; and in the latter chapter whether the human cell and DNA reveal specified complexity, information rich content, or specified complexity.

Cosmological Argument

Simultaneously an intelligent cause should lead us to a first cause, or an instigator of the cause. This First Cause Theory is also known as the Cosmological Argument as William Lane Craig, PhD in Philosophy and Theology, explains in *Mere Creation*:

> The cosmological argument aims to prove that there exists a First Cause or Sufficient Reason for the existence of the cosmos; the teleological argument aspires to show that there is an Intelligent Designer of the order in the cosmos. The teleological argument shows that the First Cause demonstrated by the cosmological argument is not some mindless ground of being but a personal, intelligent Mind; the cosmological argument shows that the Cosmic Designer is not a mere artificer or demiurge working on pre-existent materials but the Creator of all space-time reality.[12]

One version of the Cosmological Argument originated in the attempt of early Christian philosophers to rebut the Aristotelian doctrine of an eternal universe. One of its greatest proponents, the medieval Islamic theologian al-Ghazali, simply defined it as:[13]

1. Whatever begins to exist has a cause.
2. The universe begins to exist.
3. Therefore, the universe has a cause.

In defense of point number 2. Ghazali explained the impossibility of an infinite past. Because the universe has a cause then it is finite, and had to have come into being at some time in history.

William Lane Craig explains the relationship between time and this first cause:

> Given some relational theory of time, the Uncaused Cause must therefore also be timeless, at least sans the universe, since in the utter absence of events time would not exist…the timelessness of the First Cause sans the universe can be more directly inferred from the finitude of the past. Given that time had a beginning, the cause of the beginning of time must be timeless.

Finally, this Cause must also be spaceless, since it is both immaterial and timeless, and no spatial entity can be both immaterial and timeless...Hence the uncaused First Cause must transcend both time and space and be the cause of their origination.[14]

Wow! This is so breathtaking. Let's focus on Al-Ghazali's explanation: *Whatever begins to exist has a cause.* Therefore Lane is saying that the First Cause is beyond time, as the creation of the Universe began time as we know it, and beyond space; and this First Cause did not begin to exist. Therefore the First Cause always existed. The First Cause is a Necessary Being, and not a Contingency Being. This will be explained in more detail in *The Philosophy of God's Existence* chapter.

Paul Davies in *The Last Three Minutes* explains the concept of their being nothing before the Big Bang:

Remember that the expansion [of the universe] being graphed here is that of *space itself*, so zero volume doesn't mean merely that matter is squashed to an infinite density. It means that *space* is compressed to nothing. In other words, the Big Bang is the origin of space as well as of matter and energy. It is most important to realize that according to this picture there was no pre-existing void in which the Big Bang happened.[15]

Is it really so unbelievable that this First Cause could in fact be God? The Creator of the heavens and the earth. A loving Creator who loves you so much!

Problems of Evolution Without Design

Evolution is usually interpreted as excluding any hint of design in its processes. If there is any order it is due to *Natural Selection,* or nature controlling it. But what about 'negative' and 'positive' mutations? As a result we should have a large mixture of ghastly looking species. In fact what we see is an order in nature, a complexity that puzzles the evolutionist, who keeps scrambling to explain away his fears, and we also see a beauty in nature that is breathtaking!

Those who support Intelligent Design are usually believers in God, but not always. They are looking for signs of specified complexity, irreducible complexity and a reason for our very existence and to explain their doubts of macro-evolution. As a result they are led to Intelligent Design. Incidentally, they are not totally against evolution as they hold to the equilibrium that: yes it is likely that God created the universe; and that this design included micro-evolution – allowing species to adapt to different or changing environments. (Some who believe in Intelligent Design also believe that humans evolved from apes.) However many evolutionists do not hold to this equilibrium; they believe humans evolved by chance but don't recognize the possibility of a Creator. Their agenda is usually hidden but sometimes rears it's ugly head – the agenda to disprove the existence of God.

Creationists

Meanwhile another group called Creationists, are Christians that usually reject evolution outright – both micro-evolution and macro-evolution; and also support Intelligent Design. Creationists are divided into two categories: Young Earth and Old Earth Creationists. The former hold to a literal 24-hour, six days creation. But this is a little obscure since Sacred Scripture reveals that on the "third day" God created the two great lights – one to govern the day and the other the night. Though we know these are both the sun and moon, it is interesting to note that the moon merely reflects the sunlight. Therefore how could there have been a literal 24 hours when there was no sun to govern the day prior to the third day?

Moreover the Young Earth Creationists believe that Sacred Scripture is infallible. These often good-meaning Christians act as if Genesis is a scientific document. They portray a defense mechanism as they feel that all of Sacred Scripture is threatened by the theory of evolution. Therefore they seek to defend Genesis trying to justify every single word. It is understandable that they feel that the Word of God is threatened, and yet it is unfortunate that they seek to justify every single world, rather than focusing on the overall message. The complete message they could take is, for example, that God created the universe, and man was the pinnacle of God's creation.

> God said, "Let there be lights in the vault of heaven to divide day
> from night, and let them indicate festivals, days and years."
> Genesis 1:14-15

Moreover this group believes the earth to be only 6,000 years old. However, other Christians don't hold to the same literalness and are open to the universe taking millions, if not billions of years to be created by God.

The Old Earth Creationists don't hold to the literal views of the former group. They believe that the fossil record shows creation as accomplished in stages, each new appearance in the record pointing to a new moment of creation – e.g. bacteria first, followed by a long time gap and then invertebrates, then fish, followed by amphibians, and so on until the creation of man.

Both groups agree that the fossil record holds much more evidence for Creation than evolution, and that God was the Creator of the universe and life. Geisler and Brooks reveal a fascinating revelation from Sacred Scripture with the event of "God resting on the seventh day" still happening now. This is not so far fetched, with God being outside of time, then we could still be in the 7th day:

> Now God's work was all finished at the beginning of the world; as one text says, referring to the seventh day. *And God rested on the seventh day after all the work he had been doing.* And, again, the passage above says: *They will never reach my place of rest.* Hebrews 4:3-5

Furthermore, St. Augustine, in *Confessions* says that Genesis does not mention an evening and morning for the seventh day, as is mentioned on all the preceding days, this is a change of pattern from every preceding day, and so it appears to signify that the seventh day may not have ended. This is not to say that God has retired, but that he has ceased creating new species. God still creates but as Co-Creator as the Catholic Catechism beautifully describes:[16]

> Fecundity is a gift, an *end of marriage*, for conjugal love naturally tends to be fruitful. A child does not come from outside as something added on to the mutual love of the spouses, but springs from the heart of that mutual giving, as its fruit and fulfillment. So the Church, which "is on the side of life" teaches that "each and every marriage act must remain open to the transmission of life."
>
> Called to give life, spouses share in the creative power and fatherhood of God. "Married couples should regard it as their proper mission to transmit human life and to educate their children; they should realize

that they are thereby *cooperating with* the love of *God the Creator* and are, in a certain sense, its interpreters…

Asa Gray, a Congregationalist and author held to a broad concept of design and that overall nature could be understood:

> "Emergence is design by wholesale, the direction of the process by which mind and moral personality arose, which are not explainable by matter in random motion." Gray presented the idea of a Creator working through evolution to produce a gradually unfolding design; he also implied that God providentially supplies the variations in the right direction.[17]

With such an "impossibility" of life evolving by chance, as I have already covered, it points to a high probability of a Creator that has given purpose to creation. This Creator beats the odds, dealing thirteen spades in the game of life. This is the game in which the Creator can defy the odds, as He created the 'game' of life.

Paul Davies confesses that he is being drawn more and more to the realization that the universe exudes design, though he is very hesitant to attribute it to God:

> Through my scientific work I have come to believe more and more strongly that the physical universe is put together with an ingenuity so astonishing that I cannot accept it merely as a brute fact. There must, it seems to me, be a deeper level of explanation. Whether one wishes to call that deeper level "God" is a matter of taste and definition. Furthermore, I have come to the point of view that mind – i.e., conscious awareness of the world – is not a meaningless and incidental quirk of nature, but an absolutely fundamental facet of reality. [18]

Robert Jastow, an agnostic, testifies to the evidence that there are supernatural forces at work in relation to the origin of the universe and concludes his book, *God and the Astronomers,* with this wonderful analogy:

> For the scientist who has lived by his faith in the power of reason, the story ends like a bad dream. He has scaled the mountains of ignorance; he is about to conquer the highest peak; as he pulls himself over the final rock, he is greeted by a band of theologians who have been sitting there for centuries. [19]

Summary

I believe that if Young Earth Creationists studied evolution and saw that micro-evolution is in fact compatible with Christianity then they would not need to take such a literal stance. In addition I believe they could also reason that macro-evolution with God is not a threat. However, I support them when they defend the concept of a Creator. I believe there needs to be a unified voice within Christendom that says, the theory of evolution does not denounce a Creator; we accept the Earth being older than 6,000 years and don't mind if it's millions of years old; but we will not accept Neo-Darwinists (a wing of Darwinian followers) imposing their views that there is no Creator.

Nature abounds with examples of Intelligent Design, in which irreducible complexity, contingency, and specification are inherent within earthly nature and systems not only throughout our galaxy but the entire universe. If you were able to remove one component of these systems, or alter the initial laws, they would collapse. You have read in this chapter and will discover shortly that these are inherent in such examples as our galaxy, the universe, the human cell, and DNA. This points us to the instigator of this intelligent cause. Therefore, as you have read, whatever begins to exist has a cause, the Creator of our universe did not begin to exist, as there was no time in His realm. Therefore there is no cause to the existence of our Creator. Therefore God is eternal.

Chapter 5 – Bibliography

1. Isaac Newton, *Optics* New York: Dover, 1952 p344.
2. Michael J Behe, William A Dembski, Stephen C Meyer, *Science and Evidence for Design in the Universe*, Ignatius Press, San Francisco, 2000, 25-26
3. Ibid, 55
4. Ibid, 92
5. Ibid
6. Ibid, 29
7. Ibid, 36
8. ed. William Dembski, *Mere Creation*, Science, Faith and Intelligent Design, InterVarsity Press, Downers Grove, IL, 1998, 178
9. Ibid, 180
10. See Michael Behe, *Darwin's Black Box*, Simon & Schuster, New York, 1996, 74-76
11. ed. William Dembski, *Mere Creation*, Science, Faith and Intelligent Design, InterVarsity Press, Downers Grove, IL, 1998, 15
12. Ibid, 332-333

13. Ibid, 333
14. Ibid, 335
15. Paul Davies, Weidenfeld & Nicolson, *The Last Three Minutes*, London, 1994, 22
16. Catechism of the Catholic Church, Pocket Edition, St. Pauls, Australia 1995, [sections 2366 and 2367], 569
17. Ian G Barbour, Religion & Science, Historical and Contemporary Issues, SCM Press Ltd, 1998, 59
18. Paul Davies, *The Mind of God,* Penguin Books Ltd, London, 1992, 167
19. Robert Jastrow, *God and the Astronomers* (New York: Warner Books, 1978) 105-106

CHAPTER 6

UNLOCKING THE CHEMISTRY OF LIFE

Biochemistry explores the foundation stones of life – the study of the molecules that make up living tissues and cells. Simply, it's what makes you tick.

Now that we have explored the concept of Intelligent Design, let us delve into the basics of Biochemistry and discover whether there is evidence of Intelligent Design within this field. By the end of this chapter you will be able to see whether the evidence points towards the high possibility of a Creator, or whether there doesn't need to be one.

We've all heard about criminals being caught by the very evidence of DNA. Their DNA tends to be extracted from saliva (and other body fluids), human hair and even tiny flakes of skin. In fact, DNA is as unique as human fingerprints. No two people have been found to have the same DNA information.

But do we really know the intricacies and complexity of DNA? In this chapter I will explain the basics of the dynamic system of the cell, the complexity of DNA, and reveal stunning facts that you may never have pondered, or even speculated at.

Inside your body is a complex network like a sophisticated computer system that transmit, copy and delete information. The network within your body entrails complexities and processes that are phenomenally sophisticated, intriguing and wonderful.

The Cell

The first item we will check out is the cell, which can be found in all living organisms i.e. bacteria, plants, animals and humans. The cell is the foundation of your body. When gangs of cells hang out together they form tissues, and when tissues combine you get muscles, and then groups of muscles form organs.

The cell is so amazing! It is like a factory that churns out a product based on precise instructions, does repairs, gets rid of wastes, and has a security process or safety control in which it keeps the unwanted from entering, or kicks out the intruders.

The cell is a microscopic structure. Just imagine seeing only the whole PC Computer's outline under the viewing screen of a microscope. As you observe the computer running, it is obvious that there is functionality and that complex processes occur. Similarly the cell is like a PC Computer, as it is functional, intricate, complex and every part relies on another component or else the system fails (irreducible complexity).

Within your body are trillions of these cells; each one is incredibly complex and performs mind-boggling processes.

Michael Behe compares the factory-like aspect of the cells to your favourite Jeans factory (But be warned cowboy boots are not included):

> It continually manufactures new structures and gets rid of old material... new materials could be centrally made and then shipped to other compartments, like a large city making blue jeans and radios to be sent to small towns.[1]

The Cell's Structure

Now we jump straight into the make-up of the cell. Throughout this section take note of the irreducible complexity, the inherent factory like aspects; the diversity; and the dynamics of the whole cell. The following entail the cell:

1. The *cell membrane* is like the security process mentioned. It allows the cell to let in substances it needs, to expel substances it doesn't require, and to block or fight off intruders. So you could actually liken it to the bouncer at your favorite nightclub (but that doesn't mean it comes with squashed face and bulging biceps!).

2. The *endoplasmic reticulum* is a structure that spreads like tentacles throughout the cell, actually taking up a big chunk of space. It simulates a network of wires within a computer, stretching from the cell membrane, throughout the cell, and eventually to the cell nucleus; this intricate network means the *endoplasmic reticulum* allows the cell to transmit information, and proteins.

3. The *nucleus* of the cell is located at its center and can be likened to the heart of an organism, or a CPU (Central Processing Unit) of a computer. It is from the *nucleus* that information is processed and instructions for the cell to grow or replicate are issued.

    Michael Denton utilizes a factory-type analogy stating the nucleus of the cell is equivalent to the head office of a factory, containing the master blueprints. Therefore it is interesting to note that if you remove the nucleus of a cell, then the cell will actually die. Just imagine what it would be like if your cells did not contain a *nucleus*. Let's say that when you were being developed none of your cells contained a *nucleus*. Well, I am sorry to say, you would not have come into existence (what a morbid thought!). You would not have been able to even take one breath, because your organs, let alone your tissues and muscles, would not have even been able to develop.

4. *Lysosomes* are another type of structure within the cell. This structure is like your anti-virus software program on your computer. The lysosome stores the materials in which to fight off bacteria, and once the bacteria are detected the lysosome releases the material to wage war with the enemy.

5. You will also discover *mitochondria* within each cell. They produce energy that give the cells their get up and go, enabling them to function. So without *mitochondria*, your cells would not be able to replicate, perform the tasks of security or transmit the necessary information.

The systems within your cells are actually quite mind boggling. Linda Tagliaferro and Mark Bloom in *The Complete Idiot's Guide To Decoding Your Genes* reveal a startling fact about the division of the human cell:

> There are trillions of cells in the human body. About 100,000 of these cells divide every second, and each one has about 80,000 genes.[2]

Fighting Diseases

Behe explains the startling odds that an antibody has to face in order to bind to an invader of the body:

The odds of any given antibody binding to any given invader are pretty slim. To make sure that at least one kind of antibody is available for each attacker, we make billions to trillions of them. Usually, for any particular invader, it takes 100,000 to find one antibody that works.[3]

Furthermore Behe explains the process in which an antibody captures a hostage:

When an antibody on a B cell binds to a foreign molecule it triggers a complex mechanism to swallow the invader: in effect, the munitions factory takes a hostage. The antibody then breaks off a piece of membrane to make a little vesicle – a self-made taxicab. In this taxi, the hostage is brought into the B-cell factory. Inside the cell (still in the cab) the foreign protein is chopped up, and a piece of the foreign protein sticks to another protein.[4]

The dissected pieces of the invader are presented for the T cell's consideration. Behe says, "if the fit is just right, it causes the helper T cell to secrete a substance called interleukin. Interleukin is like a message from the Department of Defense to the munitions factory"[5]

Behe illustrates the staggering complexity within antibodies, "Furthermore, the sloppiness during recombination "jiggles" the segments (by crowding another amino acid into the chain, or leaving one out); this effect adds another factor of about 100 to the diversity. By mixing and matching DNA segments you get 250 x 10 x 6 x 100, which is about a million different combinations of heavy chain sequences."[6]

Once again we encounter complex factory-like processes that are vital for our very survival. The complexity of antibodies is fascinating, but it doesn't compare to what we'll explore next.

The Irreducible Complexity of the Cell

Each component of the cell is needed for it to survive. If you remove the cell membrane, endoplasmic reticulum, the nucleus, lysosomes, or mitochondria then the intricate processes integral to the cell's survival will collapse.

Therefore as you may recall, when any such irreducibly complex system collapses from removing one component of the system, then this system points to Intelligent Design and thus to an Intelligent Designer.

Isn't it incredible that scientists can not make a cell from scratch – they have to borrow from existing components. During the process of cloning they take the cell nucleus from one party and implant it into another cell. Once again they are left scratching their heads, and yet a Creator or Intelligent Designer had no trouble pre-programming the cell.

DNA

As of late, DNA features often in the news. Remarkably DNA Scientists are able to study the information encoded on your DNA. Utilizing technology and skills from the specialist field that has advanced in huge leaps and bounds in the last 10 years. The information they recover is unique to each individual – a genetic fingerprint. In this section we look at the astounding facts of DNA, which reveal the amazing complexity of machine-like workings of the cell, and in turn point significantly to an Intelligent Design, and thus an Intelligent Designer.

 DNA is an information bearing component of the cell, which is located in the cell's nucleus. The very fact that DNA is located there is vital; if the DNA was isolated from the nucleus, it would be impotent, and once again you would not be able to form past a blob as your cells could not form tissues, muscles or organs.

Information Bearing DNA

Michael Behe in *Mere Creation* explains the awesome power of information storage of DNA. Note, the reference Michael refers to is from 1989 when the home computer microprocessors were about 100 to 200 Mhz.

> The information storage density of DNA, thanks in part to nucleosome spooling, is several trillion times that of our most advanced computer chips.[7]

Linda Tagliaferro and Mark Bloom tell us that DNA in our cells is so complex that to unravel them would produce an astounding result:

If the total DNA in all the trillions of cells in one human being were laid out in a straight line, it would stretch to the sun and back more than a thousand times.[8]

Incredible! Imagine that you were stretched that far! Now that's weird! (It's OK, I won't get anyone to try to stretch you!)

Bill Gates, founder of Microsoft applauds the information rich ability of DNA, "DNA is like a computer program, but far, far more advanced than any software we've ever created."[9]

Each cell in your body has an amazing storage capacity for information, much the same as your hard drive on your computer. "A single cell of the human body contains as much information as the Encyclopedia Britannica (thirty volumes) multiplied three or four times."[10]

Wow! The cell's capacity to contain so much information is staggering. Each one of your cells is in fact a mini computer. Can we really believe this is pure chance? Can a complex system not only store such humungous amounts of information, but also transmit, transport, replicate information and defend the cell from intruders just by chance?

Sequence Complexity and Specificity of DNA

As I mentioned previously, it is the sequence or pattern that is paramount with DNA. Colson and Pearcey reveal the importance of this information and question its source:

> The chemicals in DNA are grouped into molecules (called nucleotides) that act like letters in a message, and they must be in a particular order if the message is going to be intelligible. If the letters are scrambled, the result is nonsense. So the crucial question comes down to whether the sequence of chemical "letters" arose by natural causes or whether it required an intelligent source.[11]

Similarly, Davies tells us that the precise sequence of atoms is crucial:[12]

> You can't have an arbitrary sequence because DNA is an instruction manual for making the organism. Change a few atoms and you threaten the structure of the organism. Change too many and you won't have an organism at all." Moreover he gives the fascinating odds against "producing just the proteins [of life] by pure chance are something like $10^{40,000}$ to one...the British astronomer Fred Hoyle likened the odds against the spontaneous

assembly of life as akin to a whirlwind sweeping through a junkyard and producing a fully functioning Boeing 747.

It is fundamental that DNA is joined in a specific sequence, which is also referred to as specificity. If your DNA were completely shuffled, like a deck of cards, then your DNA would be severely mutated.

Morton Jenkins in *Genetics: Teach Yourself Books,* explains the vital value of DNA:

> It is worth re-emphasizing the point that DNA truly is the key to life because:
> It controls the production of proteins.
> All enzymes are proteins
> All living processes are controlled by enzymes.[13]

Meyer in *Science and Evidence for Design in the Universe* explains the flaw of the argument that chemical attraction explains specified complexity:

> Of course, the sequences of bases in DNA do not just possess information as measured by classical Shannon information theory. These sequences store functionally specified information or specified complexity – that is, they are specified as well as complex. Clearly, however, a sequence cannot be both specified and complex if it is not at least complex. Therefore, the self-organizational forces of chemical necessity that produce redundant order and preclude complexity also preclude the generation of specified complexity (or information content) as well. Chemical affinities do not generate complex sequences. Thus, they cannot be invoked to explain the origin of specified complexity or information content.[14]

Duplication of Cells

When cells duplicate, it's analogous to identical twins, except the next cell is identical in every way including the DNA information. There are different reasons why cells duplicate, and they include: to fight diseases; to replace dead cells which die everyday (watch that sunburn – owwww!); and to enable hair, tissues, and organs to grow (just imagine your hair not growing back after you had it shaved off).

When a cell replicates itself, it is like the copy function in a Word Processor or Spreadsheet program (OK, so I'm a computer geek, lol);

you don't delete the information but copy it, leaving the original source intact (Thank God for the undo command!). The cell replicates through the *mitosis* process (the chromosomes are duplicated first). During this process the cell also copies its nucleus, and therefore the DNA residing there. In *The Complete Idiots Guide to Decoding your Genes,* the process is succinctly explained:

> When DNA is about to duplicate, it's literally as if it were splitting at the seams. The whole strand begins to unravel. The twisted ladder of the molecule untwists, and the two sides then pull apart like a molecular zipper. The rungs of the ladder – the As paired with Ts and the Cs paired with Gs – split in half, and what you have left is a long row of As, Cs, Ts, and Gs that are a missing a partner to make complete rungs on the ladder.[15]

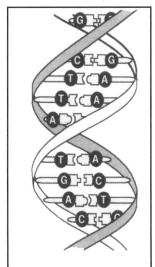

The DNA bases. Image courtesy of Neil Broom, *How Blind is the Watchmaker,* InterVarsity Press, 2001, 92

Well, I'm sure you're wondering what the heck As, Cs, Ts and Gs have to do with DNA. Just hang in there with me.

DNA has four bases A, C, T & G (A = adenine; T=thymine; G=guanine; and C=cytosine). These bases represent a four letter alphabet. In comparison Morse Code has two and for you fellow computer geeks, computers work with a binary code of two bases (0 and 1) – now that was actually a nerd test! So if you new that your already part of my club) However the bases are only mutually attracted to certain types, for example blondes (nah, just kidding, lol!). A will only pair up with T, and C will only pair up with G. Like two negative ions, if they aren't attracted then they won't do the tango.

So if the sequence in one part of the DNA chain is ATAGGC then the complimentary chain, or its partner, must be TATCCG.

If the above combination result of "TATCCG" looks confusing, just recall the previous facts of the mutual attractions, so that A is attracted to T, and G is attracted to C. Therefore from ATAGGC, the only possible attractions would give the outcome, TATCCG. We have a match!

Once the bases have paired up, the new strand twists into its twisted ladder shape, the double helix.

The fascinating fact concerning this pairing is that it's not random but predetermined, so that the DNA remains in sequence, and is not shuffled like a deck of cards (that would be catastrophic).

As mentioned above the DNA bases make up an alphabet. This alphabet helps scientists to distinguish the DNA code for particular amino acids and proteins. Tagliaferro and Bloom explain that:

> If you think of the As, Ts, Cs and Gs as letters, then combinations of these letters spell out words and sentences. These words and sentences are like the genes, which are sections of DNA that are all connected together on the DNA strand.[16]

Human Genes Vs Monkey Genes

In *The Complete Idiot's Guide to Decoding Your Genes* it is stated that we share 99.9% of the same order of DNA with other humans, but the 0.1% difference translates into several million unique spelling differences in each individual.[17]

Note the importance of that quote. Though the difference between a Chimp's genes and a human's may only be 2.0 or 3.0%, the length of the DNA is colossal – It's actually a chain of millions of nucleotides in length, and several million unique spelling differences. For sequence specificity, the nucleotides must be in a specified sequence, or else the system will collapse and the processes will cease to function and severe mutations would result. Try looking at the different combinations of the genes, and without a computer, lol, and you'll be tearing your hair out!

Therefore DNA is an information bearing code. This code is in fact highly integrated, complex, and specific. The specified complexity and irreducible complexity reveal design.

Proteins – 3D Structure

The smallest particle in existence is called an atom, for example, oxygen is an atom. And when two or more atoms combine you get a molecule, for example carbon and oxygen form carbon dioxide. (Yeah, good on ya! I know you learnt that at school. It's great that you can admit that you learnt something) Some molecules are proteins – an essential element as they represent the building blocks – the foundation stones of life – as they carry out most cell functions. They are amazingly complex as each protein molecule consists of a sequence, or long chain of amino acids; and most consist of several thousand atoms folded into an intricate 3-D structure.

There are at least 30,000 distinct types of proteins. Each is made of different combinations of the same 20 amino acids, which are arranged like letters to form chains of sequenced amino acids. In *Mere Creation* Stephen C Meyer, recounts that:

> The various chemical interactions between amino acids in any given chain will determine the three-dimensional shape or topography that the amino acid chain adopts. This shape in turn determines what function, if any, the amino acid chain can perform within the cell.[18]

A very large number and variety of different types and shapes of proteins exist, which are astonishingly versatile and undertake quite diverse and complex functions. However they can not assemble themselves, the nucleic acid, a component of DNA, is needed. Like the cell DNA can be regarded to have factory-like structures and processes, Denton says:

> While the proteins can be thought of as the working elements of a factory, the nucleic acid molecules can be thought of as playing the role of the library or memory bank containing all the information necessary for the construction of all the various machines (proteins) on the factory floor. More specifically, we can think of the nucleic acids as a series of blueprints, each one containing the specification for the construction of a particular protein in the cell.[19]

Now check out this fascinating statement by, Michael Behe. In *Mere Creation* he relates the low probability of a protein, forming by chance: He compares the possibility of attaining correct sequencing in a 100 amino acid length protein to the odds of a blindfolded man finding a single marked grain of sand hidden in the Sahara Desert not once, but a staggering 3 times! (Now you could try this if you really wanted to.)[20]

Proteins and Change

Scientist Cairns-Smith calculates the probability of chance pertaining to DNA:

> Blind chance… is very limited. Low-levels of cooperation he [blind chance] can produce exceedingly easily (the equivalent of letters

and small words), but he becomes very quickly incompetent as the amount of organization increases. Very soon indeed long waiting periods and massive material resources become irrelevant.[21]

Meyer illustrates the hurdles that must be overcome to construct even one small protein molecule of about one hundred amino acids in length:[22]

- The probability of building such a protein molecule in which all linkages of the amino acids involve peptide linkages is $(1/2)^{99}$, or roughly 1 chance in 10^{30}.
- In nature every amino acid has a distinct mirror image of itself, one left-handed version, or L-form, and one right-handed version, or D-form. Functioning proteins use only left-handed amino acids, yet the right-handed and left-handed versions occur in nature with roughly equal frequency. Therefore the probability of building our small protein molecule in which all bonds are peptide bonds and all amino acids are L-form would be roughly 1 chance in 10^{60}.
- Functioning proteins must link up in a specific sequence to be meaningful. On the assumption that all sites in a protein chain require one particular amino acid, the probability of obtaining our small protein would be $(1/20)^{100}$, or roughly 1 chance in 10^{130}.

So that's pretty small odds. How can we say that nature continually managed to achieve this without an Intelligent Designer behind it? But this pales in comparison to what Meyer reveals as the probability of the most basic form of life happening by chance:

Recent theoretical and experimental work on the so-called "minimal complexity" required to sustain the simplest possible living organism suggests a lower bound of some 250 to 400 genes and their corresponding proteins.[23] The nucleotide sequence space corresponding to such a system of proteins exceeds $4^{300,000}$. The improbability corresponding to this measure of molecular complexity again vastly exceeds 1 chance in 10^{150}, and thus the "probabilistic resources" of the entire universe.[24] Thus, when one considers the full complement of functional biomolecules required to maintain minimal cell function and vitality, one can see why chance-based theories of the origin of life have been abandoned.[25]

Michael Behe in *Darwin's Black Box* explains that amino acids combine into a, complex and specified chain which reveals its amazingly specified design:

> Proteins are made by chemically hooking together amino acids into a chain. A protein chain typically has anywhere from about fifty to about one thousand amino acid links. Each position in the chain is occupied by one of twenty different amino acids. In this they are like words, which can come in various lengths but are made up from a set of just 26 letters. As a matter of fact, biochemists often refer to each amino acid by a single-letter abbreviation-G for glycine, S for serine, H for histidine, and so forth.[26]

The above quote reveals the awesome specificity of proteins. Just dwell on the fact that a protein chain has between 50 and 1,000 amino acids, and that they must be in sequence, and then the blindfolded man analogy comes to life.

Meyer, in *Mere Creation* reveals the problems inherent in such a theory as one that relies on chance. Since the theory of Natural Selection means working with intention, and assumes there is no Creator, then once again the process is said to be run by chance. Meyer says:[27]

> Consider the probabilistic hurdles that must be overcome to construct even one short protein molecule of about 100 amino acids in length. (A typical protein consists of about 300 amino acids, and some are very much longer. Alberts et al. 1983, 118) First, all amino acids must form a chemical bond known as a peptide bond so as to join with other amino acids in the protein chain...Thus at any given site along a growing amino acid chain the probability of have a peptide bond is: $(1/2)$...The probability of building a chain of 100 amino acids in which all linkages involve peptide linkages is $(1/2)^{100}$ or roughly 1 chance in 10^{30}

Though the probability of chance is very remote, it is possible – just ask those who won the state lottery. But the probability of chance to continue to produce all the different amino acids, and for the cell to operate with DNA too, and thus to support life, is virtually impossible. In conjunction it is important to note that those who promote Intelligent Design use this data as corroborative evidence, and taking specified complexity, irreducible complexity and obvious design, contingency and the mathematical probabilities involved then there is such compelling evidence for Intelligent Design.

Jacques Monod, Nobel laureate and molecular biologist, revealed the importance of DNA and thus revealing Intelligent Design when he said, "you absolutely needed a code".[28] Therefore to have a code you must have a programmer.

Protein Folding

Integral to the working of a protein is the precise 3-D shape that it folds into. In order for it to bind to another protein, the shape is paramount so that they will fit each other with hand-in-glove or a jigsaw puzzle fit. Additionally for the two to combine there must be a positively charged amino acid on one protein, and a negatively charged amino acid on its partner. This complex folding into a 3-D shape would be like seeing a paper folded in origami. Researching proteins and the sequencing of amino acids in conjunction with the amazing complexity and specificity makes us question what powerful mind and design is behind it.

Behe, in *Mere Creation,* explains the complex and scrupulous shaping of the protein molecules:

> For a functioning protein, it's 3D shape gives it a hand-in-glove fit with other molecules in the cell, enabling it to catalyze specific chemical reactions or to build specific structures within the cell. The proteins histone 3 and 4, for example, fold into very well-defined 3D shapes with a precise distribution of positive charges around their exteriors. This shape and charge distribution enable them to form part of the spool-like nucleosomes that allow DNA to coil efficiently around itself and store information.[29]

This hand-in-glove compatibility, is like the kids game or educational tool where the object is to put specifically shaped toys into particular holes, but only some will actually match its corresponding hole. Alternatively, reflect on the fact that wrenches will only work with certain sized nuts. Without this complex compatibility the protein molecules would not be able to function adequately; there would be no opportunity for the proteins to connect properly with the molecules, and so your tissues, muscles or organs would not form at all. Therefore you would not exist.

Proteins are unique. Here is yet another genetic fingerprint as we recall that your DNA is also one of a kind. Morton Jenkins reveals the uniqueness of the proteins within an organism:

As with fingerprints, no two individuals have identical sets of proteins, since their synthesis is under the control of unique combinations of genes.[30]

Blood Clotting

Another complex function of the protein molecule is blood clotting. Michael Behe explores this amazing process in-depth in *Darwin's Black Box*. The blood clotting system needs many interdependent protein parts in order to function – if any of the parts are lacking, then the process collapses, and the blood does not clot at the right time or at the right place, or even at all. Hence this reveals irreducible complexity.

Behe provides an analogy of blood clotting being like the creation of patchwork. I would like to use the image of a finely spun web, which traps the fly or unsuspecting insect. The protein meshwork entraps blood cells that form the clot. Moreover there is one protein, *fibrinogen* which makes the fibres for the patchwork or web, while almost all the others control the timing and placement of the blood clot. Therefore if the clot is in the wrong place blood could be cut off from a major organ, such as the heart, and you would die. Behe explains the significance of the location for a blood clot:

> If blood congeals at the wrong time or place, though, then the clot may block circulation as it does in heart attacks and strokes. Furthermore, a clot has to stop bleeding all along the length of the cut, sealing it completely. Yet blood clotting must be confined to the cut or the entire blood system of the animal might solidify, killing it. Consequently, the clotting of blood must be tightly controlled so that the clot forms only when and where it is required. [31]

Just imagine what would happen if you cut yourself and the blood actually ceased to clot. Yes, you would bleed to death, and then would be 6 feet underground.

Fibrinogen is one of the integral proteins that exist in blood plasma. Behe explains the mechanics of this blood clotting:

> Then another protein, called thrombin, slices off several small pieces from two of the three pairs of protein chains in fibrinogen. The trimmed protein-now called fibrin2-has sticky patches exposed on its surface that had been covered by the pieces that were cut off. The sticky patches are precisely complementary to portions of

other fibrin molecules. The complementary shapes allow large numbers of fibrins to aggregate with each other…neither do fibrins stick randomly: Because of the shape of the fibrin molecule, long threads form, cross over each other, and (much as a fisherman's net traps fish) make a pretty protein meshwork that entraps blood cells. This is the initial clot (Figure 4-2). The meshwork covers a large area with a minimum of protein; if it simply formed a lump, much more protein would be required to clog up an area.[32]

So how does the system of Blood Clotting wind up without the entire animal solidifying? Behe explains, that "a plasma protein called antithrombin binds to the active (but not the inactive) forms of most clotting proteins and inactivates them." A second way that the clot is localized is "through the action of protein C. After activation by thrombin, protein C destroys accelerin and activated antihemophilic factor."[33]

We can thus detect Intelligent Design – the proteins are activated, deactivated and the blood clot is localized so as not to cause damage elsewhere. If the wrong protein was activated or deactivated, the consequences would be catastrophic. Furthermore Behe says:

> the blood-clotting system fits the definition of irreducible complexity. That is, it is a single system composed of several interacting parts that contribute to the basic function, and where the removal of any one of the parts causes the system effectively to cease functioning. The function of the blood clotting system is to form a solid barrier at the right time and place that is able to stop blood flow out of an injured vessel. The components of the system (beyond the fork in the pathway) are fibrinogen, prothrombin, Stuart Factor, and proaccelerin…in the absence of anyone of the components, blood does not clot, and the system fails.[34]

Brillouin using a great analogy illustrates the fascinating fact that a living organism can heal its own wound:

> The living organism heals its own wounds, cures its sicknesses, and may rebuild large portions of its structure when they have been destroyed by some accident. This is the most striking and unexpected behavior. Think of your own car, the day you had a flat tire, and imagine having simply to wait and smoke a cigar while the hole patched itself and the tire pumped itself to the proper pressure, and you could go on. This sounds incredible. It is, however, the way

nature works when you "chip off" while shaving in the morning. There is no inert matter possessing a similar property of repair.[35]

Shaky Chemical Evolution Theory

Behe reveals that with the discovery of complexity and specificity serious difficulties have emerged for the chemical evolution theory. He refers to the difficulties facing macro-evolution in relation to biochemistry, that is, amino acids, cells, DNA, and proteins all evolving without any help from an Intelligent Designer. Behe explains that:

> Amino acids alone do not make proteins, any more than letters alone make words, sentences or poetry. In both cases the sequencing of the constituent parts determines the function or lack of function of the whole. In the case of human languages the sequencing of letters and words is obviously performed by intelligent human agents. In the cell the sequencing of amino acids is directed by the information – the set of biochemical instructions – encoded on the DNA molecule.[36]

Behe compares the sequencing of letters and human words by human minds with the sequencing of amino acids. Exploring the processes behind amino acids and the amazing complexity and specificity inherent in the processes makes us ponder what powerful mind is involved. The complexity of the imbedded information, is critical in it's sequence, size and an integral part of the cell – it would cause the system to collapse if it were inhibited, or removed.

First Principal Concerning Microbiology

Meyer, explains that every naturalistic model of the origin of information has failed, and that the First Cause principal beckons:

> Thus mind or intelligence or what philosophers call "agent causation" now stands as the only cause known to be capable of creating an information-rich system, including the coding regions of DNA, functional proteins and the cell as a whole.[37]

Mascot of Intelligent Design – Flagellum

One tiny part of nature, which can only be viewed under a microscope reveals fascinating design. It has become somewhat of a mascot to the Intelligent Design movement. Behe unveils enticing design inherent within these bacteria:

> The flagellum is quite literally an outboard motor that some bacteria use to swim. It is a rotary device that, like a motorboat, turns a propeller to push against the liquid, moving the bacterium forward in the process. It consists of a number of parts, including a long tail that acts as a propeller, the hook region, which attaches the propeller to the drive shaft, the motor, which uses a flow of acid from the outside of the bacterium to the inside to power the turning, a stator, which keeps the structure stationary in the plane of the membrane while the propeller turns, and bushing material to allow the drive shaft to poke up through the bacterial membrane. In the absence of the hook, or the motor, or the propeller, or the drive shaft, or most of the forty different types of proteins that genetic studies have shown to be necessary for the activity or construction of the flagellum, one does not get a flagellum that spins half as fast as it used to, or a quarter as fast. Either the flagellum does not work, or it does not even get constructed in the cell. Like a mousetrap, the flagellum is irreducibly complex. And again like the mousetrap, its evolutionary development by "numerous, successive, slight modifications" is quite difficult to envision. In fact, if one examines the scientific literature , one quickly sees that no one has ever proposed a serious candidate to meet Darwin's criterion.[38]

Some of the flagellum motors run an at a phenomenal speed of 100,000 rpm. Moreover, it only takes a quarter turn to stop, shift direction, and turn 100,000 rpm in the other direction! The complexity, specification and irreducible complexity inherent is obvious. This even hints at the combustible engine being an invention that humanity was meant to discover to enjoy the splendor of land, the oceans, the skies and the universe. Moreover, it's as if we mechanically cloned from nature, without even knowing it.

Some of the problems of giving a purely naturalistic explanation – and excluding God – of the origin of this motor-like mechanism are given by Behe:[39]

- A cilium contains over two hundred different kinds of proteins
- The bacterial flagellum, in addition to the proteins already discussed, requires about forty other proteins for function.
- The exact roles of most of the proteins are not known, but they include signals to turn the motor on and off

• As the number of required parts increases, the difficulty of gradually putting the system together skyrockets

Moreover Behe gives this crushing knock out punch to the macro-evolutionists when he says, "no scientist has *ever* published a model for the gradual evolution of this extraordinary molecular machine."[40] Behe speaks highly and sincerely of his evolution-minded colleagues. Though his challenge is genuine, I can't foresee anyone taking it up. If someone does try such a mind-boggling feat, I'll let you know.

The Human Brain

You thought that computers were amazing creations, but in fact in comparison our brains are truly sensational! You are able to think, and thus communicate as a result of mere electrical or chemical impulses. This is how the information is passed from your brain to your muscles, for example, instructing your fingers to move. But what is truly scintillating is the amount of neurons, also known as nerve cells, within your brain; there are estimated to be 100 billion of them These neurons actually communicate and transfer information to each other. Moreover it is estimated that there are over 1,000,000,000,000,000 connections in the brain (this is more than the estimate of stars in the universe). Therefore remove these neurons or connections and the brain will cease to function; once again irreducible complexity is revealed.

For further information about the brain check out these websites: http://serendip.brynmawr.edu/bb/neuro/neuro98/202s98-paper1/ O'Hare.html; http://sunsite.kth.se/art/96/stoc/index.html; http://sunsite.kth.se/art/96/stoc/physionomy.html

Unknown Frontier

Neil Broom, a Biochemist from Auckland University, tells us that the lay reader should not be left with the impression that the process concerning the cell and proteins is completely understood:

In fact our current knowledge of protein manufacture reveals layer upon layer of ever increasing complexity and mystery at the cellular level. For example, we really do not know how the ribosome actually functions, nor how it could have arisen in the first place, bearing in mind that it is itself constructed from specific RNA and protein molecules. Then there is the question of protein shape which can be exceedingly complex. The ability of proteins to function as enzymes (think of an enzyme as a molecular version of a mechanical assembling or dismantling tool) is critically dependent on their being able to fold successfully into a precise 3-D configuration as the raw amino acid chain emerges from the ribosome.[41]

Morton Jenkins reveals that though scientists are still trying to explore, duplicate or manipulate the workings of the body, they can not match from scratch, the intricacies of the human body:

> Our bodies are chemical factories that carry out thousands of chemical reactions with a precision, speed and efficiency that could never be rivaled by chemists in laboratories. The laboratory chemist will take months to synthesize relatively simple organic compounds. By contrast, a single bacterium can synthesize all the chemicals that it needs to make a copy of itself in twenty minutes! [42]

Wow! Astounding! Scientists rack their brains, stressing out for months, and yet phenomenally, in 20 minutes a single bacterium does it naturally. This inherent pre-programming baffles scientists, and yet it is evidence of Intelligent Design.

Conclusion

We sum up with a quote from Myers regarding the origin of information:

> During the last forty years, every naturalistic model proposed has failed precisely to explain the origin of the specified genetic information required to build the living cell. Thus, mind or intelligence, or what philosophers call "agent causation", now stands as the only cause known to be capable of generating large amounts of specified complexity or information content (from nonbiological precursors).[43]

It's so easy to isolate components of the cell and forget the overall complexity and specificity of the interacting components of the system as they work elaborately, relying upon each other. Neil Broom states that it is important to remember the big picture within the dynamics of a cell:

> ...each individual step in the entire molecular process, whether it be making of a particular protein, or the replication of the gene itself, is not a result of the gene's isolated activity, but arises from the functioning of an entire living cell or organism.[26]

In this chapter we have encountered the components of the cell which reveal such intricate systems that reveal irreducible complexity and specificity, and point to Intelligent Design. From the awe-inspiring processes of the cell and DNA to Blood Clotting, we can only but conclude that God has designed these processes in order that we could survive and thrive.

Do you really believe that by pure chance, i.e. via macro-evolution and without a Creator, that complex amino acids, and proteins evolved in such a way as to be able to have blood clots, and also that they were able to protect the species so precisely without letting the rest of the organism's blood clot? Just think what would happen to an animal if it didn't have this complex act of order and purpose of the proteins. That's right, it would die.

This whole Irreducible Complexity within Biochemistry leads one to query whether Darwin would have held to macro evolution if he had access to the knowledge that we have today of the cell and DNA. I think this tremendous complexity, wonderful order and inherent evidence for Intelligent Design would have led him to seriously doubt macro evolution, while retaining the theory of micro-evolution.

The make-up of your physicality is via your DNA. What you look like – muscles, organs, facial features – is determined by your DNA. And yet your DNA is a staggeringly, mouth-watering complexity. Your DNA bears an information rich system which reveals Intelligent Design. If someone played scrabble with the nucleotides on your DNA as you were forming in your mother's womb, not only would they have torn out their hair trying to put them back into sequence, but you would not have formed past a blob.

DNA reveals an irreducibly complex and specified system. The incredible amount of information that can be stored in DNA flies in the face of macro evolution. But we are also faced with the amino acids, proteins and the entire cell that is needed for DNA, and DNA for these components. Remove the DNA from the cell, and the cell will not function; no cells will replicate and therefore no tissues, muscles or organs will form. This irreducible complexity once again points to an amazing pre-programmed system, and thus points to Intelligent Design.

Therefore the cell, with its factory-like processes, complexity and irreducible complexity reveals Intelligent Design and thus an intelligent mind behind it; and thus a Creator. If you remove any of the components, whether of the cell, or reconfigure the amino acids, then the entire system crashes. When we explore DNA we encounter a labyrinth-type complexity – one which is information rich.

　DNA reveals Intelligent Design with the information rich bearing DNA which shows mindlike originality and purpose. Therefore DNA reveals that you have a Creator.

Chapter 6 – Bibliography

1. Michael Behe, *Darwin's Black Box*, The Free Press, New York, 1996, 103
2. Linda Tagliaferro and Mark V Bloom, *The Complete Idiot's Guide To Decoding Your Genes,* New York Alpha Books, 1999, 74
3. Michael Behe, *Darwin's Black Box*, Simon & Schuster, New York, 1996, 121
4. Ibid, 122-123
5. Ibid, 123
6. Ibid, 129
7. ed. William Dembski, *Mere Creation*, Science, Faith and Intelligent Design, InterVarsity Press, Downers Grove, IL, 1998, 120
8. Linda Tagliaferro and Mark V Bloom, *The Complete Idiot's Guide To Decoding Your Genes,* New York, Alpha Books, 1999, 69
9. B Gates, *The Road Ahead,* Boulder, Col.: Blue Penguin, 1996, 228.
10. Colson & Pearcey, *Now How Shall We Live*, Illinois, Tyndale House Publishers Inc, 1999, 75
11. Ibid
12. Paul Davies, *The Fifth Miracle: The Search for the Origin of Life,* Penguin Books, New York, 1998, 64-65
13. Morton Jenkins, Genetics: Teach Yourself Books, Hodder Headline Plc, Illinois, 1998, 111
14. Michael J Behe, William A Dembski, Stephen C Meyer, *Science and Evidence for Design in the Universe*, Ignatius Press, San Francisco, 2000, 90
15. Linda Tagliaferro and Mark V Bloom, *The Complete Idiot's Guide To Decoding Your Genes,* New York, Alpha Books, 1999,
16. Ibid, 73
17. Ibid
18. ed. William Dembski, *Mere Creation*, Science, Faith and Intelligent Design, InterVarsity Press, Downers Grove, IL, 1998, 120
19. Michael Denton, *A Theory In Crisis,* Checy Chase: Adler & Adler Publishers Inc. 1986, 239
20. Quoted from *Mere Creation:* which cited Behe 1994. Experimental support for regarding functional classes of proteins to be highly isolated from each other. In *Darwinism: Science or Philosophy,* ed. J Buell and G Hearn, p68-69.
21. AG Cairns–Smith, *The Life Puzzle* (Edinburgh: Oliver and Boyd, 1971) 91-96
22. Michael J Behe, William A Dembski, Stephen C Meyer, *Science and Evidence for Design in the Universe*, Ignatius Press, San Francisco, 2000, 74-75
23. E. Pennisi, "Seeking Life's Bare Genetic Necessities", *Science* 272 (1996): 1098-99; A. Mushegian and E. Koonin, "A Minimal Gene Set for Cellular Life Derived by Comparison of Complete Bacterial Genomes", *Proceedings of the National Academy of Sciences*, USA 93 (1996): 10268-73; C. Bult et al.,

"Complete Genome Sequence of the Methanogenic Archaeon, *Methanococcus Jannaschi*", *Science* 273 (1996): 1058-72

24. W Dembski, *The Design Inference: Eliminating Chance through Small Probabilities,* Cambridge: Cambridge University Press, 1998), 67-91, 175-223.
25. Michael J Behe, William A Dembski, Stephen C Meyer, *Science and Evidence for Design in the Universe*, Ignatius Press, San Francisco, 2000, 76
26. Michael Behe, *Darwin's Black Box*, The Free Press, New York, 1996, 52
27. ed. William Dembski, *Mere Creation*, Science, Faith and Intelligent Design, InterVarsity Press, Downers Grove, IL, 1998, 125
28. H Judson, *Eighth Day of Creation*, New York: Simon and Schuster, 1979, 611
29. ed. William Dembski, *Mere Creation*, Science, Faith and Intelligent Design, InterVarsity Press, Downers Grove, IL, 1998, 120?
30. Morton Jenkins, Genetics: Teach Yourself Books, Hodder Headline Plc, Illinois, 1998, 93
31. Michael Behe, *Darwin's Black Box*, The Free Press, New York, 1996, 79
32. Ibid, 80
33. Michael J Behe, William A Dembski, Stephen C Meyer, *Science and Evidence for Design in the Universe*, Ignatius Press, San Francisco, 2000, 88
34. Michael Behe, *Darwin's Black Box*, The Free Press, New York, 1996, 86
35. L. Brillouin, 'Life, Thermodynamics, and Cybernetics', in *Modern Systems Research for the Behavioural Scientist.* Ed. W Buckley, Aldine, Chicago, 1968, 154
36. ed. William Dembski, *Mere Creation*, Science, Faith and Intelligent Design, InterVarsity Press, Downers Grove, IL, 1998, 121
37. Ibid, 124-125
38. Michael J Behe, William A Dembski, Stephen C Meyer, *Science and Evidence for Design in the Universe*, Ignatius Press, San Francisco, 2000, 134-5
39. Michael Behe, *Darwin's Black Box*, Simon & Schuster, New York, 1996, 72-73
40. Ibid, 72
41. Neil Broom, *How Blind is the Watchmaker?* Theism or atheism: should science decide?, Ashgate Publishing, Brookfield, Vermont, 1998, 116
42. Morton Jenkins, Genetics: Teach Yourself Books, Hodder Headline Plc, Illinois, 1998, 93
43. Michael J Behe, William A Dembski, Stephen C Meyer, *Science and Evidence for Design in the Universe*, Ignatius Press, San Francisco, 2000, 92-3
44. Neil Broom, *How Blind is the Watchmaker?* Theism or atheism: should science decide?, Ashgate Publishing, Brookfield, Vermont, 1998, 87-88

For further reading re Michael Behe, inlucindg his on-line articles see: www.arn.org/behe/behehome.htm

CHAPTER 7

CLUTCHING AT STRAWS

This chapter is aptly named, "Clutching At Straws" as some of the theories that macro-evolutionists cleave to, are so far fetched and beyond reason, that they are trying to sustain their theory by clutching at straws. If the macro-evolution theory had not been preserved by public opinion, the media, and especially enthusiastic 'disciples' then it would have been thrown into the garbage can a long time ago.

One of the theories of evolution is that all animals have a common ancestor – macro-evolution. Evolutionists believe that birds evolved from winged dinosaurs – the earliest known bird was the Archaeopteryx.[1]

Evolution of Birds

In the case of the evolution of birds, we come up against a brick wall, due to the complexity and the diversity of these creatures. An example of this complexity is with the bird's breathing apparatus of the birds. Michael Denton reveals that:

> In all other vertebrates the air is drawn into the lungs through a system of branching tubes which finally terminate in tiny air sacs, or alveoli, so that during respiration the air is moved in and out through the same passage.
>
> In the case of birds, however, the major bronchi break down into tiny tubes which permeate the lung tissue. These so-called parabronchi eventually join up together again, forming a true circulatory system so that air flows in one direction through the lungs.
>
> This unidirectional flow of air is maintained during both inspiration and expiration by a complex system of interconnected air sacs in the bird's body which expand and contract in such a way so as to ensure a continuous delivery of air through the parabronchi. The existence of this air sac system in turn has necessitated a highly specialised and unique division of the body cavity of the bird into several compressible compartments. Although air sacs occur in certain reptilian groups, the structure of the lung in birds and the overall functioning of respiratory system is quite unique.[2]

If you managed to grasp all that, then I am very impressed! Indeed, the systems described are so complex and unique that no lung in any other vertebrate species is known that in any way approaches the avian system, hence it's uniqueness. Therefore we are faced with the question; How could such a unique respiratory system happen by chance? The maintenance of the respiratory function is absolutely vital to the life of a species; the slightest malfunction can lead to death within minutes. So imagine that purely by chance the bird's ancestor had a different respiratory system and by Darwin's theory, gradually with intermediate steps, along with time, the respiratory system evolves. If this was so, then the poor creature would most probably have been doomed to death. The more we explore in-depth the biology of creatures, the more we realize how absurd macro-evolution is.

Miller's Experiment

Some evolutionists postulate that life came to exist from a pre-biotic cocktail, based on an American chemist, Stanley Miller who worked in collaboration with his research supervisor, Harold Urey.

Neil Broom explains Miller's experiment:

> It consisted of heating a mixture of the common gases methane, hydrogen and ammonia together with water in a laboratory flask. This flask contained a pair of tungsten electrodes providing a spark discharge to simulate the probable action of lightning. After several days Miller observed the formation of a discoloured residue which, on analysis, was found to contain several types of amino acids - fundamental building blocks of proteins, the primary substance of living systems.[3]

TIME Magazine praised Miller and Urey saying, "If their apparatus had been as big as the ocean, and if it had worked for a million years instead of one week, it might have created something like the first living molecule."[4]

In *When Skeptics Ask* Norman Geisler and Ron Brooks refute this hypothesis by resorting to the law of entropy:

> Also, the energy needed from the sun and cosmic radiation are damaging to the very substances produced. Under the conditions required for life to have arisen spontaneously, it is more likely that the elements would be destroyed faster than they could be produced.[5]

Entropy basically means, "a measure of the amount of energy unavailable for work in a thermodynamic system"[6] The first law of thermodynamics is that "no matter or energy is either being created or completely destroyed."[7] The second law says that "every system left to its own devices always tends to move from order to disorder, its energy tending to be transformed into lower levels of availability, finally reaching a state of complete randomness and unavailability for further work."[8]

Sean O'Reilly utilizing entropy refutes the macro-evolutionist's hypothesis that an infinite universe is the answer:

> The first law speaks to the finite nature of the universe of matter. If we listen to the implications of its finite nature and all that science has to tell us about the high degree of order which it has exhibited, we should conclude that its existence and the evident conservation of its finite mass-energy are not likely to be self-explanatory, or to be explained by science, since it too is limited, is finite. The second law contains a direction, an "arrow of time", aimed at the ultimate heat death of the Universe, with its total mass-energy unchanged in quantity, but totally unavailable for further work. It also clearly implies that the Universe cannot be infinitely old since if it were, it would be already dead.[9]

O'Reilly then deals what I term the killer blow to macro-evolution theory:

> The second law also directly contradicts evolutionary theory; if language has any meaning, both cannot be true. Evolution theory requires a universal principle of upward change; the entropy law is a universal principle of downward change. The latter has been proved to apply in all systems tested so far; the former cannot even be tested scientifically.[10]

Therefore as we learnt at the beginning of this book, Natural Selection only works on positive, or upward changes. However, entropy works via downward change, and so without the hand of God, our universe will eventually die out. Don't worry it won't happen during your, or your children's lifetime, as the sun still has an estimated life left of 5 billion years.

Pre-biotic Cocktail Experimental Flaws

Remarkably, Miller himself now denounces his famous study; he still tries to prove macro-evolution though.

Broom illustrates the flaws of Miller's experiment, in relation to DNA:

> Another fundamental objection to the 'protein first' hypothesis is
> that it is difficult to see how a protein might actually replicate itself.
> Recall that DNA consists of two intimately related strands of nucleic
> acid chains in which there is a complementary matching between
> the bases on these two strands...By contrast, in the complex folded
> 3-dimensional shape of most protein enzymes there is no local amino
> acid-to-amino acid pairing or complementarity. There is therefore
> no obvious way by which the crucial amino acid sequence defining
> a given protein can be communicated to a new set of amino acids so
> as to provide a mechanism for faithful molecular replication.[11]

Moreover you will recall in the *Unlocking the Chemistry of Life*
chapter that amino acids, the building blocks of life, do not produce
life in themselves. Just having several types of amino acids do not
lead to proteins. As Michael Behe stipulates in *Darwin's Black Box:*

> Proteins are made by chemically hooking together amino acids
> into a chain. A protein chain typically has anywhere from about
> fifty to about one thousand amino acid links. Each position in the
> chain is occupied by one of twenty different amino acids.[12]

Therefore Miller's experiment does not prove that proteins appeared
from a pre-biotic cocktail as the result of the formation of several
types of amino acids.

Planets: A Smithsonian Guide, The story of Our Solar System states
that Earth's early atmosphere was actually comprised of:

> Carbon dioxide, nitrogen, hydrogen, water vapor, and other *volatile*
> elements (that vaporize at relatively low temperatures) [13]

Once again we are left scratching our heads over the fact that Miller's
highly controlled experiment only comprised the gases methane,
hydrogen and ammonia and these gases were in compacted state for the
experiment. Someone has to be wrong here. In fact Miller graciously
concedes that he erred with the whole theory. It seems more likely that
the earth's early atmosphere was not limited to the gases of Miller's
experiment: methane, hydrogen and ammonia. Therefore we can
conclude that it is very unlikely that complex life, could have evolved
from such a pre-biotic cocktail.

Monkeying Around

The best case in point of the absurdity concerning some macro-evolutionists' arguments is Thomas Huxley's famous analogy:

> Six monkeys tapping away mindlessly on their typewriters for millions of years would eventually write all the books in the British Museum! Another version has a team of chimps typing the complete work of Shakespeare, taking of course a comparably enormous length of time.[14]

You don't have to be a rocket scientist to understand how completely far from the truth this aforementioned statement is. Why not just render a similarly ridiculous analogy of giving the monkeys pens instead of typewriters? Then just give them a million years, and expect them to at least write the complete alphabet instead of the complete works of Shakespeare. If the pens don't clog up by then, or the monkeys die of boredom, then I wouldn't give a monkeys *** of hope for them to write anything legible.

The brilliant author, CS Lewis captures remarkably this absurd way of thinking:

> To the modern man it seems simply natural that an ordered cosmos should emerge from chaos, that life should come out of the inanimate, reason out of instinct, civilization out of savagery, virtue out of animalism.[15]

Because we are intellectual and highly creative beings and can formulate specified sentences (specified complexity), along with the ability to reason that people like Shakespeare could create such masterpieces. Even if you gave me a typewriter and a million years, I wouldn't be able to reciprocate the wonderful unique ability of Shakespeare.

Macro-Evolution Forced Upon Us

It is a travesty that such a twisted theory as macro-evolution is forced into our homes, and also upon children as they learn at school. One of the leading personalities of science, David Attenborough seeks to impose such a view as he tries to envision what earth would have been like as it underwent birth-pangs in order to bring forth life:

The planet then was radically different in almost every way from the one we live on today. The clouds of water vapour that had surrounded it had condensed to form seas, but they were still hot. We are not sure how the land masses lay but they certainly bore no resemblance in either form or distribution to modern continents. Volcanoes were abundant, spewing ash and lava. The atmosphere was very thin and consisted of swirling clouds of hydrogen, carbon monoxide, ammonia and methane. There was little or no oxygen. This mixture allowed ultraviolet rays from the sun to bathe the earth's surface with an intensity that would be lethal to modern animal life. Electrical storms raged in the clouds, bombarding the land and the sea with lightning [16]

Moreover Attenborough using the example of Miller's experiment, claims that with the passage of time, millions of years, and in conjuncture with additional elements, possibly from outer space, it would be possible for the eventual development of the first replicating DNA molecules, and so of life itself.

I find it astonishing that though the scientific community doesn't hold to such an experiment, with its strictly controlled nature such as only three gasses being used, this experiment allows for several types of amino acids, which is only a microscopic part of a living organism. If we used a baking analogy, such as baking bread, we know that if we only add yeast and water we do not get bread. Therefore if we just add several types of amino acids and time, we would only get several types of amino acids. Similarly, Neil Broom says "No living organism can be represented by a single molecule any more than a clay brick can represent a house!"[17] It is imperative that the protein requires a multitude of amino acids to be arranged in a meaningful sequence, not just a blob of protein. Therefore Millers experiment only revealed a limited number of amino acids, like finding a single clay brick without the spouting, the ceiling, or roof and saying it is a house.

To build a house for example, using intelligent design, thought, purpose and creativity goes into the design and building; it is the same with Intelligent Design – therefore the same for any created thing (Contingent Being). God has invested his thoughts, purpose, planning and creativity into the design of the universe, the design of you and me.

Controlled Experiments

Some scientists conjure up their experiments to suit themselves, as if they have a hidden agenda. Some of the ways they doctor the experiments are by careful control of temperature, various solutions, and precise timing and sequencing during each step of the experiment. Philosopher Naomi Oreskes reveals this is the case:

> But just as we may wonder how much the characters in a novel are drawn from real life and how much is artifice, we might ask the same of a model: How much is based on observation and measurement of accessible phenomena, how much is convenience?[18]

Gerard Joyce conducted experiments on the theory of evolving RNA and DNA molecules and reveals the manipulation inherent in the experiment:

> Darwinian evolution fundamentally involves the repeated operation of three processes: selection, amplification and mutation. Selection, whether it occurs naturally or artificially, is a winnowing process that separates the "haves" from the "have-nots." In nature the haves among organisms are those that survive to reproductive age, find a suitable mate and produce viable offspring. In the laboratory the haves are molecules that meet whatever criterion is imposed by the experimenter.[19]

Richard Dawkins, contradicts himself when he depicts genes as selfish and purposeful, yet asserts that they just are and don't have foresight.

Richard Dawkins and Bernd-Olaf Küppers used a computer in a rather contrived manner, to prove the theory of Natural Selection. Meyer explains:

> Both use a computer to demonstrate the efficacy of prebiotic Natural Selection. Each selects a target sequence to represent a desired functional polymer. After creating a crop of randomly constructed sequences and generating variations among them at random, their computers select those sequences that match the target sequence most closely. The computers then amplify the production of those sequences, eliminate the others (to simulate differential reproduction), and repeat the process. As Küppers puts it, "Every mutant sequence that agrees one bit better with the meaningful or reference sequence…will be allowed to reproduce more rapidly."20. In his case, after a mere thirty-five generations, his computer succeeds in spelling his target sequence, "NATURAL SELECTION".[21]

While Dawkins similarly adopts an algorithm to prove the theory of Natural Selection. I'm tempted to say that he's weaseled his answer out. You'll get my pun shortly. In his book, *The Blind Watchmaker*, Dawkins creates the following computer simulation and his target sequence is obtained in short order:[22]

1. WDL·MNLT·DTJBKWIRZREZLMQCO·P
2. WDLTMNLT·DTJBSWIRZREZLMQCO·P

10. MDLDMNLS·ITJISWHRZREZ·MECS·P

20. MELDINLS·IT·ISWPRKE·Z·WECSEL

30. METHINGS·IT·ISWLIKE·B·WECSEL

40. METHINKS

The theory of Natural Selection allows for this staging of the process. But as we covered in the Intelligent Design chapter when we are dealing with language we are encountering specified complexity. Additionally, there is blatant intent behind the experiment; therefore Natural Selection is supposed to know what the outcome will be; in other words it has foresight. But foresight is only a mind-like quality, and this reveals Intelligent Design. Moreover we know that regarding the human language intelligent design is the behind any book, including this one. The designer must have human mind-like qualities. Therefore if Natural Selection is true, then it reflects the mind-like qualities of a Creator, and when we tie this in with the Big Bang evidence – this Creator is most likely to be God.

Evidence Against Macro-Evolution

Throughout *God: Fact or Fiction?* I have covered several flows of the theory of macro-evolution. These weaknesses include such areas as the improbability of life occurring by chance, the Big Bang revealing the likelihood of a Creator, the mindlike qualities inherent in the theory of Natural Selection, the uniqueness , high creativity, abstract thought, and reasoning of humans. But there is much more evidence to reveal.

As covered earlier there are limits for which some species can actually change:

The concept of genetic variation shows the immense variety which exists in the genes of each kind of type. It recognizes, however that there are limits or boundaries (e.g. cats will always be cats, dogs will always be dogs) which prevent change into a "higher" entity with a radically new genetic structure. [23]

But the problems facing the macro-evolutionist do not stop there. They escalate with Percival Davis, once a staunch supporter of macro-evolution, stating:

Moreover, if an organism is first highly bred, and then allowed to breed freely, offspring quickly revert to the original form. The natural tendency in living things is to stay within definite limits. Although recombination is often cited as a source of new traits for evolution to work on, it does not produce the endless, vertical change necessary for evolution. Recombination is merely reshuffling of the existing genes.

The only known means of introducing genuinely new genetic material into the gene pool is by mutation, a change in the DNA structure. Gene mutations occur when individual genes are damaged from exposure to heat, chemicals, or radiation. Chromosome mutations occur when sections of the DNA are duplicated, inverted, lost, or moved to another place in the DNA molecule...Mutations do not create new structures. They merely alter existing ones. [24]

The following statements refute Dawkins by utilising Microbiology with the sequences inherent in DNA. First Murray Eden, an engineering academic at Massachusetts Institute of Technology reveals that:

Clearly, we have the evidence available to us, namely that we are alive, and the evidence that life has developed to this state in a relatively small number of generations...What I am claiming is simply that without some constraint on the notion of random variation, in either the properties of the organism or the sequence of the DNA, there is no particular reason to expect that we could have gotten any kind of viable form other than nonsense. [25]

Secondly Neil Broom reveals that:

It is easy to see why many origin-of-life scientists believe that these or similar molecules were the most likely candidates for providing the first rudimentary living system. We are also confronted with a cunning molecular conspiracy of 'aiding and abetting' between these different molecular species – to make proteins we need proteins to be already in existence. To make DNA and RNA we need proteins, and to make proteins we need DNA and RNA. It is a genuine 'chicken and egg' problem and it continues to pose major conceptual difficulties for those committed to a hard-line naturalism.[26]

Therefore we see irreducible complexity in the relationship between the proteins, DNA and RNA. Take any of them out of the equation and the processes collapse entirely. Furthermore Neil Broom reveals the flaws of macro-evolution in relation to the genetic code:

> Thus any mechanism for evolution that depends ultimately on random changes to the genetic code as a source of biological novelty would appear to be largely incompatible with what we know about complex information systems.[27]

As you have learnt information systems are highly specified or structured. A genetic code is a blueprint and can't be messed with. The specific order of the information is paramount, otherwise the cell will not be able to replicate, and fight diseases.

Keane summarises the problems inherent in the macro-evolution theory:

> Numerous aspects can readily be cited for which Evolution Theory requires immense odds: The generation of living cells from non-living matter, the survival of these cells in an unsuitable chemical environment, the origin of photosynthesis, the dependence on extremely rare beneficial mutations, the need for evolution in both male and female forms at each new level of evolution, the many-times repeated evolution of eyes in unrelated species, the repeated evolution of flight, the existence of ducts associated with the fetal human heart – all these aspects and many more are dependent upon one chance in many, many millions being successful – not just once, but time and time again.[28]

Summary

Man has forgotten the above; that an irreducibly complex and fine tuned cosmos has come from apparent chaos – The Big Bang; that life has come from the creation of space, time, matter and energy and therefore God's command; that civilization has come from savagery, and virtue shows itself when we could be just looking out for ourselves. Man has forgotten that there is a Creator, and therefore he bursts forth with an absurd statement like saying monkeys, typewriters and time = creativity and intellect! Even Darwin has said that time on its own is insufficient for evolution.

Miller's experiments are Intelligent Design – controlled Intelligent Design. He controlled the experiments to get the outcome he wanted. Then surprise surprise, he now recants on those very experiments. And most scientists agree that there is not proof for the pre-biotic soup theory – life did not evolve from such a conglomeration.

As there are obviously many "Clutching at Straws" examples; in *God: Fact or Fiction: Volume 2* I will endeavor to provide more. But now we move onto the evidence within the fossil record.

Chapter 7 – Bibliography

1. http://www.cnn.com/TECH/science/9806/23/feathered.dinosaur/ [posted 24 June 1998]
2. Michael Denton, *A Theory In Crisis* (Checy Chase: Adler & Adler Publishers Inc. 1986, 210-11
3. Neil Broom, *How Blind is the Watchmaker?* Theism or atheism: should science decide? Ashgate Publishing Ltd, 1998, p96
4. *TIME*, May 25, 1953, 82
5. Norman Geisler and Ron Brooks, *When Skeptics Ask*, Victor Books, Illinois, 1990, 223
6. Collins Pocket English Dictionary, London, 1986, 286
7. Gerard Keane, *Creation Rediscovered*, Evolution and The Importance of The Origins Debate, Tan Publishers, 1999, 130
8. Ibid
9. Sean O'Reilly, *Bioethics and the Limits of Science,* Front Royal, VA: Christendom Publications, 1980, 56-7
10. Ibid
11. Neil Broom, *How Blind is the Watchmaker?* Theism or atheism: should science decide? Ashgate Publishing Ltd, 1998, 120-121
12. Michael Behe, *Darwin's Black Box*, The Free Press, New York, 1996, 52
13. Thomas Watters, *Planets: A Smithsonian Guide*, MacMillan, 1995, 71
14. Sir James Jeans, *The Mysterious Universe*, MacMillan, New York, 1930, 4
15. CS Lewis,
16. D. Attenborough; *Life on Earth,* Collins and BBC, 1979, 19
17. Neil Broom, *How Blind is the Watchmaker?* Theism or atheism: should science decide? Ashgate Publishing Ltd, 1998, 96
18. N Oreskes, K Shrader-Frechette, and K Belitz; *Science* Vol. 263, 1994, 641-646
19. Scientific American, December, 1992, 48

20. B. Küppers, "The Prior Probability of the Existence of Life", in L Krüger, G Gigerenzer, and MS Morgan, eds., *The Probabilistic Revolution* (Cambridge: MIT Press, 1987) 366
21. Michael J Behe, William A Dembski, Stephen C Meyer, *Science and Evidence for Design in the Universe*, Ignatius Press, San Francisco, 2000, 80-1
22. Richard Dawkins, *The Blind Watchmaker,* Norton, New York, 1986, 47-8
23. Gerard Keane, *Creation Rediscovered*, Evolution and The Importance of The Origins Debate, Tan Publishers, 1999, 25
24. Percival Davis, *et al., Of Pandas and People: The Central Question of Biological Origins,* Haughton Publishing Company, Dallas, 1989, 11
25. M. Eden, "Inadequacies of neo-Darwinian evolution as a scientific theory', in *Mathematical Challenges to the Neo-Darwinian Interpretation of Evolution.* Eds. P. S Moorland and M.M Kaplan, Wistar Institute Press, Philadelphia, 1967, 14.
26. Neil Broom, *How Blind is the Watchmaker?* Theism or atheism: should science decide? Ashgate Publishing Ltd, 1998, 117-118
27. Ibid, 165
28. Gerard Keane, *Creation Rediscovered*, Evolution and The Importance of The Origins Debate, Tan Publishers, 1999, 32

CHAPTER 8

UNCOVERING TRANSITIONAL SPECIES?

When we think of fossils, we tend to bring to mind images of crustaceans carefully dug out of the ground, or alternatively some may think of parents or grand parents as living fossils – another generation. Seriously though, Paleontology is the study of fossils; Paleontologists have discovered remnants of plants, organisms, humans, and animals to name just a few. However before we enter into this area of Intelligent Design we must be aware of the flaw that Michael Denton exposes in relation to the discovery of transitional fossil skeletons:

> To demonstrate that the great divisions of nature were really bridged by transitional forms in the past, it is not sufficient to find in the fossil record one or two types of organisms of doubtful affinity which might be placed on skeletal grounds in a relatively intermediate position between other groups. The systematic status and biological affinity of a fossil organism is far more difficult to establish than in the case of a living form, and can never be established with any degree of certainty. To begin with, 99% of the biology of any organism resides in its soft anatomy, which is inaccessible in a fossil.[1]

This type of argument leads us to question whether what we have been taught to believe, e.g. man evolving from apes, or ape-like creatures is in fact true. For every fossil discovery it is very important to note whether Paleontologists have recovered an entire specimen, or merely fragments. Also of importance, is whether they have recovered samples that contained the soft anatomy that could be studied in the minutest detail so that it could be compared with humans today. How could scientists know what the animal/human even looked like? Yet in most science textbooks there are illustrations depicting the Neanderthal and its transitionary relatives as if it was obvious they had a certain texture, colour and length of hair. Why is there apparent evidence of a transitional species of man which is ape-like, and yet no evidence of other transitional or intermediary species?

Gish reveals the plethora of fossils that have been discovered in conjunction with the rapidity in which the animals were struck down. This is truly mind-boggling:

> It is impossible to account for most of the important geological formulations according to uniformitarian principles. These formations include the vast Tibetan Plateau, 750,000 square miles of sedimentary deposits many thousands of feet in thickness and now at an elevation of three miles; the Karoo formation of Africa, which has been estimated by Robert Broom to contain the fossils of 800 billion vertebrate animals; the herring fossil bed in the Miocene shales of California, containing evidence that a billion fish died within a four-square mile area, and the Cumberland Bone Cave of Maryland, containing fossilized remains of dozens of species of mammals, from bats to mastodons, along with the fossils of some reptiles and birds – including animals which now have accommodated to different climates and habitats from the Artic region to tropical zones. ..The fossil record, rather than being a record of transformation, is a record of mass destruction, death, and burial by water and its contained sediments.[2]

Evidence of Transitional Species?

Darwin himself claimed the paramount importance of intermediate fossils:

> By the theory of Natural Selection all living species have been connected with the parent-species of each genus, by differences not greater than we see between the natural and domestic varieties of the same species at the present day; and these parent-species, now generally extinct, have in their turn been similarly connected with more ancient forms; and so on backwards, always converging to the common ancestor of each great class. So that the number of intermediate and transitional links, between all living and extinct species, must have been inconceivably great. But assuredly, if this theory be true, such have lived upon the earth.[3]

Denton reveals the alarming amount of conversion needed for species to evolve into another species. It's important to note here that Darwin stressed that Natural Selection works very slowly. Yet where is the evidence for these thousands of transitional species? Denton states that:

> Considering how trivial the differences in morphology usually are between well-defined species today, such as rat-mouse, fox-dog,

and taking into account all the modifications necessary to convert a land mammal into a whale - forelimb modifications, the evolution of tail flukes, the streamlining, reduction of hindlimbs, modifications of skull to bring nostrils to the top of the head, modification of trachea, modifications of behaviour patterns, specialised nipples so that the young could feed underwater (a complete list would be enormous) - one is inclined to think in terms of possibly hundreds, even thousands, of transitional species on the most direct path between hypothetical land ancestor and the common ancestor of modern whales.[4]

The obstacles facing the theory of macro-evolution are now piling up. But the claim is that a land mammal eventually evolved into a whale. But the changes needed go beyond what Denton has illustrated. They include changes to: their thermal insulation – you try and stay hundreds of feet underwater; breathing; sight (ability to see underwater and in the dark); hearing – you must know it's difficult to hear anything clearly underwater – and yet whales communicate to each other; and navigation.

As Denton said, a complete list of changes needed between the land mammal and the whale would be enormous. Gish uncovers more evidence:

All mammals, living or fossil, have a single bone, the dentary, on each side of the lower jaw, and all mammals, living or fossil, have three auditory ossicles or ear bones, the malleus, incus, and stapes. In some fossil reptiles the number and size of the bones of the lower jaw are reduced compared to living reptiles. Every reptile, living or fossil, however, has at least four bones in the lower jaw and one auditory ossicle, the stapes. There are no transitional forms showing, for instance, three or two jaw bones, or two ear bones. No one has explained yet, for that matter, how the transitional form would have managed to chew while his jaw was being unhinged and rearticulated, or how he would hear while dragging two of this jaw bones up into his ear.[5]

Keane deals the final blow to the theory that fish evolved into reptiles – this can also be used to refute that land mammals evolved into whales:

In all fishes, living or fossil, the pelvic bones are small and loosely embedded in muscle. There is no connection between the pelvic bones and the vertebral column. None is needed. The pelvic bones do not and could not support the weight of the body.[6]

Denton highlights the sudden appearance of vertebrate fossils within the fossil record which refutes evolution:

> The first members of each major group appear abruptly, unlinked to other groups by transitional or intermediate forms.[7]

He explains that starting about 400 million years ago a high proportion of known fish groups, including many extinct fish groups, and many representatives of modern fish forms (e.g. lungfish, coelacanths and sturgeons), appear in the fossil record:

> The first representatives of all these groups were already so highly differentiated and isolated at their first appearance that none of them can be considered even in the remotest sense as intermediate with regard to other groups. The story is the same for the cartilaginous fish - the sharks and rays - which appear first some 50 million years later than most other fish groups. At their first appearance they too are highly specialised and quite distinct and isolated from the earlier fish groups. No fish group known to vertebrate paleontology can be classed as an ancestor of another; all are related as sister groups, never as ancestors and descendants.[8]

Denton claims a similar pattern repeating itself about 350 million years ago, with each group being distinct and hence no group can be rightly classed as the ancestor of any other group.

He reveals that the virtual complete absence of intermediate and ancestral forms from the fossil record is widely recognized today by many leading paleontologists (geologists who deal with prehistoric life through the study of fossils).

One excuse evolutionists use is that the gaps in the fossil record could and would be filled when rock strata of prehistoric life was found. However geologists have discovered rock layers of all divisions going back 500 million years and of all the species they have uncovered, no transitional forms have been found. Preston Cloud, a specialist in this field, explains:

> 2. The "Lipalian" gap does not exist: sequences of sedimentary rock transitional from Precambrian into Cambrian appear to be present in Australia, the southern Great Basin, perhaps British Colombia, perhaps Arctic Canada, the Appalachian region, the eastern Baltic, Siberia, and possibly Africa. 3. An explanation that calls on the

absence of Precambrian littoral and intertidal sediments is invalid; such deposits, as well as deeper water sediments, are well represented in the Precambrian, although their proportions vary...One should expect to find after-death imprints of such organisms even if not tracks or burrows and some organisms, such as brachiopods, could hardly exist except in context with a shell.[9]

Cloud explains that he knows of colleagues who have searched through some 55 tons of hard quartzite by having it quarried free, and seven tons of selected blocks carefully split into thin slabs for investigation. While they have searched, though in vain, for "unequivocal metazoan fossils through thousands of feet of sediments"[10] at many different locations, they have uncovered no fossil transitional species.

Prehistoric Fish Found Alive

In 1938, there was a fascinating discovery by fishermen in the Indian Ocean. Their astounding catch included a species which was believed to have been extinct for 100 million years, the coelacanth (a relative of the also extinct species, Rhipidistia). Peter Forey in *Latimeria: A Paradoxical Fish* explains that there have been many fossil coelacanths and:

> on the basis of osteological features, their systematic position as near relatives of the extinct rhipidistians and as tetrapod cousins had become part of "evolutionary fact", perpetuated today in textbooks. Great things were therefore expected from the study of the soft anatomy and physiology of *Latimeria*. With due allowance for the fact that *Latimeria* is a truly marine fish, it was expected that some insight might be gained into the soft anatomy and physiology of that most cherished group, the rhipidistians. Here, at last, was a chance to glimpse the workings of the tetrapod ancestor. These expectations were founded on two premises. First, that rhipidistians are the nearest relatives of tetrapods and secondly, that *Latimeria* is a rhipidistian derivative.[11]

Many macro-evolutionists racked their brains to discover how the coelacanth could have survived outside of water and hence evolved into a tetrapod (species with four legs). But the results proved very disheartening as Barbara Stahl relates:

> the modern coelacanth shows no evidence of having internal organs preadapted for use in a terrestrial environment. The

outpocketing of the gut that serves as a lung in land animals is present but vestigial in Latimeria. The vein that drains its wall returns blood not to the left side of the heart as it does in all tetrapods [though it was expected to] but to the sinus venosus at the back of the heart as it does directly or indirectly in all osteichthyans except lungfishes. The heart is characteristically fish-like in showing no sign of division into left and right sides, and the gut, with its spiral-valved intestine, is of a type common to all fishes except the most advanced ray-fins.[12]

Hence, the soft anatomy, especially that of the heart, intestine and brain, was not what was expected of a tetrapod ancestor. A discovery like this is proving that not all creatures in fact evolve as much as the macro-evolutionists claim. Many would say that over these 400 million years the coelacanth would have evolved further. They have already claimed that it evolved from the tetrapod but the results are in fact to the contrary.

Fossil discoveries also disproved another theory or element of macro-evolution; that millions of years ago the 'ancestors' of today's species were much more basic. It was proved that the creatures unearthed were in fact already highly complex.

Back to the gaps in the fossil record. Paleontologist, Schindewolf explains his view of the lack of evidence. He "discussed the gaps in the fossil record as recording not the frustrations of an incompletely preserved fossil record but the realities of the process of evolution. For Schindewolf, the gaps in the fossil record demonstrated clearly the incorrectness of Darwinian gradualism as an explanation of evolutionary change."[13]

Summary

For a species to evolve into another, such as a land mammal into a whale, there would have to be huge modifications. This includes modification of the forelimbs, reduction of existing limbs, and not to forget there would have to be a major overhaul of the heart and every other component such as blood vessels, the brain, and the formation of gills. Such an overhaul of a species would take hundreds, if not thousands of transitional species. Paleontologists have revealed that no such evidence has been discovered, which Darwin claimed should exist.

If there were no transitory species, and macro-evolution was involved, then would there not have to be an evolutionary leap, a major evolutionary change, with many simultaneous changes to the species? Wouldn't the leap of evolution, need a creator to cause it? How could such a huge leap be effected when we see that when a species is supposed to have evolved a number of attributing organs need to have evolved at the same time, such as the organs of the Giraffe if it indeed evolved from the short necked species? The sudden leap of evolution theory without God in fact seems more implausible than the gradual theory of evolution. How could there be such a leap of evolution from such species as bacteria to fish, to amphibians, to mammals, and humans? With the evidence already covered this does in fact seem a rather implausible theory.

The discovery of a fish (a coelacanth) which was believed to have been extinct, for 100 millions years, has dealt a blow to macro-evolutionists; the comparison with many fossil coelacanth proved that the fish has not evolved as evolutionists would have wanted. In fact there was no proof that it had evolved from the land, though many macro-evolutionists claimed this.

Here is more corroborative evidence that the theory of macro-evolution is not fool proof, and that the evidence claimed by Darwin does not exist. Is it not more feasible that a Creator in fact made the species, and that omitting a Creator, creates a fallacy?

Chapter 8 – Bibliography

1. Michael Denton, *A Theory In Crisis,* Checy Chase: Adler & Adler Publishers Inc. 1986, 177
2. Gish, *Evolution, The Fossils Say No!,* p61
3. Darwin, op cit, p309
4. Michael Denton, *A Theory In Crisis,* Checy Chase: Adler & Adler Publishers Inc. 1986, 174
5. Gish, *Evolution, The Fossils Say No!,* p85
6. Gerard Keane, *Creation Rediscovered,* Evolution and The Importance of The Origins Debate, Tan Publishers, 1999, 112
7. Michael Denton, *A Theory In Crisis,* Checy Chase: Adler & Adler Publishers Inc. 1986, 164
8. Ibid
9. Cloud, P.E (1968) "Pre-Metazoan Evolution and the Origins of the Metazo", in *Evolution and Environment,* ed E.T Drake, Yale University Press, New Haven, pp 1-72, see p25-6.
10. Ibid, see p26.
11. Forey, P.L (1980) "*Latimeria:* A Paradoxical Fish", *Proc. Of the Roy, Soc. Of London,* B208: 369-84, see p369.
12. Stahl, B.J. (1974) *Vertebrate History: Problems in Evolution,* McGraw-Hill Book Co, New York, 146
13. Jeffrey Schwartz, *Sudden Origins,* Chichester, Wiley, New York, 1999, 296

CHAPTER 9

THE WONDER OF THE UNIVERSE

The universe galvanizes in us such feelings of wonder, humility and awe. Dr. Hugh Ross in his brilliant book *Creation and Time* links the universe with creation:

> Ours is the first generation that has witnessed the measuring of the universe, including its date of birth. In demarking the universe, astronomers in many respects are measuring the creation. In measuring the creation, they are determining several of the characteristics of the Creator, even certain aspects of His personality.[1]

We are in exciting times as science discovers more impressive secrets and aspects of our world, galaxy and the universe. The universe reflects God in many ways, and so certain aspects of God and His personality are revealed. Let's start with the power, or awesomeness of God. As we see the immensity of creation we can ponder the fact that God didn't create for cheap thrills, or to boost his ego. If God created the whole universe He is all powerful. Furthermore if man is superior to other creatures (highly creative, abstract thought, reasons between right and wrong, manipulates the environment) then the universe was created for humanity. Therefore one of the Creators' expression of love was to create the universe for his creation – us. He knew that we would get a huge kick out of first gazing at the stars and planets, and then endeavouring to explore them. Just think what adventure our ancestors had in building ships to traverse the world's oceans and discovering new frontiers. This creation of the universe is just one expression of God's love, and a big one at that! As technology advances in leaps and bounds we really only begin to see the immensity and wonderful order, and irreducible complexity (there's that word again) within the universe. It is like we are unwrapping a cosmic gift (actually we are), and the giver is our loving Creator. So as we come to see this gift in all its sparkling beauty we now need to figure out how it works. But we must not forget it is a gift, and it has been given to us in love.

The vastness of space is gigantic! Or Should I say mega-gigantic! Just take this concept; Light travels at the rate of 186,000 miles per second (300,000 km/sec). Therefore a light year (the distance light travels in a year) is about 6 million million miles (9 million million km). When we compare the size of the Milky Way galaxy (our galaxy) of about 100,000 light-years across, we see the immensity of this one galaxy among about 100 billion galaxies.

So when we see a newspaper article on a nebular that is 7,000 light years away, then it is in fact 6 million million x 7,000 = 42 million million miles (using the calculation above) which is really mind blowing! What is also astonishing is what you learnt at school (I hope), that the universe is continuing to expand.

There is another mind-blowing concept to remember; the Nebula though it is 7,000 light years away, we are observing something that is 7,000 x 6 million million miles away, or 7,000 years in the past.

Chet Raymo in *An Intimate Look At The Night Sky* reveals some stunning facts about the constellation Canes Venatici, or the Whirlpool Galaxy:

> Modern photographs show a dazzling double coil of tightly spiraling arms sprinkled with stars and streaked with dark lanes of dust. The Whirlpool Galaxy is 15 million light-years distant and contains at least 100 billion stars. It is very much like our own Milky Way Galaxy, from which it is receding at 340 miles per second as part of the general expansion of the universe. Tonight it will be 30 million miles farther away than last night.[2]

Intricacies of the Big Bang

Stephen Hawking writes, "If the rate of expansion one second after the Big Bang had been smaller by even one part in a hundred thousand million million the universe would have recollapsed before it even reached its present size."[3]

Wow! Just think how precise the Big Bang actually had to be! No scientist could ever hope to come to such an atomic precision.

As you reflect on your childhood moments of gazing at the stars with all its thrill and wonder, it seemed as endless as counting grains of sands on the beach. However now astronomers have estimated the number of stars in our galaxy. The Milky Way has about 200 - 700 billion stars. However this number could grow, as the ability to detect the very dimmest of stars (red dwarfs) improves.[4] We can now comprehend even more the awesome splendor of our universe.

Age of the Universe and the Earth

Have you every pondered on the possible ages of the universe and the earth? Carl Sagan, author of *Pale Blue Dot* reveals the likely answers:

> Ages rolled by before the Earth began. More ages will run their courses before it is destroyed. A distinction needs to be drawn between how old the Earth is (around 4.5 billion years) and how old the Universe is (about 15 billion years since the Big Bang). The immense interval of time between the origin of the Universe and our epoch was two-thirds over before the Earth came to be.[5]

That's so amazing! Though God didn't have to, He chose to take time in creating the universe and the Earth.

Though the universe is said to be about 10-15 billion years old[6], Paul Davies testifies that it is hard to be precise because:

> The measurements are difficult to perform precisely and are subject to a variety of errors. Even though modern telescopes have greatly increased the number of galaxies investigated, the expansion rate is still uncertain to within a factor of two, and is the subject of lively controversy.[7]

Amir D Aczel in *God's Equation* reveals some startling research undertaken on the cosmos.(p.XIII) Firstly, he explains that Esther M. Hu, head of a team of astronomers at the University of Hawaii glimpsed through Keck telescopes the most distant object visible in the universe - a galaxy 13 billion light years away. Also as a result she deduced the galaxy was receding from us at a mind-blowing speed of 95.6 percent of the speed of light. Therefore not only is the universe expanding, but it is expanding at a phenomenal rate.

In addition Aczel explains that the unthinkable was a reality; incredible as it sounds, the expansion rate of the universe was in fact accelerating:

> Perlmutter, could not ignore what his data were telling him. The faraway supernovae - along with their galaxies - were receding from Earth at rates that were *slower* than expected. These rates

were slower than the rate of recession of the more *nearby* galaxies. This could mean only one thing, he concluded: the universe was accelerating its expansion....Perlmutter was befuddled. He had started this whole project years earlier hoping to measure the rate of *deceleration* of the universe – he never really expected our universe to be expanding *faster* all the time.[8]

As a result Perlmutter stumbled across a major discovery, which he hadn't expected, one which would lead him to other conclusions:

What Saul Perlmutter found puzzling here was the apparent exceptional quality of his data. He had half-expected his data to be corrupted by the usual observational errors. ...This phenomenon told Perlmutter that there was little or no dust between the observers on Earth and their exploding stars halfway back to the Big Bang, and thus the observations were of exceptionally high quality. What the data were telling him had to be believed - the universe was expanding faster and faster. And this meant something frightening: our universe is infinite.[9]

Wow! The universe was expanding at a faster rate all the time, as if a Creator had his foot on the cosmic accelerator. This thought is very frightening if you don't believe in God.

Secondly, Neta A Bahcall, a professor of astronomy at Princeton University studied the mass density of the universe and Amir Aczel explains that:

All the studies Neta and her colleagues have conducted over the past decade indicate that our universe has low mass - as little as 20 percent of the minimum mass density required to eventually stop the universe expansion.[10]

Hang on a minute! So that means that there isn't enough mass detected to even slow down the expansion of the universe. Therefore it gives what Aczel says is "strong indications that the universe will expand forever."[11]

But Perlmutter was not the only scientist to discover this awesome result. At the meeting of the American Astronomical Society on January 1998 a rival team of astronomers "presented findings - based on different methods of analysis - with the same puzzling inference. Astronomers Netal Bahcall and Xiaohui Fan of Princeton University, who studied massive galaxy clusters several billion light years from Earth, announced results that could also imply an ever-expanding universe."[12]

Both Aczel and Perlmutter are referring to an infinite universe, as it will expand forever. There was the Big Bang, from the infinitely small space and yet the expansion seems to be expanding forever. This is exciting for Christians and yet scary for atheists. There has to be a designer, and I would like to add, and this leads us to the Creative, and Loving Creator as the universe was created as an expression of His love. The splendour, awesomeness, design, specified complexity, and fine-tuning of the universe testifies to this.

Anthropic Principles

The Anthropic Principle is the principle where the physical structure of the universe is precisely what it must be in order to support life.

Using this principle, Freeman Dyson claims that an intelligent mind could be behind the functioning of the universe:

> I conclude from the existence of these accidents of physics and astronomy that the universe is an unexpectedly hospitable place for living creatures to make their home in. Being a scientist, trained in the habits of thought and language of the 20th century rather than the 18th, I do not claim the architecture of the universe proves the existence of God. I claim only that the architecture of the universe is consistent with the hypothesis that mind plays an essential role in its functioning.[13]

Wow! Here is a scientist saying that the setup and processes of the universe are consistent with the possibility of mind, hence Intelligent Design is playing an essential role.

In *Mere Creation*, in the chapter called Big Bang Model Refined by Fire, Hugh Ross describes 29 characteristics of the universe that must be fine-tuned for any kind of physical life to be possible. These characteristics reveal the inherent irreducible complexity within the universe. A couple of sources you can use are *The Fingerprint of God* (1989); and a more extensive list is in *The Creator and the Cosmos (1995)* – though I have used Hugh Ross' contribution in *Mere Creation*.. First I will list only 10 of the most fascinating ones, in order to give you a glimpse of the order that is in the universe:[14]

- *age of the universe* – if older: no solar-type stars in a stable burning phase in the right part of the galaxy;

if younger: solar-type stars in a stable burning phase would not yet have formed.

- *expansion rate of the universe* – if larger: no galaxy formation; if smaller: universe collapses prior to star formation
- *initial uniformity of radiation* – if smoother: stars, star clusters and galaxies would not have formed;
  if coarser: universe by now would be mostly black holes and empty space
- *gravitational force constant* – if larger: stars would be too hot and would burn up quickly and unevenly
  if smaller: stars would be so cool that nuclear fusion would not ignite, thus no heavy element production
- if larger: insufficient chemical bonding; elements more massive than boron would be unstable to fission
  if smaller: insufficient chemical bonding
- *mass density of the universe* – if larger: too much deuterium from Big Bang, hence stars burn too rapidly
  if smaller: insufficient helium from Big Bang, hence too few heavy elements forming
- *ratio of number of protons to number of electrons* – if larger: electromagnetism dominates gravity preventing galaxy, star and planet formation
  if smaller: electromagnetism dominates gravity preventing galaxy, star and planet formation
- *number of effective dimensions in the early universe* – if smaller: quantum mechanics, gravity and relativity could not co-exist, and life would be impossible
  if larger: quantum mechanics, gravity and relativity could not co-exist, and life would be impossible
- *velocity of light* – if larger: stars would be too luminous
  if smaller: stars would not be luminous enough

Incredibly, there are another 45 characteristics which specifically relate to the fine tuning of our Galaxy in order to support life. These characteristics reveal the inherent irreducible complexity within our galaxy. I have listed only 12 such characteristics:[15]

- *galaxy size* – if too large: infusion of gas and stars would disturb sun's orbit and ignite too many galactic eruptions
  if too small: insufficient infusion of gas to sustain star formation for long enough time
- *galaxy type* – if too elliptical: star formation would cease before sufficient heavy element buildup for life chemistry
  if too irregular: radiation exposure on occasion would be too severe and heavy elements for life chemistry would not be available

- *galaxy location* – if too close to a rich galaxy cluster: galaxy would be gravitationally disrupted
  if too close to very large galaxy(ies): galaxy would be gravitationally disrupted
- *Jupiter mass* – if greater: earth's orbit would become unstable
  if less: too many asteroid and comet collisions would occur on earth
- *proximity of solar nebula to a supernova eruption* – if farther: insufficient heavy elements for life would be absorbed
  if closer: nebula would be blown apart
- *parent star distance from center of galaxy* – if farther: quantity of heavy elements would be too great; stellar density would disturb planetary orbits
- *age [of planet e.g. earth]* – if too young: planet would rotate too rapidly
  if too old: planet would rotate too slowly
- *thickness of crust [i.e. earth]* – if thicker too much oxygen would be transferred from the atmosphere to the crust
  if thinner: volcanic and tectonic activity would be too great
- *asteroidal and cometary collision rate* – if greater: too many species would become extinct
  if less: crust would be too depleted of materials essential for life
- *carbon dioxide level in atmosphere* – if greater: runaway greenhouse effect would develop
  if less: plants would be unable to maintain efficient photosynthesis
- *quantity of forest and grass fires* – if too many: too much destruction of plant and animal life
  if too few: not enough charcoal returned to soil, limiting biomass and diversity of life
- *gravitational interaction with a moon* – if greater: tidal effects on the oceans, atmosphere and rotational period would be too severe
  if less: orbital obliquity changes would cause climatic instabilities; movement of nutrients and life from the oceans to the continents and vice versa would be insufficient; magnetic field would be too weak.

Additionally Jupiter reflects the Anthropic Principle for the following reasons:

- If it was larger earth's orbit would be unstable
- If it was smaller then too many comets would collide with earth.

Obviously something has fine-tuned the universe so that complexity and exactness could happen in our galaxy and universe. Isaac Newton explains that:

Though these bodies may, indeed, persevere in their orbits by the mere laws of gravity, yet they could by no means have at first derived the regular position of the orbits themselves from those laws...[Thus] this most beautiful system of the sun, planets, and comets, could only proceed from the counsel and dominion of an intelligent and powerful being.[16]

The Sun

There are many characteristics of the universe that we owe our lives to, and thus to our wonderful Creator. The fascinating fact about the sun is that it is located 93 million miles from us and is a vital part of life; without it, we would not exist!

Jack Zirker, in *Journey from the Center of the Sun* reveals the power of the sun and how sudden emissions have seriously impacted on our lives. He explains such an event of a coronal mass ejection:

On March 13, 1989, the sun ejected ten billion tons of hot hydrogen gas toward the earth. After a trip of three days this huge mass struck the earth's magnetic field. The impact caused huge electrical currents to surge in the power lines of eastern Canada. Within a few seconds, transformers smoked and relays melted. The entire electric power grid of Quebec shut down. Millions waited in the dark for power to be restored.[17]

While scientists can only predict by a matter of days when such an occurrence is likely within a few days, they can not predict precisely when such an ejection is to occur.

The Birth and Incredible Stamina of the Sun

Jack Zirker explains the how the sun is believed to have been formed:

Astronomers believe that the sun was born in a huge interstellar cloud of molecular hydrogen gas, some 5 billion years ago. The cloud slowly collapsed under its own gravity, spinning faster and faster as it shrank, much as a skater spins when she folds her arms. Gradually, a flat disk developed at the edges of the cloud, from which all the planets eventually formed. At the center of the cloud, the proto-sun continued to shrink, heating up as gravity compressed the gas. After several million years, thermonuclear processes ignited in the sun's core and it began to shine as a real star. Theorists calculate that it has at least 5 billion years left before it runs out of fuel.[18]

Moreover Zirker depicts the sun as having a mass that is a million times that of earth's. Wow! Now that's huge. In addition it also loses a "million tons a second in the form of sunlight and has been doing that with no perceptible shrinkage, for over four billion years!" [19] Now that you have an inkling of the sun's power, check out this fascinating statistic from Zirker which is related to solar energy, "In one second the sun emits enough energy to supply the United States for *four million years!*" [20]

Chet Raymo, in *An Intimate Look At The Night Sky* explains that we are actually daily being bombarded by particles shot at us directly from the sun:

> They key lies in the insubstantial neutrino (which is released as two protons fuse and one turns into a neutron). Neutrinos are strange little particles. They are about as close to being nothing as something can be and still be something. They have no charge and possibly no mass. However, they carry energy, and they zip along at the speed of light. Because they are wisps of almost nothingness, they interact with ordinary matter hardly at all. Most of the neutrinos created at the center of the Sun fly straight up through the Sun's overlying layers. Within seconds of their birth they are launched into space, and eight minutes later some of them collide with the Earth. Go outside and face the Sun (don't look at it directly!). Feel the heat on your skin. Sense the light on your closed eyelids. The heat and the light were created at the Sun's core millions of years ago. But as you stand there in the sunlight, trillions of neutrinos fly through your body every second, neutrinos created at the center of the Sun only eight minutes earlier. You are utterly transparent to these tenuous particles; they stream through you unimpeded. For that matter, the planet Earth is transparent; at night the solar neutrinos fall upon the other side of the planet, whisk right through the body of the Earth, and penetrate your body from underneath the bed![21]

Raymo reveals that it is difficult to catch neutrinos, but not impossible. In the United States, Canada, Japan and Italy there are vast underground chambers of pure water which when a neutrino hits, it releases a tiny flash of light. Computers record the flashes of light, and scientists pour over the results.

Zirker unveils the details about these underground facilities:[22]

> Picture a tank 48 feet long and 20 feet in diameter, filled with cleaning fluid, and buried a mile underground in a gold mine. Such a contraption hardly fits one's picture of a modern elementary particle physics experiment. Nevertheless this is what Raymond Davis's neutrino detector looks like It contains 600 tons of perchlorethelene, a volatile compound rich in the chlorine isotope, ^{37}Cl.

The Sun's order?

Zirker explains the sun's amazing order and in turn we observe what reveals irreducible complexity:

> Now in the sun, the *temperature gradient*, not the pressure gradient, drives the flow of energy through the resistant (opaque) plasma. The rate of energy flow is fixed, once and for all time, by the nuclear generation processes in the core. That amount of energy *must* escape or the sun will explode. On the other hand, the opacity of each layer, which resists the flow is determined by that layer's temperature and density. The sun has to adjust the temperature in each layer in such a way that the *gradient* across each layer is sufficient to drive the flow of energy through the opacity of that layer. It manages somehow to solve this complicated problem without the aid of a computer.[23]

Do we have to worry about the sun expending all it's energy and dying within the next few million years? While such a thought would be rather terrifying, we can be rest assured that scientists believe there is still another five billion years of life in her yet!

Planets and Guardians

Jupiter and Saturn are a couple of planets that are intrinsic to our existence. They are so fundamental that they have actually saved our lives. Ken Crosswell in *Planet Quest* states that:

> Long ago, Jupiter and Saturn cleaned the solar system of most cometary debris, including comets that may have been quite large, possibly as large as planets. Consequently, catastrophic impacts – such as the one that killed the dinosaurs and most other species living 65 million years ago – now occur only rarely. In the early solar system, said Wetherill, Jupiter and Saturn worked as a team,

playing ball with comets and passing them back and forth from one planet to the other, boosting the comets' velocities. Most of the comets got cast clear out into interstellar space, while some were deposited in the Oort cloud, the vast comet reservoir that surrounds the solar system....In 1994, the world witnessed a dramatic event that symbolized Jupiter's role as protector of terrestrial life: the planet took a direct hit from Comet Shoemaker-Levy 9, an impact that left Jupiter's atmosphere scarred for months. Had the planet not intervened, the comet might someday have collided with Earth.[24]

Without these two planets Earth would most probably be hit by thousands of cometry debris, including the comets themselves. These two guardians most probably enabled life to develop and flourish without being interfered with by this space debris. Cross explains another affect Jupiter and Saturn has with protecting earth:

Without Jupiter and Saturn, the Earth might also be buried under water. Much of the water now on Earth came from comets, and even with Jupiter and Saturn protecting the planet, seawater covers 71 percent of the Earth's surface. If Jupiter and Saturn did not exist, and comets rained down on Earth more often, the Earth might be a completely water-covered world, and any life would forever remain in the sea – another situation that might have prevented the emergence of intelligent life. Although dolphins have a fair degree of intelligence, they have not developed a written language, preventing future generations of dolphins from studying and building on the knowledge of their ancestors.[25]

The Moon and It's affect on Earth

Neil F Comins in *What if the Moon Didn't Exist?* Reveals interesting facts about the relationship of the Moon to that of the Earth:

The moon affects the earth through its gravitational attraction and through the sunlight it reflects here. The most direct gravitational effect of the moon is its influence on the ocean tides. In turn, the ocean tides pull on the moon, causing it to speed up and spiral away from the earth. These tides also slow the earth's rotation.[26]

Without the moon mankind would not have been able to keep track of the seasons, and so plantation and harvesting would have been like playing Russian Roulette.

For example, during a new moon, when the moon is between the earth and the sun, the moon and the sun pull on the oceans in the same direction and the tides are especially high. During a quarter moon (when one half of the moon's face is visible), the gravitational forces act in different directions and partially cancel each other, leading to lower tides.[27]

Design in the universe

The evidence is overwhelming for the universe to be designed by an intelligent being. Meyer reveals some of the compelling evidence:

The constants of physics, the initial conditions of the universe, and many other of its features appear delicately balanced to allow for the possibility of life. Even very slight alterations in the values of many factors, such as the expansion rate of the universe, the strength of gravitational or electromagnetic attraction, or the value of Planck's constant, would render life impossible. Physicists now refer to these factors as "anthropic coincidences" (because they make life possible for man)…many physicists have noted that the fine tuning strongly suggests design by a preexistent intelligence.[28]

Sir Fred Hoyle admits that the evidence speaks for itself:

A commonsense interpretation of the facts suggests that a superintellect has monkeyed with physics, as well as chemistry and biology, and that there are no blind forces worth speaking about in nature."[29]

Mankind comes from dust

At some funerals we hear the words that it is from "dust that we came and dust that we shall return." Chet Raymo explains that we come from cosmic dust:

Our bodies take in atoms with our food and use them to build tissue and bone under instructions from the DNA that *was* our inheritance from our parents. And where did the carrots and peas and corn and cow get their atoms? From soil and air and water. And those? The atoms of the Earth were there within the presolar nebula of dust and gas out of which the solar system was born 4.5 billion years ago.

And? And those atoms were blasted into the nebulae of the Galaxy from the heavy-element factories at the cores of massive stars that lived and died before the Sun and Earth were born.[30]

Man's Advancement

That's an amazing fact to ponder. The 'evolution' of man, and I'm talking micro-evolution, has happened because we have been able to build on the past. We have studied and built on the knowledge of our ancestors. With many discoveries in science they happened because of the mind and work of others. How could so many planets have been discovered without the telescope? How could the telescope have worked without first discovering how to make glass? It's important to note that no other creature has been able to improve so much from learning from the past. We have the ability of written records (history), the creation of multitudes of languages and now visual movie records, to make huge leaps in advancement. We are the only creatures to so successfully organize and transcend our environment – we can travel across, land, sea and even live in space. Furthermore we are the only species to uncover the laws of the universe. Yes we have taken huge leaps forward, but as we turn our back on our Creator we seem to take such huge steps backwards; thus our society struggles to cope with the effects; wars, contraception, abortion, euthanasia, divorces, escalating crime rates, absent parents, suicides are all linked to societies/cultures rejecting God. I will cover this more in my next book.

Hugh Ross transposes the above illustrations into a wonderful context of God's personality:

> As helpful as Big Bang cosmology has been in attesting to the Creator's existence and transcendence, it has provided even great service in attesting to the Creator's personality. The more we learn about the physics of the universe, the more clearly we see reflected not only the awesome power but also the mind and heart of the One who planned and initiated and sustains all things, inanimate and animate. Big bang cosmology is elucidating the universe and in so doing rendering the design of the universe irrefutable. Astronomers and physicists widely acknowledge that the only reasonable system, our planet - all ingeniously focused on the requirements for life - is the action and ongoing involvement of a personal intelligent Creator.[31]

The anthropic principle illustrates the order which the Earth depends on for its survival. Intelligent Design seems to take on even more credence when non-Christians confirm to the possibility of their being a Creator behind the design. According to science historian Frederic B. Burnham, scientists now regard the concept that God created the universe "a more respectable hypothesis today than at any time in the last hundred years." [32]

I would like to share a poem that I wrote in 1998, which encapsulates the beauty and wonder that the universe displays, and points towards an Intelligent Designer, and a Loving Creator:

GOD'S TOUCH

The beauty of nature
Astounds, captures and enthralls

From the grandeur of mountains
To the calmness and power of the sea
From the wonder of new life
To the uniqueness of creation

The Virgin forests
Swarm with wildlife
Beauty is in every living creature
The raw power of the storm
And the stillness of the lake
Are enthralling in themselves

All creation has one mark
There is one print left on all creation
That is, God's touch.

Summary

Our awe-inspiring universe reflects God in a vast number of ways. Significant evidence of Intelligent Design has been revealed through our universe. God created the universe for you, me, those that have come before us and those yet to gaze at the stars in wonder. This was an expression of God's love – a cosmic gift that has been given to us to explore. The more we delve into this gift, the more we discover the richness and hidden realities within. Our universe is so humungous! Earth is merely a drop in a vast ocean of space. And yet the Creator has given it to us – we are the stewards of the universe – a universe which is expanding faster all the time. The Anthropic Principle (the physical structure of the universe is so precise to support life) exists throughout many areas of science. Within the cosmos the laws of nature were so fine tuned for the origin of life, and the origin of our universe. If at the onset these laws were tweaked here or there, life would not have originated; the Big Bang theory reveals immaculate fine-tuning). One obvious Anthropic Principle is the sun. Without the sun we would not be alive – everything would be frozen! There would be no origin of life!

God reveals Himself to us through the splendour and awesomeness of our universe. He has given us a wonderful cosmic gift. How will we respond to such a loving Creator?

Chapter 9 – Bibliography

1. Hugh Ross, *Creation And Time*, Navpress, Colorado, 1994, 8
2. Chet Raymo, in *An Intimate Look At The Night Sky,* Walker & Company, New York, 2001, 171
3. Stephen W Hawking. *A Brief History of Time* (New York: Bantam Books, 1988, 291.
4. see FAQs on http://stardate.org (27/06/02)
5. Carl Sagan, *Pale Blue Dot*, Random House, 1994, pg 29
6. Hugh Ross, *Creation And Time*, Navpress, Colorado, 1994, 11
7. The Last Three Minutes, Paul Davies, Weidenfeld & Nicolson, London, 1994, 22
8. Amir Aczel, *God's Equation: Einstein, Relativity, and the Expanding Universe*, Four Walls Eight Windows, 1999, p 7-8
9. Ibid, 8-9
10. Ibid, xiii
11. Ibid, xiii
12. Ibid, 11
13. Freeman Dyson, *Disturbing the Universe* (New York: Harper & Row, 1979
14. ed. William Dembski, *Mere Creation*, Science, Faith and Intelligent Design, InterVarsity Press, Downers Grove, IL, 1998, 372-375
15. Ibid, 375-380
16. Isaac Newton, *Mathematic Principles of Natural Philosophy*, trans. A. Motte, ed. F. Cajori, University of California Press, Berkeley, California, 1978, 543-44
17. Journey from the Center of the Sun, Princeton University Press, Princeton and Oxford, 2002, p 1
18. Ibid, 7
19. Ibid, 7
20. Ibid, 7

21. Chet Raymo, in *An Intimate Look At The Night Sky,* Walker & Company, New York, 2001, 68
22. Journey from the Center of the Sun, Princeton University Press, Princeton and Oxford, 2002, p?
23. Ibid, 41-42
24. Ken Crosswell, Planet Quest: The Epic Discovery of Alien Solar Systems, The Free Press, New York, 1997, 167
25. Ibid, 168
26. Neil F Comins, *What if the Moon didn't exist?,* Harper Collins Publishers, 1993, 4
27. Ibid, 7
28. Michael J Behe, William A Dembski, Stephen C Meyer, *Science and Evidence for Design in the Universe*, Ignatius Press, San Francisco, 2000, 56-7
29. F.Hoyle, "The Universe: Past and Present Reflections", *Annual Review of Astronomy and Astrophysics* 20 (1982): 16
30. Chet Raymo, in *An Intimate Look At The Night Sky,* Walker & Company, New York, 2001, 144
31. ed. William Dembski, *Mere Creation*, Science, Faith and Intelligent Design, InterVarsity Press, Downers Grove, IL, 1998, 371
32. Briggs, David, "Science, Religion, Are Discovering Commonality in Big Bang Theory,"

CHAPTER 10

EVIDENCE UNCOVERED BY THE SANDS OF TIME

Now that we have explored the evidence from non-biblical sources, we can now scrutinize the evidence uncovered from the study of Archeology. Archaeology is corroborative evidence that enhances the credibility of the writers who gave us painstaking and meticulous details within the New Testament. In itself it is a science and reveals the life of ancient people through excavations. Therefore in this chapter I seek to give you a glimpse of a fraction of the evidence revealed by this science pertaining to Sacred Scripture and characters revealed therein. (I would appreciate for a future book any materials or sources that you the reader may stumble across.)

There are in fact hundreds of thousands of archaeological sites that have been located within the places mentioned in Sacred Scripture. Each year this number expands with more discoveries, the re-exploration of old sites, and recalculations are made of locations and data specified in Sacred Scripture.

Problems Facing Archaeology

Archaeology stumbles upon several obstacles especially within the Biblical lands. Archaeologist Randall Price reveals some of them in *The Stones Cry Out:*

> *Only a fraction of the surveyed sites have been excavated.* This may be surprising to some people, but archaeology, even in Israel – where it is tied to the national tourist economy – does not receive high priority. Israeli government budgets go mostly towards military applications, securing the country against terrorism, or developing a still-young nation. Archaeologists, most of whom are not salaried as archaeologists but as professors, must raise their expedition money from private sources. And most of their workers are volunteers who must pay their own expenses to excavate. For these reasons, less than 2 percent of the surveyed sites in Israel have been excavated. [1]

So there we have it. So few sites have been excavated in certain locations, especially the Middle East. Unfortunately discoveries also languish for many years in museums left unloved and most importantly untranslated. Many discoveries are never published due to lack of resources and expertise. Randall estimates that of the known 500,000 cuneiform texts left in museum storage, only about a fraction, i.e. 10% have ever been published.

Biblical People and Places Confirmed

There is an abundance of archaeological evidence confirming the reliability of Sacred Scripture – pertaining to events, conquests, falls of kingdoms, characters, cities buildings, that are all mentioned in Sacred Scripture; the details reveal lost cultures and practices of ancient peoples – and can be found throughout the Old Testament and the New Testament.

The unprecedented discoveries began in the 1840's and uncovered cities, enormous palaces cuneiform archives (wedge shaped symbols e.g. Babylonian and Persian). Israel Finkelstein and Neil Asher Silberman in *The Bible Unearthed* reveal the dynamic discoveries:

> Places like Nineveh and Babylon, previously known primarily from the Bible, were now seen to be the capitals of powerful and aggressive empires whose artists and scribes thoroughly documented the military campaigns and political events of their time. Thus references to a number of important biblical kings were identified in Mesopotamian cuneiform archives-the Israelite kings Omri, Ahab, and Jehu and the Judahite kings Hezekiah and Manasseh, among others.[2]

In 1945 archaeologists stumbled across a rare treasure in a dig at the ancient Assyrian city of Calah (now Nimrud) – The Black Obelisk of King Shalmaneser III. They were astounded to discover that the obelisk depicted Jehu, King of Israel from 841 – 814 BC. Randall Price details the discovery:[3]

> The stone was a four-sided polished block (obelisk) of black limestone 6.5 feet high. On each side panel of the obelisk were carved five registers of relief sculptures depicting various scenes of tribute brought to the Assyrian court. In addition, above and below the panels on all sides were almost 200 lines of cuneiform

text. Once the cuneiform text was translated it was found that they catalogued 31 military campaigns by the Assyrian monarch Shalmaneser III. The detailed relief sculptures of tribute and tribute-bearers beautifully picture many different styles of clothing, costly articles, and even exotic animals for the Assyrian zoo. However, the big surprise came when the lines above one register showing a figure kneeling before the Assyrian king were translated:

Tribute of Jehu, son of Omri. Silver, gold, a golden bowl, a golden beaker, golden goblets, pitchers of gold, tin, staves for the hand of the king [and] javelins, [Shalmaneser] received from him.

The discovery of one Israelite King was quite a feat, however the discovery of a "photo" of hundreds of Israelites within an actual biblical event is breathtaking! Randall Price reveals that the "photo" came from a distant land (in relation to Israel) of Assyria and explains that:

It originated as a 90-foot-long mural decorating a ceremonial suite in the palace of the Assyrian king Sennacherib at Nineveh. The palace was excavated by Henry Layard, and the mural, made of panels of relief sculptures, is today housed in the British Museum. On the reliefs are accurate and realistic depictions of the battle between the Assyrians and the people of Lachish, which occurred during the Assyrian conquest of Judah in 701 BC (see 2 Kings 17:5-6; 2 Chronicles 32:1). The scene shows (from left to right) the Assyrian camp, their siege and conquest of the city with Assyrian troops storming the walls, the torture of some of the city's inhabitants, and finally the exile of the prisoners and their presentation before Sennacherib, who was seated on this throne in front of his camp.[4]

This account echoes the Biblical account from the 2nd book of Kings and the 2nd book of Chronicles:

Shalmaneser king of Assyria made war on Hoshea who submitted to him and paid him tribute.
2 Kings 17:3

After these loyal actions, Sennacherib king of Assyria advanced and invaded Judah, and laid siege to the fortified towns, intending to demolish them.
2 Chronicles 32:1

2 Chronicles continues with the account of Sennacherib's pompous attitude and downfall as a result of insulting Israel, especially Yahweh.

While the earliest record of Israel outside Sacred Scripture was discovered in Egypt. A stele depicted the campaign of Pharaoh Mernetptah (son of Ramesses II) in Canaan at the end of the 13ᵗʰ Century BCE:

> The inscription tells of a destructive Egyptian campaign into Canaan, in the course of which a people named Israel were decimated to the extent that the pharaoh boasted that Israel's "seed is not!" The boast was clearly an empty one, but it did indicate that some group known as Israel was already in Canaan by that time. In fact, dozens of settlements that were linked with the early Israelites appeared in the hill country of Canaan around that time.[5]

One of the major archaeological discoveries was the uncovering of 26,000 Assyrian tablets found in the palace of Ashurbanipal. In When Skeptics Ask it is noted:

> Several of these records confirm the Bible's accuracy. Every reference in the Old Testament to an Assyrian king has proven correct. Even though Sargon was unknown for some time, when his palace was found and excavated, there was a small painting of the battle mentioned in Isaiah 20.[6]

In the book of Isaiah in the Old Testament, as mentioned above, we see that the above is confirming the existence of the Israelites and Sargon, king of Assyria, along with what happened to Israel:[7]

> The year the general-in-chief, sent by Sargon king of Assyria, came to Ashdod and stormed and captured it at that time Yahweh spoke through Isaiah son of Amoz and said, "Go, undo the sackcloth round your waist and take the sandals off your feet." And he did so, and walked about naked and barefoot. Yahweh then said, "As my servant Isaiah has been walking about naked and barefoot for the last three years as a sign and portent for Egypt and Cush, so the king of Assyria will lead the captives of Egypt and the exiles of Cush…"

This confirms Sargon's existence as mentioned in Sacred Scripture. God told the prophet Isaiah that Israel's persecutors would in turn become persecuted. Therefore among the interesting discoveries was

Sennacherib's record of the siege of Jerusalem. Isaiah prophesied that it would not be conquered and Sennacherib found a way to save face – by omitting 'small' details of Hezekiah's entrapment:

> As to Hezekiah, the Jew, he did not submit to my yoke, I laid siege to 46 of his strong cities, walled forts, and to the countless small villages in their vicinity... I drove out of them 200,150 people, young and old, male and female, horses, mules, donkeys, camels, big and small cattle beyond counting and considered them booty. Himself I made a prisoner in Jerusalem, his royal residence, like a bird in a cage. [8]

> *But as for Ha-za-qi-ia-u* (Hezekiah), the Jew, who did not bow in submission to my yoke, forty-six of his strong walled towns and innumerable smaller villages in their neighbourhood I besieged and conquered (cf. 2 Ki.18:13) by stamping down earth-ramps and then by bringing up battering rams, by the assault of foot-soldiers, by breaches, tunneling and sapper operations...He himself I shut up like a caged bird within Jerusalem his royal city. [9]

> In the fourteenth year of King Hezekiah, Sennacherib king of Assyria advanced on all the fortified towns of Judah and captured them.
> 2 Kings 18:13

In 2 Kings 18:28 the Assyrian cupbearer-in-chief taunts the people of Jerusalem, "'"Listen to the word of the great king, the king of Assyria. The king says this, "Do not let Hezekiah delude you. He will be powerless to save you from my clutches. Do not let Hezekiah persuade you to rely on Yahweh by saying: Yahweh is sure to save us; this city will not fall into the king of Assyria's clutches.

2 Kings 19:35 reveals the fate of the Assyrian Army care of Yahweh's justice – an angel of Yahweh struck down 185,000 men.

Randall Price interprets the motive for such an Assyrian inscription:

> What can we observe in Sennacherib's account of his siege against Jerusalem? First, we find his affirmation that Jerusalem was surrounded without any hope of rescue or escape. Sennacherib had exacted tribute from King Hezekiah and had militarily shut him up "like a bird in a cage." Second, we find his confirmation that while he had surrounded Jerusalem, he could not conquer the city. The best he could say was that he besieged it – *nothing more!* And we can be sure that if he could have said more he would have, for his list of conquests both precede and follow his attack on Jerusalem.

It was not the Assyrian way to record a disaster, so in the typical fashion of a Near Eastern monarch who could only boast for posterity but never admit a failure, Sennacherib's silence speaks volumes.[10]

Though the Assyrian records are silent about the outcome of Hezekiah, Sacred Scripture is not. It is written:

> Hezekiah fortified his city,
> And laid on a water-supply inside it;
> With iron he tunneled through the rock
> And constructed storage-tanks.
> In his days Sennacherib invaded
> and sent Rabshakeh;
> he lifted his hand against Zion,
> and boasted loudly in his arrogance.
> Then their hearts and hands trembled,
> they felt the pangs of a woman in labour,
> but they called on the merciful Lord,
> stretching out their hands towards him.
> Swiftly the Holy One heard them from heaven
> and delivered them by the agency of Isaiah;
> he struck the camp of the Assyrians
> and his Angel annihilated them.
> Ecclesiasticus 48:17-21

Sodom and Gomorrah

Randal Price in *The Stones Cry Out* unveils archaeological discoveries of a site of which are highly likely to be the city of Sodom that is mentioned in the book of Genesis. In Genesis 19 Lot is hosting a couple of angels, but the local townsfolk of Sodom, both young and old, want to rape his guests (now that's an evil bunch in Sodom!). Because not even 10 righteous men could be found there God destroys the town and a nearby town called, Zoar is spared and Lot flees there.

Excavations of the site Babe dh-Dhra revealed fascinating details about Sodom:

> The excavations revealed that the fortification wall surrounding the city was some 23 feet thick! It was uniquely segmented and the last segment had a gateway flanked by twin towers. Within this walled area was an interior city of mud-brick houses along the northwest side and a Canaanite temple with a semicircular altar and numerous cultic objects. Outside the townsite they found an enormous cemetery with thousands of buried people...But

something else caught the attention of the excavators: the evidence of extensive destruction by fire. The townsite was covered by a layer of ash many feet in thickness. The cemetery also revealed ash deposits, charred posts and roof beams, and bricks that had turned red from the intense heat. What caused this fire?[11]

Archaeologist, Bryant Wood reveals the answer:

The evidence would suggest that this site of Babe dh-Dara is the biblical city of Sodom. Near that site, about a kilometer or so away, archaeologists found a vast cemetery indicating that at one time there was a very large population living there at this place...But during that last phase, they buried their dead in these buildings made of mud bricks built right on the surface of the ground...they had been burned – from the inside out....But as they investigated exactly how this burning took place, they had to change their opinion on this. In one particular instance when they were excavating one of these charnal houses, they cut what we call a balk through that building as they were digging so that they had a vertical cross section of that house and the destruction, and what they discovered was that the fire started on the roof of the building, then the roof burned through, collapsed into the interior and then the fire spread inside the building. And this was the case in every single charnel house that they excavated.[12]

Wood states that this is a bizarre occurrence and extremely difficult to explain apart from the Scriptural explanation. The cemetery is separate from the town and yet the buildings have been burned from the top down. The town site and the cemetery were covered in ash, and the most likely explanation is that God did rain down fire and brimstone to punish the wickedness of the people who would not change their ways.

The sun rose over the horizon just as Lot was entering Zoar. Then Yahweh rained down on Sodom and Gomorrah brimstone and fire of his own sending. He overthrew those cities and the whole plain, with all the people living in the cities and everything that grew there.
Genesis 19:23-25

King David

In 1993 at the biblical site, Tel Dan in northern Israel, a momentous discovery was revealed, an inscription confirming the existence of King David:

It was the "House of David" inscription, part of a black basalt monument, found broken and reused in a later stratum as a building stone. Written in Aramaic, the language of the Aramean kingdoms of Syria, it related the details of an invasion of Israel by an Aramean king whose name is not mentioned on the fragments that have so far been discovered. But there is hardly a question that it tells the story of the assault of Hazael, king of Damascus, on the northern kingdom of Israel around 835 BCE. This war took place in the era when Israel and Judah were separate kingdoms, and the outcome was a bitter defeat for both. The most important part of the inscription is Hazael's boasting description of his enemies:

[I killed Jeho] ram son of [Ahab] king ofIsrad, and [I] killed [Ahaz]iahu son of Jehoram king of the House of David. And I set [their towns into ruins and turned] their land into [desolation].

This is dramatic evidence of the fame of the Davidic dynasty less than a hundred years after the reign of David's son Solomon. The fact that Judah (or perhaps its capital, Jerusalem) is referred to with only a mention of its ruling house is clear evidence that the reputation of David was not a literary invention of a much later period. Furthermore, the French scholar Andre Lemaire has recently suggested that a similar reference to the house of David can be found on the famous inscription of Mesha, king of Moab in the ninth century BCE, which was found in the nineteenth century east of the Dead Sea. Thus, the house of David was known throughout the region; this clearly validates the biblical description of a figure named David becoming the founder of the dynasty of Judahite kings in Jerusalem.[13]

Professor Avraham, director of the Nelson Glueck School of Biblical Archaeology of the Hebrew Union College was the archaeologist who made this amazing discovery, the crowning moment of his career. This one inscription also confirmed the existence of Scriptural figures, such as Jehoram, Ahab and Ahaz. He states:

In a wall constructed somewhere around the end of the ninth to the beginning of the eighth century B.C we found a fragment inscribed in Aramaic. Its lines speak of warfare between the Israelites and the Arameans, which from the Bible we know was constant between Israel and Damascus [during this period]. In this fragment a king of Damascus, Ben Hadad, is apparently victorious. He has killed someone and taken prisoners and horsemen... But what was really thrilling was to find that he defeated a "king of Israel of the House of David"! So here you have the mention of the "House of David" in an Aramean inscription dated...about 150 years after the days of King David. The following year in another scene of excavation we found two more pieces and these two pieces link to the first one and give us the names of these kings. The king of Israel that is referred to is "Jehoram"...who is the son of Ahab. The king of the House of David [Judah] is "Ahaziahu" [Ahaziah], who is also mentioned in the Bible...the exciting thing here is that you have a historical stele referring to historical events of which the Bible speaks at great lengths [2 Kings 8:7-15; 9:6-10].[14]

Archaeologist Yigael Yadin in *The Art of Warfare,* relates how armed with foreknowledge (intricate scriptural details), they were able to amaze and impress their laborers and uncover the Megiddo gate which had been built by King Solomon:

Before proceeding further with the excavation, we made tentative markings of the ground following our estimate of the plan of the gate on the basis of the Megiddo gate. And then we told the labourers to go ahead and continue removing the debris. When they had finished, they looked at us with astonishment, as if we were magicians or fortune-tellers. For there, before us, was the gate whose outline we had marked, a replica of the Megiddo gate. This proved not only that both gates had been built by Solomon but that both had followed a single master plan.[15]

Isn't it remarkable that they could estimate plans by using Sacred Scripture which literally pointed them to the right location.

Crucifixion Confirmed

Archaeology also confirms the details of crucifixion which was the barbaric torture and means of capital punishment used by the Romans, as mentioned in Sacred Scripture, as the discovery of a gravesite in Jerusalem in 1968 uncovered the secret, revealing 35 bodies. Historians believe this was the result of their involvement in the Jewish revolt against Rome in 70 A.D:

The inscription identified one individual as Yohan Ben Ha'galgol. Studies of the bones performed by osteologists and doctors from the

Hadassah Medical School determined the man was 28 years old...
What intrigued archaeologists were the evidences that this man had
been crucified in a manner resembling the crucifixion of Christ. A
seven-inch nail had been driven through both feet, which were turned
outward so the nail could be hammered inside the Archilles Tendon.

Archaeologists also discovered that nails had been driven through
his lower forearms. A victim of a crucifixion would have to raise and
lower his body in order to breathe. To do this, he needed to push up
on his pierced feet and pull up with his arms. Yohan's upper arms
were smoothly worn, indicating this movement.[16]

The disciple John records that in order to expedite the death of a prisoner,
executioners broke the legs of the victim so that he could not lift himself
up to breathe by pushing with his feet (John 19:31-34). Yohan's legs were
found crushed by a blow, broken below the knee.

It was the Day of Preparation, and to avoid the bodies' remaining on
the cross during the Sabbath – since that Sabbath was a day of special
solemnity – the Jews asked Pilate to have the legs broken and the
bodies taken away. Consequently the soldiers came and broke the
legs of the first man who had been crucified with him and then of the
other. When they came to Jesus, they saw he was already dead, and
so instead of breaking his legs one of the soldiers pierced his side
with a lance; and immediately there came out blood and water.
John 19:31-34

New Testament Evidence

There has been some fascinating evidence uncovered which most likely
proves the existence of the disciple and apostle, St. Peter. In *Son of God*,
Angela Tilby reveals the following:

The fishing town of Capernaum has been extensively excavated; it
was little more than a cluster of homes along the lake front The
evidence is quite strong for the site of Peter's house. There was clearly
Christian devotion on this site before Queen Helena's travels in the
fourth century when many more holy places were discovered. We
know that Christians were living here because there are records of
conflicts between Jews and Christians. A pilgrim called Egeria,
towards the end of the fourth century, reported that the house of the
'prince of the apostles' had been made into a church. An excavation

of the area took place a hundred years ago, and the archaeologists found the remains of a fifth-century church.

Underneath was an earlier church that had been built round the remains of a first-century house. In the rubble of the original house remnants of fishing equipment were discovered. The house clearly belonged to a fisherman, and it turned out to be one of a number of small, poorly built houses, only distinguished from those around it by the fact that the walls were plastered. Archaeologists found fragments of plaster on which simple Christian prayers had been inscribed, such as 'Lord Jesus Christ help your servant' and 'Christ have mercy'. These are testimony that the house had some significance for early Christians. It is likely that they met for worship here, and it is certainly possible that the reason this house was chosen was because local people had handed on the memory that the house had once belonged to Peter.[17]

How Remarkable! They were able to recover what is highly likely to be the disciple, St. Peter's house. The early Christians often protected their sacred sites by building a Church upon it.

We also have evidence of the existence of the Jewish High Priest Caiaphas whom prophesied that Jesus would die for the nation (John 11:49-52), and then judged Jesus with the chief priests and the whole Sanhedrin before handing Jesus over to Pilate (Matthew 26:59-60, 63-66).

One of them, Caiaphas, the high priest that year, said, "You do not seem to have grasped the situation at all; you fail to see that it is to your advantage that one man should die for the people, rather than that the whole nation should perish." He did not speak in his own person, but as high priest of that year he was prophesying that Jesus was to die for the nation – and not for the nation only, but also to gather together into one the scattered children of God. John 11:49-52

The chief priests and the whole Sanhedrin were looking for evidence against Jesus, however false, on which they might have him executed. But they could not find any, though several lying witnesses came forward...And the high priest said to him, "I put you on oath by the living God to tell us if you are the Christ, the Son of God." Jesus answered him, "It is you who say it. But, I tell you that from this time onward you will see the *Son of man seated at the right hand of the Power and coming on the clouds of heaven.*" *[see Psalm 110:1 and Daniel 7:13]* Then the high priest tore his clothes and said, "He has blasphemed. What need of witnesses have we now? There! You have just heard the blasphemy. What is

your opinion?" They answered, "He deserves to die."
Matthew 26:59-60, 63-66

Randall price recounts the discovery of the remains of Caiaphas in Jerusalem's Peace Forest during November, 1990:[18]

> The discovery was made when the roof of the burial chamber collapsed and revealed 12 limestone ossuaries. One of the ossuaries was exquisitely ornate and decorated with incised rosettes. Obviously it had belonged to a wealthy or high-ranking patron who could afford such a box. On this box was an inscription. It read in two places *Qafa* and *Yehosef bar Qayafa* ("Caiaphas," "Joseph, son of Caiaphas"). [See Zvi Greenhut, "Caiaphas' Final Resting Place," *Israel Hilton Magazine* (Spring 1993), 16]

Summary

In this chapter we briefly explored the fascinating science of Archaeology in which the sands of time have uncovered evidence which confirms many places, characters, buildings, and events which were revealed in Sacred Scripture. We have explored proof of the existence of such historical people as the Israelite Kings: Omri, Ahab, Jehu, Hezekiah and David. Additionally, discoveries have confirmed the existence of the Assyrian Kings Shalmaneser III, Sargon and Sennacherib and the Pharaoh Mernetptah. It was also fascinating to cover what was highly likely to be the remains of the city of Sodom; evidence of crucifixion; and what was highly likely to be St. Peter's house.

Archaeologist and Rabbi, Nelson Glueck, reveals the valuable relationship between archaeology and Sacred Scripture:

> As a matter of fact, however, it may be stated categorically that no archaeological discovery has ever controverted a biblical reference. Scores of archaeological findings have been made which confirm in clear outline or in exact detail historical statements in the Bible. And by the same token, proper evaluation of biblical descriptions has often led to amazing discoveries. They form tesserae in the vast mosaic of the Bible's almost incredibly correct historical memory.[19]

Therefore we have been able to prove that those who say Sacred Scripture is a complete fabrication are speaking in ignorance. Though not all the places and characters of Sacred Scripture have been proved, it is like a huge jigsaw and so the sands of time have been able to confirm that some of the characters and events of the Bible did actually take place.

For those who think there is an inseparable gap between science and religion, the results of two separate surveys gave astonishing results. Sociologist James Leuba conducted a survey in 1914 which revealed that 40% of American scientists believed in the existence of God. Then more than 80 years later, Edward Larson, UGA professor of law and history conducted the survey again. How many American scientists do you think believed in God's existence? 20%? Or how about 10%? Wrong! It would seem that the number would be much smaller in the new survey. But, remarkably the number of scientists who now believed in God had not changed. In fact it was 40%.

Furthermore when Larson conducted more than 100 individual interviews to for more comprehensive answers as to American scientists religious beliefs. The results showed that all of them believed in evolution, none believed in creationism, and some believed in an altruistic God.

Now let us move onto the next section of *God: Fact or Fiction?* as we progress from science to the aspect of religion, or belief in a Creator. In this section you will be able to see that God has been revealed to us through Divine Revelation. Hopefully this section will be as rewarding as this one. But before you make it to the next section, I have put in here some photos care of NASA for you to marvel and wonder at. As you read this next section I hope you do so with an open mind. Well, you've made it this far haven't you? So, enjoy!

Chapter 10 – Bibliography

1. Randall Price, *The Stones Cry Out* Harvest House Publishers, Oregon, 1997, 46-47
2. Israel Finkelstein and Neil Asher Silberman, *The Bible Unearthed*, Free Press, New York, 2001, 18
3. Randall Price, *The Stones Cry Out* Harvest House Publishers, Oregon, 1997, 77
4. Ibid, 79
5. Israel Finkelstein and Neil Asher Silberman, The Bible Unearthed, [year] pg57
6. When Skeptics Ask, 199
7. Translation by A. Leo Oppenheim in *Ancient Near East Texts*, ed. by James B. Pritchard (Princeton: The Princeton Press, 1950) 288
8. DOTT – (texts of Shalmaneser III of Assyria), 67
9. Israel Finkelstein and Neil Asher Silberman, *The Bible Unearthed*, p129

10. Randall Price, *The Stones Cry Out* Harvest House Publishers, Oregon, 1997, 273
11. Ibid, 1997
12. Ibid, 1997
13. Interview Randall Price and Avraham, October 17, 1996.
14. Yigael Yadin, The Art of Warfare in Biblical Lands, p 288
15. [email brendanr@ihug.co.nz if you need this reference]
16. www.probe.org/docs/arch-nt.html, 3/10/2002
17. Angela Tilby, *Son of God*, Hodder and Stoughton, London, 2001, 67-68
18. Randall Price, *The Stones Cry Out* Harvest House Publishers, Oregon, 1997, 303
19. Nelson Glueck, *Rivers in the Desert: A History of the Negev* (New York: Farrar, Straus and Cudahy, 1959), 31

SECTION II

RELIGION

CHAPTER 11

TRUTH: OBJECTIVE OR SUBJECTIVE?

Mankind longs for truth; the quest has led many to a priceless conclusion. The journey has helped them to contemplate whether truth is actually subjective or objective. The questions they faced included, "Is truth something that is the same for everyone? Is it objective or subjective? Does truth change? Is truth relative? Does truth reflect characteristics of a Creator" As you traverse this chapter, you will encounter some great grounding to whether truth is in fact, objective or subjective and universal. First we look back in history in regards to truth:

> To say that the truth is not, or need not be, what we suppose assumes two things that have, of late, been questioned: that there is a truth of the matter, and that we might find it out, if only to the extent of finding what it isn't.[1]

Sextus Empiricusa, philosopher, in the third century summarised the Skeptical philosophers by stating that "if we say there is no truth, then in that at least we are liars: if we cannot find the truth, what right have we to say we can't?"[2]

There are two different categories of truth: Truth that concerns itself with matters of fact; and truth that concerns itself with moral actions. The first category has existed since the dawn of creation, and thus the beginning of space, time, matter and energy; the second has existed since man first walked the earth, and thus made moral decisions.

Objective Truth

Do we really believe the notion that, "Since you perceive it to be true, then it is true?" With truths concerning simple matters of fact we can answer this question with a simple test. You could take a chair, climb on it and say to yourself, "If I step off this chair, I will not fall, since I don't believe in gravity. After all I can't see or touch gravity – it is beyond my senses."

Well my friend, welcome to reality – welcome to the human race. Most of us know what will happen when we step off the chair. Note this is an example, so please don't sue me! I don't want to become a pauper or vagabond.

Logic

The term, logic comes from *logos* meaning *word*. Logic relates to reality through language. When something is logical it has an intrinsic objective truth or worth. No matter what we think e.g. "I don't believe in gravity!", the logical truth does not change, only our perception does. Though obviously our perception can change, truth itself does not.

But as Geisler & Brooks explain truth can not contradict itself:

> Now all logic can be reduced to one single axiom – the law of non-contradiction. This law says that no two opposite statements can both be true at the same time in the same sense. Logicians usually simplify that to A is not non-A. If we try to deny that, we get, "Two contradictory statements can be true," or "A is not [not non-A]." Both of these statements have a problem. They assume what they are trying to deny. In the first, it still assumes that there can be truth without the law of non-contradiction. But if opposites can be true then there is no difference between true and false, so this statement cannot be true, as it claims to be.[3]

Therefore when two politicians say something that contradicts each other, for instance, one says, "I did not do it" and the other says, "He did do it", then we know by the law of non-contradiction that one of them is lying or very mistaken.

Moral Truth

Issues of morality are however much more complex than simple matters of fact. This is due to their intangibility (you can't touch them). Moral Truths are actions that we deem to be either good or evil. We can deny the existence of this type of truth in theory, however most rational people would accept that certain types of actions exist that are fundamentally good or evil, for example, giving to the poor would be classed by most as a good action, while murder or rape on the other hand would be viewed by most to be an evil action.

Can the moral truth of these actions change over time? Let us take the example of moral actions that have been wrong for thousands of years, but yet today are considered to be morally neutral and in some cases even morally good. Many things in today's world were deplored by our parents and grandparents generation, e.g. abortion, homosexuality (acting on feelings, practicing), prostitution (prostitutes are now called sex workers and sadly now a legal profession here in New Zealand), contraception (the first Church to relax it's moral view was the Anglican Church in 1930 though it said that the "primary and obvious method is complete abstinence from intercourse (as far as may be necessary) in a life of discipline and self-control lived in the power of the Holy Spirit." But then the conference weakened it's moral stance by saying "in those cases where there is such a clearly felt moral obligation to limit or avoid parenthood, and where there is a morally sound reason for avoiding complete abstinence, the Conference agrees that other methods may be used, provided that this is done in the light of the same Christian principles. The Conference records its strong condemnation of the use of any methods of conception control from motives of selfishness, luxury, or mere convenience." - see http://www.anglican communion.org/acns/archive/1930/1930-15.htm) sex outside of marriage and euthanasia (the active killing of someone using a lethal injection). These were deplored because as a moral truth they were revealed to be wrong . But now in the 21st century many people accept them as OK. For example, abortion has historically been seen as abhorrently evil, and yet only in the last 40 years has it become morally neutral and now it has been deemed to be a basic human right for women and even children. (The International Planned Parenthood Federation, in 2002 distributed a brochure claiming that the United Nations Convention on the Rights of the Child's right to life, and right to health, can be interpreted to mean that children should have access to abortion.)

If these examples above, are in fact truths, can they change? The simple answer is, no. The morality of these actions does not change over time, for example murder was wrong 5,000 years ago, 2,000 years ago, 500 years ago, 50 years ago, and is still wrong today. Truth does not change, and has not changed, but people's perception of right and wrong has changed dramatically in our life-time.

Alternatively it could be argued that these "horrible" things that our grandparents were against, are now deemed OK, and that it was our grandparents' generation who were wrong. But when you really research these subjects it is the moral truth underlying them that is critical. For the example concerning abortion, it is the taking of a human life. The unborn baby is actually deprived of the chance to live. For me, seeing a graphic video of what happens in an abortion, first opened my eyes up to this truth.

Moreover is we take the example of the 'gang' rape punishment meted out to a woman in Afghanistan in 2002. Most people would know this gross violation of the woman was wrong – even if any court said it was OK. This is what we call a moral truth. So truth does not change, but people's perception of truth does.

This also relates to faith. It is so true about what we believe in. Often we believe a rumor about another faith. Unless we study that faith we should not entertain or believe in those rumors. For instance you have most probably heard the rumor, Muslims accept terrorism – i.e. blowing themselves up and taking infidels with them. But the terrorists believed (their perception) that the infidel would go to hell, and they would go to heaven. The Muslim Faith does not teach this, but only a small proportion of radicals do – they are the militant fundamentalists. Another rumor you may have heard is that Catholics worship Mary, the mother of God. But when you discuss this with a Catholic who knows what he is talking about, or read the Catholic Catechism then you will discover that Catholics honor Mary, but do not worship her – they do not treat her as more important than God. This concept relating to Mary and other teachings of the Catholic and Orthodox Churches have been discussed in more depth in my first two books: *Set Free!* and *Born to be Free.*

Moral truth urges us to do what is right via our conscience. But our free will gives us the ability to heed the call:

> In dealing with our own questionable behavior we seek ways to excuse ourselves, or we suggest reasons why others should not judge us so harshly. We function within a universe that makes moral demands on us moment by moment. We experience the "I ought to" moral force in our lives as a daily even hourly experience, challenging us to act in ways often contrary to our most powerful bodily impulses. How we *actually* behave may be very different to how we believe we *ought* to behave. The existence of a moral law impinging on almost every aspect of our behaviour, urging us to do right and making us feel uncomfortable when we do wrong, is a fundamental aspect of human experience and relies crucially on the

reality of free will. We are constantly faced with choosing to obey or disobey the inner voice of this moral law. Our response to this law is fundamentally different from the way we respond to the so-called material laws that act in a relentless mechanical sense. We cannot say no to gravity but we are free to disobey the moral law.[4]

Iain Mackenzie in *The Dynamism of Space* explains that humility and not pride is needed when we encounter truth:

> Something of *humility* of mind is required, not only in letting the mind be informed by the external verities, but also in pondering the fact that the truth of an object resided in that object before I began speaking about it, resides there when I am speaking about it, and will remain there long after I have spoken about it. But above all, that truth of that object will remain exactly what it is in its integrity whatever I say about it.[5]

In our search for truth, if we proceed with humility we will find it and its splendor. But if we proceed with pride we will be blinded to the truth and will not recognize it as such.

Free Will

It is a fact that humans have free will. This is not something that is tangible, and so agnostics would probably deny this. Gerard Keane in *Creation Rediscovered* explains:

> Human beings are creatures made by God and subject to His laws, which have been made known by Divine Revelation. Since human beings consist of both body and soul, they are destined for eternal existence in the timeless world after death. Though man lives in a world beset by confusion, greed and sorrow, it is possible to rise above the difficulties of this life. We have been given a free will by God, and can become truly "set free" by choosing to live in conformity with God. Most importantly, human beings can discern objective truth.[6]

If we did not have Free-Will we would be mere robots:

> The simplest argument for the existence of free will is observation of how we use words. We praise, blame, command, counsel, exhort and moralize to each other. Doing these things to robots is absurd.

We do not hold machines morally responsible for what they do, no matter how complicated the machines are. If there is no free will, all moral meaning disappears from language – and from life.[7]

Free will is who we are – part of our essence. Without free will we would not be humans, we would obey our Creator without questioning. Life would definitely not have the same pleasures that we experience as a result of free will. We choose to love someone, and when they choose to respond we are left with such a wonderful feeling. Without free will we would not have that aspect of pleasure. Moreover, without free will we could not respond freely to God's offering His love to us, the offering of a loving relationship with Him – as a result we could not have the experience of growing in love whether within a human relationship or loving God, but merely obey without any feeling of love. Free will is a beautiful gift from God. It makes up our essence. It makes us who we are.

Relativism

The theory of Relativism says that truth is not objective, but subjective. It claims, "Whatever is true for you, may not be true for me." It also says you can not judge one morality against another. If you say, "All is relative," or "Relativism is better than absolutism," or "truth is subjective not objective", you are stating something that assumes an absolute value that contradicts relativism. As C.S Lewis explains:

> The moment you say that one set of moral ideas can be better than another, you are, in fact, measuring them both by a standard, saying that one of them conforms to that standard more nearly than the other. But the standard that measures the two things is something different from either. You are, in fact, comparing them both with some Real Morality, admitting that there is such a thing as real Right, independent of what people think, and some people's ideas get nearer to that real Right than others.[8]

In other words to say that "All is relative" or "Relativism is better than absolutism," or "Truth is subjective not objective" is to assume that some real or absolute right exists, which is impossible using the theory of relativism. Bryan Magee, in *The Story of Philosophy* illustrates the flaw in this theory and the universality of truth:

It is indefensible to maintain that something could be the right thing to do for me and yet wrong for somebody else in identical circumstances: if it is right for me it must be right for anyone else in the same position. This means that, just as the empirical world is governed by scientific laws that have universal application, so the moral world is governed by moral laws that have universal application. And it means that morality is founded on reason, as science is founded on reason.[9]

But there is an advantage in believing in relativism, you can never be wrong – how convenient! Whenever you have a discussion, you can be pig-headed and say, "Truth is relative" or, "You are right and I am right." Therefore with this line of reasoning, Hitler was right to do what he did, as his truth was to rule the world, at the expense of others. This defies logic.

The disadvantage of the theory of relativism is that if it were true you could never learn anything, because this involves moving from a false belief to a true one. Once again this defies logic.

Truth can be made to be relative or subjective when taken out of context, or the meaning is reinterpreted.

Skepticism

The theory of Skepticism is the philosophy that we should doubt whether anything can be known. But this philosophy is like a house built on unstable foundations. With the slightest shake the philosophy crumbles. Geisler and Brooks share a witty and hilarious example showing how we can deal with skeptics:

> One great philosopher had an effective way to deal with skepticism. When encountered by people who claimed to doubt everything, he would ask, "Do you doubt your own existence?" If they answered yes, then he would point out that they must exist in order to doubt and *that* certainty should remove their doubts. If they answered no, then he could show them that there are at least some things which are beyond doubt. To counter this assault on their doctrines, the skeptics decided to simply remain silent. Then they would not be caught in this trap. The philosopher was not shaken though. At that point, he simply said, "I guess there is nobody here after all. I may as well go talk to somebody who exists." And he walked away. [10]

Another example from the same authors is a great rebuttal when a strong skeptic or relativist tries to come at you with their point of view:

> Finally, we find that even those who say that there is no moral order expect to be treated with fairness, courtesy and dignity. If one of them raised this objection and we replied with, "Oh shut up. Who cares what you think?" we might find that he does believe there are some moral "oughts". Everyone expects others to follow some moral codes, even those who try to deny them. But moral law is an undeniable fact.[11]

In other words even the skeptic or relativist believes in truth If they do not perceive something as true then they reject it – just as they may reject that truth is absolute.

Experience

There are many truths that we learn by experience. We learn something is hot, by "trial and error", usually a painful one. When growing up we also learn that most things have consequences; if we disobey our parents we will be punished. We also learn truths by observing others – we may observe our brothers or sisters getting in trouble for doing something wrong, so we learn we should not emulate what they did if we are ever faced with a similar situation. We also learn from good experiences, such as, what we can do to please our parents, and what is helpful for them. We learn how to love, through our growing up years, even if they are tough times, there is always some aspect of love to be learnt. Another truth that we have all learnt is the law of gravity; if we step off something, into thin air, from a great height, we will fall, or if we trip over, we will also fall, and we know it usually hurts.

There are other truths that we can learn from experience. The written word has enabled us to learn from the experiences of others. Science has been able to take gigantic leaps, especially in the last century, due to the written word. Another example of the written word is Sacred Scripture which contains so many experiences from others, and is a living word – that is God still acts through that word, He longs for us to read it, so that He can speak through that word. To open up the meaning of Sacred Scripture, that is to help us to interpret it, is one aspect that God intended for the Church; included with this is that the Early Church Fathers, also known as the "Apostolic Fathers", who are a group of early Christian writers who testify to the faith of the early Church (dating from the Apostles to about AD 749). Therefore we have the ability to learn truth through experience. (see my 2nd book for more examples. I intend to write a book based on their lives and God's wisdom that shines from their experiences)

The Ontological Argument

The Ontological Argument is the philosophy of the nature of being. One of it's most ardent proponents and possibly its inventor was St. Anselm (1033-1109), Archbishop of Canterbury for 16 years. Bryan Magee utilizes the wisdom shared by this medieval philosopher:

> Imagine, he says, the greatest, most perfect being possible. If the being you think of has every desirable attribute except that of existence, it is not the greatest or most perfect possible, because obviously a being that exists is both greater and more perfect than one that does not. Therefore the greatest, most perfect possible being must exist.[12]

Just think where we'd be scientifically if we didn't have the written word to build on – we would not have so many of the scientific discoveries. Most of the famous pioneers were able to build their ideas from written word, from the ideas of others.

Rene Descartes devised a new version of the ontological argument for the existence of God. Bryan Magee refers to Descartes and what he declared:

> I know myself, he says, to be a very imperfect being, ephemeral and perishable, and finite, and yet I have in my mind the concept of an infinite being, eternal and immortal, perfect in every way; and it is impossible that anything should be able to create something greater than itself out of its own resources; therefore this perfect being must exist, and must have implanted in me an awareness of itself, like a craftsman's signature inscribed on an example of his handiwork.[13]

Therefore for something to be the greatest, most perfect being it must exist – also known as the Necessary Being – and it must not be created by something less perfect. In addition the awareness of the perfect being must be open to man's discovery. Therefore this imperishable soul of ours was created to find the truth, and therefore find God and let the Trinity dwell therein. Yes God has made it possible for us to discover Him. Kant's philosophy was that we can never know for certain that anything exists if we can't see it. If you recall, this is the theory of Relativity. Magee states that this does not rule out the Creator:

"of the existence of God, and of immortal souls. It is important to realize that it does not rule out the existence of God, only *knowledge* of the existence of God. As Kant himself famously put it, he had ruled out knowledge in order to make room for faith.[14]

When man says there is no God, this does not rule out the existence of God. Only man's knowledge of God's existence is wrong. In other word's it's man's perception that's wrong – we can't stop God existing by ignoring Him or denying Him.

Does Truth Reflect a Creator?

When we look at the concept of truth, and indeed of most of creation, the physical and the laws, we can see evidence of personality. Our very existence reveals God as loving God who has created us as his crown of creation. Let's explore the aspect that God is a moral God. We are moral creatures – we live by moral choices, training our consciences to make the right decisions in relation to what is right or wrong:

The existence of a moral law in the mind of a moral Lawgiver shows us that God is a moral Being. He is neither beyond morality (like some kings [or politicians or celebrities] think they are) nor beneath morality (like a rock). He is by nature moral. This means that part of what He knows is the difference between right and wrong. But we can take this one step further: He is not only moral; He is good. We know that part of what He created was people, and persons are good, in and of themselves. The fact that persons always expect to be treated better than things shows that. Even someone denying that people have value at least expects you to value his opinion as a person. But whatever creates good things must be good itself (a cause can't give what it hasn't got). So God is not only moral, He is good.[15]

As well as God being moral we can also reason that God is truth, peace, joy, truth, etc. Therefore, let's go to His Word to explore references to His truth, including truth about the nature of God and man's longing for truth.

First of all let's look at an example where God is revealed as truth:

> Jesus said to him, "I am the way and the truth and the life. No one comes to the Father except through me."
> John 14:6

So Jesus is saying that He is the truth. Since He is the Son of God, and part of the Trinity (as mentioned in the chapter, *Personal God*), then He is the source of truth, He is truth.

Scripture That Attests to Truth

At the heart of my previous books was the theme of freedom. The truth indeed will set you free!

> Jesus then said to those Jews who believed in him, "If you remain in my word, you will truly be my disciples, and you will know the truth, and the truth will set you free."
> John 8:31-32, [Jesus then says that everyone who commits sin is a slave of sin.]

It's remarkable how the following scripture relates to the concept that time had a beginning:

> Paul, a slave of God and apostle of Jesus Christ for the sake of the faith of God's chosen ones and the recognition of religious truth, in the hopes of eternal life that God, who does not lie, promised before time began, who indeed at the proper time revealed his word in the proclamation with which I was entrusted by the command of God our saviour.
> Titus 1:2

Some people claim that God can do anything. But the following scripture shows that God can't do anything against His nature:

> So when God wanted to give the heirs of his promise an even clearer demonstration of the immutability of his purpose, he intervened with an oath, so that by two immutable things, in which

it was impossible for God to lie, we who have taken refuge might be strongly encouraged to hold fast to the hope that lies before us. Hebrews 6:17-18
This is the one who came through water and blood, Jesus Christ, not by water alone, but by water and blood. The Spirit is the one that testifies, and the Spirit is truth.:..Whoever does not believe God has made him a liar by not believing the testimony God has given about his Son.
1 John 5:6,10

Now let's return to the idea that God is moral; "Our contention is that the moral law is rooted in God's good and loving nature. This is not an ultimate beyond God, but within Him. And it is impossible for God to will something that is not in accordance with His nature. God is good and cannot will evil arbitrarily. So there is no dilemma."[16]

The following Scripture reveals that the pillar of truth is in fact the Church:

I write this to you in the hope that I may be able to come to you soon; but in case I should be delayed, I want you to know how people ought to behave in God's household – that is, in the Church of the living God, pillar and support of the truth.
1 Timothy 3:14-15

Summary

In this chapter we have pondered that truth is indeed objective and universal, while the perception of truth is subjective. Truth itself has not changed while people's perception of truth has. We are faced with moral truths which do not change of themselves – the perception has changed for man's convenience or gain, e.g. abortion, euthanasia, homosexuality, and sex outside of marriage. Relativism is a weak theory when it is revealed that truth is objective, therefore what is true for you, is also true for me in the same type of situation.

A fascinating project you can undertake is to scrutinize all the Churches and discover whether any have not changed their moral truths.

Experience can lead us to truth, e.g. when growing up we learn not to touch the stove after we have been burnt. This experience gives us knowledge and truth. In relation to morals we can also learn from experience and knowledge. For example, someone intentionally hurts us and hopefully we don't want to do the same to someone else, and so we think twice when faced with a similar situation.

Knowledge of the truth also comes from reading God's living word, Sacred Scripture, in which truth and the source of truth are revealed, and we can come to true humility to embrace the truth.

Therefore we can reason from Revelation that God is truth; and so it is true that Jesus is the Son of God, the Messiah, and that he created humanity as the crown of creation as gift of His tremendous love.

Chapter 11 – Bibliography

1. Anthony Kenny, *The Oxford History of Western Philosophy,* Oxford University Press, 1994, 8
2. Ibid
3. Norman Geisler and Ron Brooks, *When Skeptics Ask,* Victor Books, Illinois, 1990, 270-271
4. Neil Broom, *How Blind is the Watchmaker?* Theism or atheism: should science decide?, Ashgate Publishing, Brookfield, Vermont, 1998, 199
5. Iain Mackenzie, The Dynamism of Space, The Canterbury Press, Norwich, 1995, 31
6. Gerard Keane, *Creation Rediscovered,* Evolution and The Importance of The Origins Debate, Tan Publishers, 1999, 173-174
7. Peter Kreeft & Ronald Tacelli, *Handbook of Christian Apologetics*, InterVarsity Press, Illinois, 1994, 137
8. C.S Lewis, *Mere Christianity* (New York: Macmillan Co., 1943, 25
9. Bryan Magee, The story of Philosophy, (The Essential guide to the history of western philosophy, DK Publishing, 1998, 137
10. Norman Geisler & Ron Brooks, *When Skeptics Ask*: A Handbook on Christian Evidences, Victor Books, USA, 1990, 266
11. Ibid, 24
12. Bryan Magee, The story of Philosophy, (The Essential guide to the history of western philosophy, DK Publishing, 1998, 57
13. Ibid, 87
14. Ibid, 222
15. Norman Geisler & Ron Brooks, *When Skeptics Ask*: A Handbook on Christian Evidences, Victor Books, USA, 1990, 27
16. Ibid, 30

CHAPTER 12

ON THE WINGS OF FAITH AND REASON

This chapter encompasses some key characteristics that differentiate us humans from the animal kingdom; and so I have utilised the encyclical letter[1], *Fides Et Ratio, On the Relationship between Faith and Reason* written by Pope John Paul II, as he has covered the subject in extraordinary detail. Hopefully you will find this chapter quite enthralling. He profoundly states that "Faith and Reason are like two wings on which the human spirit rises to the contemplation of truth"; and that "God has placed in the human heart a desire to know the truth – in a word, to know Himself [God]."[2] (cf. Exodus 33:18; Psalm 27:8-9, 63:2-3; John 14)

Faith

The Collins Pocket Dictionary explains faith as "unquestioning belief esp. in God, religious tenets, etc" and "complete trust or confidence."[3]

"The acceptance of the word of another, trusting that one knows what the other is saying and is honest in telling the truth...It is called divine faith when the one believed is God, and human faith when the persons believed are human beings."[4]

We all put our faith in something or someone. For example we all *believe* the sun will rise in the morning though we have no way of truly *knowing* it will. In addition we put our faith in contraptions such as bunji jumps, as we trust nothing will go wrong. We put our faith in our family and friends, such as our spouse or our parents. God is our Heavenly Father and so we have the obligation to search, trust and so put our faith in Him.

More radically, Thomas Aquinas, one of the greatest minds of the Medieval times recognized that nature, philosophy's proper concern, could contribute to the understanding of Divine Revelation. Faith therefore has no fear of reason, but seeks it out and has trust in it. Just as grace builds on nature and brings it to fulfillment, so faith builds upon and perfects reason.[5]

It was so important for Christianity to proclaim the gospel and deepen the understanding of faith:

> For them, the first and most urgent task was the proclamation of the Risen Christ by way of a personal encounter which would bring the listener to conversion of heart and the request for Baptism. But that does not mean that they ignored the task of deepening the understanding of faith and its motivations. Quite the contrary.[6]

Some people think that it's a cop-out to leave anything to the area of faith, such as you will read in the chapter on miracles. But, let's take the atom – can you see it? You believe it because someone has told you that it is true. There are many things that you believe because someone else tells you something that you can't know for yourself, for instance, you have an ailment but you can't tell exactly what it is, so you go to a doctor to seek his enlightenment.

It's possible to deepen one's faith. This can be done through different means. The first is to ask God for more faith, and the second is to put your faith into action – thus trusting God. This too is like two wings of a bird. Instead of complaining, get into a habit of thanking God for everything – that is trust. This does not mean you blindly accept everything that comes your way. But it means having a grateful heart! If you look at your relationship to your best friend or lover, you realize that your relationship deepens when you put your trust in each other. Here is your opportunity to trust more in your Creator.

Reason

The Collins Pocket Dictionary explains reason as among other things, "an explanation or justification of an act, idea, etc; the ability to think, draw conclusions, etc; to think logically about; to argue or infer [he reasoned that the method was too costly.]"[7]

> What human reason seeks "without knowing it" (cf. Acts 17:23) can be found only through Christ: what is revealed in him is "the full truth" (cf. Jn 1:14-16) of everything which was created in him and through him and which therefore in him finds its fulfillment (cf. Col 1:17).[8]

Within the human heart there is a space for the divine and Pope John II illustrates St. Paul's discourse with the Athenian Philosophers:

> The Apostle accentuates a truth which the Church has always treasured: in the far reaches of the human heart there is a seed of

desire and nostalgia for God. The Liturgy of Good Friday recalls this powerfully when, in praying for those who do not believe, we say: "Almighty and eternal God, you created mankind so that all might long to find you and have peace when you are found".(*Ut te semper desiderando quaererent et inveniendo quiescerent*": *Missale Romanum.*) There is therefore a path which the human being may choose to take, a path which begins with reason's capacity to rise beyond what is contingent and set out towards the infinite.[9]

It "was the task of the fathers of philosophy to bring to light the link between reason and religion.", while the Fathers of the Church "entered into fruitful dialogue with ancient philosophy, which offered new ways of proclaiming and understanding the God of Jesus Christ."[10]

One of the greatest minds of the Catholic Church, Saint Augustine searched for truth among different philosophical schools, but none of them revealed the truth. However, when he encountered the truth of Christian faith he discovered the strength for radical conversion. St. Augustine later became Bishop of Hippo and produced the "first great synthesis of philosophy and theology embracing currents of thought, both Greek and Latin."[11]

At this point it is pertinent to quote Vatican II, an ecumenical (universal) council of the Catholic Church (1962-1965) which was called for by Pope John XXIII. It's main mission was to "more effectively preserve and present the sacred deposit [teachings handed on by Jesus and his apostles] of Christian doctrine."[12] The Council says:[13]

The sacred Synod professes that "God, the first principle and last end of all things, can be known with certainty from the created world, by the natural light of human reason" (cf. Rom. 1:20). It teaches that it is to his Revelation that we must attribute the fact "that those things, which in themselves are not beyond the grasp of human reason, can, in the present condition of the human race, be known by all men with ease, with firm certainty, and without the contamination of error."[14]

Faith and Reason

The definition given by the Catholic Pocket Dictionary explores Faith and Reason in greater depth than the Collins Dictionary, and thus to a greater depth of reality:

The relationship between human response to God's revelation and use of human native intelligence. This relationship is mainly of three kinds, where the role of reason is to assist divine faith: 1. reason can establish the rational grounds for belief by proving God's existence, his authority or credibility as all-wise and trustworthy, and by proving that God actually made a revelation since he confirmed the fact by working (even now) miracles that testify to God's having spoken to human beings, especially in the person of Jesus Christ; 2. reason can further reflect on what God has revealed and thus come to an even deeper and clearer understanding of the divine mysteries; and 3. reason can both show that the mysteries of faith are in harmony with naturally known truths and can defend their validity against the charge of being contrary to reason.[15]

Therefore through reason the existence of God can be proved. St. Thomas Aquinas explained that this could be done via 5 key proofs – motion, efficient cause, possibility and necessity, gradation to be found in things, and governance of the world. These will be explained in further detail in *Philosophy of God's Existence* chapter. But for now we will show an example of reason using the Causation, or Efficient Cause proof:

Causation

In the world of sensible things we find there is an order of efficient causes. There is no case known (neither is it, indeed, possible) in which a thing is found to be the efficient cause of itself; for so it would be prior to itself, which is impossible. Now in efficient causes it is not possible to go on to infinity, because in all efficient causes following in order, the first is the cause of the intermediate cause, and the intermediate is the cause of the ultimate cause, whether the intermediate cause be several, or one only, Now to take away the cause is to take away the effect. Therefore, if there be no first cause among efficient causes, there will be no ultimate, nor any intermediate, cause. But if in efficient causes it is possible to go on to infinity, there will be no first efficient cause, neither will there be an ultimate effect, nor any intermediate efficient causes; all of which is plainly false. Therefore it is necessary to admit a first efficient cause, to which everyone gives the name 'God'.[16]

Once again we are brought back to the question: Who caused God? We can reason the answer, that something had to cause the existence of our universe. You will recall that something had to cause the Big Bang, something outside of space, time, matter and energy – a first cause. This first cause we reason to be God.

The systems of irreducible complexity, in conjunction with the evidence of specified complexity reveal the powerful mind behind creation, and possibly Natural Selection. The Big Bang similarly reveals God – who else could create such a complex, awe-inspiring and breathtakingly immense universe?

As explained at the beginning of this Chapter, "Faith and Reason are like two wings on which the human spirit rises to the contemplation of truth" Therefore if we pluck the feathers of just one of the wings, e.g. reason, then we are relying on merely faith to explain truths. Not only would the bird be freezing, and look ultra weird, it would be unable to fly. It would be like you flapping your arms when you were a kid trying to fly, and that represents faith, as if you expected to believe in faith alone. Faith is vital, like each wing of the bird is vital, but it must be in harmony with reason. On the contrary we could pluck the feathers of faith and expect people to believe merely on reason. But once again we need both in order to contemplate the fullness of truth. The Enlightenment was such a situation in which faith was thrown out and people tried to rely purely on reason. Ironically this attitude is what happened with the Fall of mankind through Adam and Eve – they chucked out faith, instead of trusting in God, and relied only on reason.

In proving God's existence we see His character reflected in what he has created – due to the purpose and end result. In revealing his nature God shows the amazing and wonderful love that He has for mankind – therefore for you personally. I will cover this more in-depth in the chapter on Personal God.

The First Vatican Council (1869-1870) affirmed "emphatically that there exists a knowledge which is peculiar to faith, surpassing the knowledge proper to human reason, which nevertheless by its nature can discover the Creator. This knowledge expresses a truth based upon the very fact of God who reveals himself, a truth which is most certain, since God neither deceives nor wishes to deceive."[17]

St. Anselm (AD 1033 – 1109), who became the Archbishop of Canterbury, in his *Proslogion* explains that he was led to use both faith and reason to believe in God:

O Lord, you are not only that than which nothing greater can be conceived, but you are greater than all that can be conceived…if you were not such, something greater than you could be thought, but this is impossible."[18]

Faith and reason work together in perfect harmony (I know it sounds like a song, lol). Proverbs 16:9 explains this vitality, "The human heart may plan a course, but it is Yahweh who makes the steps secure". The Pope elaborates on this scripture:

with the light of reason human beings can know which path to take, but they can follow that path to its end, quickly and unhindered, only if with a rightly tuned spirit they search for it within the horizon of faith. Therefore, reason and faith cannot be separated without diminishing the capacity of men and women to know themselves, the world and God in an appropriate way.[19]

Quest for Meaning

Essential to life as a human is the quest for meaning. We want purpose, meaning and hope in our lives. It's fascinating that the words "know yourself" were carved on a temple portal at Delphi. This quest for meaning is so much a part of ourselves. When we don't know who we are, we are lost, often visionless, like a ship mercilessly being tossed by the relentless and unforgiving waves. To not know oneself is to cower in fear of what life may bring us, and so we lack hope.

The themes of *Set Free!* and *Born to be Free* revealed that freedom comes as a result of knowing God and knowing yourself. In the chapter, *Personal God* you will read who is the source of our hope. It is in our discovery of the meaning of life that we discover true freedom.

While we have explored philosophy (Greek = love of wisdom), the same subject asks the question of life's meaning. It reveals that the desire for truth is part of human nature itself:

human beings seek to acquire those universal elements of knowledge which enable them to understand themselves better and to advance in their own self-realisation. These fundamental elements of knowledge spring from the *wonder* awakened in them by the contemplation of creation.[20]

The meaning of life is love. We all want to love and be loved, it is an innate desire of ours. Additionally love requires sacrifice – limits our freedom for someone else:

> Only truth about oneself can bring about a real engagement of one's freedom in relation with another person. It is a giving of oneself, and giving of oneself means exactly to limit one's own freedom for the sake of another person. The limitation of one's freedom could be something negative and painful, were it not for love, which transforms it into something positive, happy and creative…Will strives towards goodness, and freedom is a prerequisite of will. Freedom, therefore, is for love, since it is through love that man participates in goodness. This is the basis for its principal position in the moral order, in the hierarchy of values, and the hierarchy of proper longing and desires of man. Man needs love more than he needs freedom, since freedom is only a medium, whereas love is a purpose. Man desires, however, true love, because only when it is based on truth can an authentic engagement of freedom be made possible.[21]

In the search for meaning, we discover who we are, and have the ability to wonder is integral to this journey. The following statement sadly has an ironic ring to it as we consider those who cease to wonder or enjoy life:

> Without wonder, men and women would lapse into deadening routine and little by little would become incapable of a life which is genuinely personal.[22]

Focusing on the "genuinely personal" I would like to highlight the aspect of intimacy. We can not truly love ourselves and others if we have lost the wonder of creation, life and God. Therefore without this true love and wonder we are reduced to mere animals – no destiny, no wonder of life, thus living a deadening routine – bored with life and devoid of hope.

Revelation

The definition given by the Pocket Catholic Dictionary is fascinating, and so I will quote most of it:

> Disclosure by God of himself and his will to the human race. The disclosure comes to human beings by way of communication,

which implies the communicator, who is God; the receiver, who is the human being; and a transmitter or intermediary. Depending on the intermediary, there are in general two main forms of revelation, commonly called natural and supernatural (Divine).

If the intermediary is the world of space and time, the revelation is said to be natural. In this case, the natural world of creation is the medium through which God communicates himself to humankind. Moreover, humanity's natural use of reason is the means by which it attains the knowledge that God wishes to communicate. It is therefore natural twice over, once in the objective source from which human beings derive knowledge of God and divine things, and once again in the subjective powers that a person uses to appropriate what God is revealing in the universe into which humanity has been placed.

Supernatural revelation begins where natural revelation ends. It is in the character of a grace from God who has decided to communicate himself in a manner that far exceeds his manifestation through nature.[23]

An example of natural revelation is that God left the ability for humanity to discover through reason and intellect the laws of nature. Thence, mankind was able to create some wonderful inventions, such as mathematics, physics, electricity, the combustion engine, etc. Without mathematics you would not have the amazing pyramids, or any of the most complex buildings, as engineering itself would be virtually impossible. These laws of nature are not here by chance.

Only a good God would reveal His nature and allow the laws of nature to be discovered by his creation. Hence this is one part of the evidence that man is the pinnacle of creation. Animals can not discover these laws – they don't have the intellect do so – but man, can. God has allowed for truth to be discovered in science, religion and philosophy.

While God spoke to mankind indirectly through the inspired prophets, especially in the Old Testament times, he chose to speak to man differently through Christ. Jesus was God Himself speaking as man to His fellow humans; this is Divine Revelation. Yes God chose to become man to speak to us, and to free us. This will be elaborated upon, in the chapter, *Personal God*.

Vatican Council II explained the importance of supernatural, or Divine Revelation:

It pleased God in his goodness and wisdom, to reveal himself and to make known the mystery of his will (cf. Eph. 1:9). His will was that men should have access to the Father, through Christ, the Word made flesh, in the Holy Spirit, and thus become sharers in the divine nature (cf. Eph. 2:18; 2 Pet. 1:4). By this revelation, then, the invisible God (cf. Col 1:15; 1 Tim. 1:17), from the fullness of His love, addresses men as his friends (cf. Ex. 33:11;Jn.15;14-15), and moves among them ((cf. Bar. 3:38), in order to invite and receive them into his own company...The most intimate truth which this revelation gives us about God and the salvation of man shines forth in Christ, who is himself both the mediator and the sum total of Revelation.[24]

The Old Testament speaks of people who couldn't discover God as "naturally stupid" – today we call this ignorance (lack of specific knowledge):

Yes, naturally stupid are all who are unaware of God,
and who, from good things seen, have not been able to discover Him-who-is,
or by studying the works, have not recognized the Artificer.
Wisdom 13:1

While St. Paul in the New Testament said, "For what can be known about God is perfectly plain to them, since God has made it plain to them: ever since the creation of the world, the invisible existence of God and his everlasting power have been clearly seen by the mind's understanding of created things. (Rom 1:19-20)

From the aforementioned quote concerning natural revelation "through space and time" we can say that God reveals himself through science naturally (as covered in Intelligent Design), and through the person of Jesus Christ, supernaturally. We have seen Divine Revelation through the words and miracles and person of Christ.

Jesus perfected Revelation "by fulfilling it through his whole work of making himself present and manifesting himself: through his words and deeds, his signs and wonders, but especially through his death and glorious Resurrection from the dead and finally his sending of the Spirit of truth".[25]

Revelation, "impels reason continually to extend the range of its knowledge until it senses that it has done all in its power, leaving no stone unturned."[26]

Philosophy and Theology meet through Revelation as it "stirs thought and seeks acceptance as an expression of love." This revealed truth is an "anticipation of that ultimate and definitive vision of God which is reserved for those who believe in him and seek him with a sincere heart. The ultimate purpose of personal existence, then, is the theme of philosophy and theology alike. For all their difference of method and content, both disciplines point to that "path of life" (Psalm 16:11) which, as faith tells us, leads us in the end to the full and lasting joy of the contemplation of the Triune God.[27]

In the section on Divine Revelation the Second Vatican Council explains the natural path we should take:

> "The obedience of faith" (Rom. 16:26; cf. Rom. 1:5; 2 Cor. 10:5-6) must be given to God as he reveals himself. By faith man freely commits his entire self to God, making "the full submission of his intellect and will to God who reveals," and willingly assenting to the Revelation given by him. Before this faith can be exercised, man must have the grace of God to move and assist him; he must have the interior helps of the Holy Spirit, who moves the heart and converts it to God, who opens the eyes of the mind and "makes it easy for all to accept and believe the truth." The same Holy Spirit constantly perfects faith by his gifts, so that Revelation may be more and more profoundly understood.[28]

The Pope says, "Man cannot grasp how death could be the source of life and love; yet to reveal the mystery of his saving plan God has chosen precisely that which reason considers "foolishness" and a "scandal"".[29] Therefore many things of the gospel, when scrutinized with pure reason, are incomprehensible, and that's why we need to use faith too when exploring Divine Revelation. But if we don't have faith, we should ask God for the gift; if we have a small amount of faith, we need to ask God to increase it. Humanity finds it difficult to grasp that Jesus death could be source of life. Just reflect, how could death be the source of life? God gave us Divine Revelation through the prophets, and so it was revealed that the Messiah would die for the sins of mankind and that the Messiah would bring salvation.

Returning to our imagery of the wings of faith and reason, Revelation could be likened to that of the heart of the bird. Without the heart, and therefore without God revealing himself to us by both natural and Divine Revelation , we would not be able to believe in Him, and especially in Christ, as God would not have revealed His son to us. In addition Revelation could be like the tail of the bird, without which we would be aimless and hopeless, and thus could not soar to where we wanted to.

Mysteries

In point 3 under Faith and Reason, it is stated that "mysteries of faith are in harmony with naturally known truths". In conjunction with mysteries there are mysteries of science, and mysteries of the universe that mankind still continues to explore and identify. The farthest reaches of space will continue to be a mystery, and yet there are aspects of the universe that we have been able to unravel. In juxtaposition the mysteries of faith have been unraveled by successive generations – from the Church Fathers, Saints, and the Church Councils, the Holy Spirit has revealed certain depths of the mysteries of faith. However these mysteries are so deep that we may not be able to fully comprehend them until heaven – that is, unless God chooses to reveal their fullness.

The Pocket Catholic Dictionary explains mystery as:

> A divinely revealed truth whose very possibility cannot be rationally conceived before it is revealed and, after revelation, whose inner essence cannot be fully understood by the finite mind. The incomprehensibility of revealed mysteries derives from the fact that they are manifestations of God, who is infinite and therefore beyond the complete grasp of a created intellect. Nevertheless, though incomprehensible, mysteries are intelligible. One of the primary duties of a believer is, through prayer, study and experience to grow in faith, i.e. to develop an understanding of what God has revealed (Greek: mysterion, something closed, a secret)[30]

Proverbs 25:2 explains it appropriately, "To conceal a matter, this is the glory of God, to sift it thoroughly, the glory of kings." Pope John Paul II explains the unique relationship that humans have:

> In God there lies the origin of all things, in him is found the fullness of the mystery, and in this his glory consists: to men and women there falls the task of exploring truth with their reason, and in this their nobility consists.[31]

In Psalm 139:17-18 the Psalmist expresses deeply how awesome is the knowledge of God:

> How hard for me to grasp your thoughts,
> how many, God, there are!
> If I count them, they are more than the grains of sand;
> If I come to an end, I am still with you.

The Pope carries on the explanation of the unique relationship mankind has by saying:

> The desire for knowledge is so great and it works in such a way that the human heart, despite its experience of insurmountable limitation, yearns for the infinite riches which lie beyond, knowing that there is to be found the satisfying answer to every question as yet unanswered.[32]

The he draws us back to the aspect of mystery as he says mysteries "contain a hidden truth to which the mind is drawn" and that the sign of the Eucharist embodies, "the indissoluble unity between the signifier and signified makes it possible to grasp the depths of the mystery."[33]

We use Faith and Reason to entrust ourselves to the Creator, or as some people put it to commit ourselves to God. Therefore we use our whole person as we use our intellect.

Summary

Therefore God reveals Himself, His character and substance, while mankind identifies what already exists, but what he has not seen or known before. Mankind discovers the finger print of God the Creator through the Big Bang and Intelligent Design and using reason we can deduce that God created primarily for mankind, the pinnacle of His creation – the purpose for creation.

When we use faith in conjunction with our reason we see more of what God has revealed. Therefore faith and reason are integral to us as human beings and differentiates us from all other creatures. They both lead us on the quest for meaning, and guiding and supporting us on the quest for truth – the quest for God.

Chapter 12 – Bibliography

1. http://www.vatican.va/holy_father/john_paul_ii/encyclicals/index.htm
2. http://www.vatican.va/edocs/ENG0216/_INDEX.HTM
3. Collins Pocket English Dictionary, Wm Collins Sons & Co. Ltd, Glasgow, 1986
4. Johns A Hardon, SJ, Pocket Catholic Dictionary (Abridged edition of Modern Catholic Dictionary), Image Book, Doubleday, 1985, 142
5. http://www.vatican.va/edocs/ENG0216/_INDEX.HTM, section 43
6. Ibid, section 38
7. Collins Pocket English Dictionary, Wm Collins Sons & Co. Ltd, Glasgow, 1986

8. http://www.vatican.va/edocs/ENG0216/_INDEX.HTM, section 34
9. Ibid, section 24
10. Ibid, section 36
11. Ibid, section 40
12. Johns A Hardon, SJ, Pocket Catholic Dictionary (Abridged edition of Modern Catholic Dictionary), Image Book, Doubleday, 1985, 123-125
13. Ed. Austin Flannery, OP, Vatican Council II – The Conciliar and Post Conciliar Documents, Costello Publishing Company, New York, 1988 Revised, 752
14. First Vatican Council, *Dogmatic. Constitution on Catholic Faith*, c.2 (on Revelation): *Denz* 1785 and 1786 (3004 and 3005)
15. Johns A Hardon, SJ, Pocket Catholic Dictionary (Abridged edition of Modern Catholic Dictionary), Image Book, Doubleday, 1985, 142-143
16. Summa Theologica, I, 2, 3
17. http://www.vatican.va/edocs/ENG0216/_INDEX.HTM, section 8
18. Proemium and Nos. 1, 15: *PL* 158, 223-224; 226; 235
19. http://www.vatican.va/edocs/ENG0216/_INDEX.HTM, section 16
20. http://www.vatican.va/edocs/ENG0216/_INDEX.HTM, section 4
21. See Karol Wojtyla, *Love and Responsibility*, quoted by Fr. Andrew N Woznicki in *A Christian Humanism: Karol Wojtyla's Existential Personalism* (New Britain, CT: Mariel Publications, 1980), 28
22. http://www.vatican.va/edocs/ENG0216/_INDEX.HTM, section 4
23. Johns A Hardon, SJ, Pocket Catholic Dictionary (Abridged edition of Modern Catholic Dictionary), Image Book, Doubleday, 1985, 370-371
24. Ed. Austin Flannery, OP, Vatican Council II – The Conciliar and Post Conciliar Documents, Costello Publishing Company, New York, 1988 Revised, 750
25. http://www.vatican.va/edocs/ENG0216/_INDEX.HTM, section 10
26. http://www.vatican.va/edocs/ENG0216/_INDEX.HTM, section 14
27. http://www.vatican.va/edocs/ENG0216/_INDEX.HTM, section 15
28. Ed. Austin Flannery, OP, Vatican Council II – The Conciliar and Post Conciliar Documents, Costello Publishing Company, New York, 1988 Revised, 752
29. http://www.vatican.va/edocs/ENG0216/_INDEX.HTM, section 23
30. Johns A Hardon, SJ, Pocket Catholic Dictionary (Abridged edition of Modern Catholic Dictionary), Image Book, Doubleday, 1985, 275
31. http://www.vatican.va/edocs/ENG0216/_INDEX.HTM, section 17
32. http://www.vatican.va/edocs/ENG0216/_INDEX.HTM, section 17
33. http://www.vatican.va/edocs/ENG0216/_INDEX.HTM, section 13

CHAPTER 13

EVIL: DOES IT EXIST?

As of late, when one thinks of evil, one infamous date is brought to mind, 11 September 2001. Most of us can even recall how we heard of the ghastly event, and exactly what we were doing at that time. But can we really class this as evil? To do so, we need to look at the concept of evil and what it actually means.

The *Collins Pocket English Dictionary* defines evil as being "morally wrong (wicked); harmful; unlucky (disastrous) and the noun wickedness is sin; and anything that causes harm, pain, etc."[1]

It's fascinating that the Catholic Pocket Dictionary explains evil as, "the absence of what ought to be there."[2] Therefore if you take away love, and replace it with hate, then that is evil. Or take away any of the good characteristics of God, for example, love, patience, mercy, compassion, and understanding and replace that with something that shouldn't be there e.g. envy (not being satisfied with what God has given us), hatred, pride, lust, adultery, unforgiveness – once again you are left with evil; what ought to be there, is not there, and has been replaced by a fake substitute – the source of this substitute, is like the substitute itself, it is evil – hence the father of evil, the devil.

Evil can be divided into two categories: moral evil and natural evil. First let's explore the former.

Moral Evil

We can describe moral evil as being an action or intention with the desire to cause harm or pain to yourself or others. This is related to the above definition where it explains the absence of what ought to be there, e.g. if you had the intention to hit someone and make them hurt, then you are replacing a good intention with a bad. So therefore where you should be doing something good for your neighbor, instead you are doing something bad.

If you take the example of Adam and Eve, we discover that humanity loved God. Then after God created the world, and Adam and Eve, the father of lies comes into the picture. Note that the serpent was known formerly as Lucifer, meaning the angel of light, but he turned away from God's graciousness and love, refusing to serve his Creator and betrayed God, taking a third of the angels with him. Thus man believes the lies of Satan, disobeying and rejecting God, and thus breaking the bond of trust, the bond of love:

> Now the serpent was the most cunning of all the animals that the LORD God had made. The serpent asked the woman, "Did God really tell you not to eat from any of the trees in the garden?" The woman answered the serpent: "We may eat of the fruit of the trees in the garden; it is only about the fruit of the tree in the middle of the garden that God said, "You shall not eat it or even touch it, lest you die. But the serpent said to the woman: "You certainly will not die! No, God knows well that the moment you eat of it your eyes will be opened and you will be like gods who know what is good and what is bad." Genesis 3:1-5 (New American Bible)

It is important to note here that the serpent first seeks to bring evil into the world by replacing trust of God with disbelief. The serpent also twists the truth; you will see that the consequence of allowing evil into their lives is a spiritual death, and the truth is that their eyes will be opened; they will lose their innocence, and indeed be able to choose evil or good, where once evil did not exist.

> The woman saw that the tree was good for food, pleasing to the eyes, and desirable for gaining wisdom. So she took some of its fruit and ate it; and she also gave some to her husband, who was with her, and he ate it. Genesis 3:6 (New American Bible)

Therefore the eyes of Adam and Eve were opened to good and evil. They hid from God because they were afraid. Maybe their fear caused them to realize that they had wronged their Creator by disbelieving and disobeying Him. This is how evil entered the world. Man replaced love and trust of their Creator with disbelief, disobedience and distrust – the bond of trust, and thus love was shattered. Humanity thus replaced love with evil.

Suffering and Evil

The very existence of the evil and suffering in the world is one of the major, if not the most used excuses that people utilize when revealing why they don't believe in God. Evil is dependent on suffering, though not all suffering is evil. The fact is, without evil, there would not be the level of suffering that there is – perhaps suffering would not exist.

The questions that many people ask are: If God is all loving, why is there suffering in the world? If God truly loves us why does he let evil things happen to good people?

But when we put these "superficial lenses" on we are blocked from one beautiful truth. Yes God is all loving; He embraced suffering, an excruciating suffering more than most of us could endure. Jesus knew he was going to suffer, and he embraced suffering so that you and I could be reconciled to God. Without his suffering the doorway to eternal life would not have been opened to us. In the next chapter I will dwell more on this fact of God's plan to redeem humankind. But for now, let's contemplate that Jesus embraced the way of suffering, yes he was afraid (he sweated great drops of blood) – maybe his fear was related to being separated from God the Father during this time of suffering – Jesus took the sins of mankind upon himself – all past sins, and all future sins and He thus felt abandoned on the Cross.

The power of the Cross transcends time, as God is not bound by time; He is outside of time. Therefore the power of the Cross is as powerful today as it was when Jesus was crucified.

Jesus knows what it is like to suffer – but our suffering pales in comparison. Also our sufferings are only temporal, as Jesus sufferings on the Cross were temporal. It is so liberating to know that our current suffering is only limited to earth, and that when we obtain Heaven, we will not suffer anymore, and most of all, our time in Heaven is just the beginning of a wonderful place that we enter into for eternity. Pope John Paul II puts it so beautifully when he says, "Where might the human being seek the answer to dramatic questions such as pain, the suffering of the innocent and death, if not in the light streaming from the mystery of Christ's Passion, Death and Resurrection? [3]

Suffering can also lead us closer to God. It is through other people's love and concern that God can be revealed to those suffering. Jesus showed us the way – he embraced suffering:

> The Spirit himself joins with our spirit to bear witness that we are children of God. And if we are children, then we are heirs, heirs of God and joint-heirs with Christ, provided that we share his suffering, so as to share his glory.
> Romans 8:16-17

Therefore suffering is very much a part of life as humans. We can either draw closer to God through the suffering, or we can become bitter towards God. It is only through sharing suffering that we can share God's glory. This isn't a fatalistic mentality that we don't seek help from health professionals, but it is a matter of attitude and not grumbling and feeling sorry for oneself, but embracing the suffering.

Peter Kreeft reveals three things about evil:

> First, evil is not a *thing*, an entity, a being. All beings are either the Creator or creatures created by the Creator. But every thing God created is good, according to Genesis. We naturally tend to picture evil as a thing – a black cloud, or a dangerous storm, or a grimacing face, or dirt. But these pictures mislead us.[4]

Therefore it is when we choose to turn away from God, and give into hidden desires, or what are known as the seven deadly sins – pride, avarice, lust, envy, gluttony, anger and sloth – then we take upon us evil. In turning away from our Creator we are freely choosing evil. The fact is that we owe our very existence to God. Then why do we sometimes act like he doesn't exist?

> Second, the origin of evil is not the Creator but the creature's freely choosing sin and selfishness. Take away all sin and selfishness and you would have heaven on earth. Even the remaining physical evils would no longer rankle and embitter us. Saints endure and even embrace suffering and death as lovers embrace heroic challenges. Furthermore, the cause of physical evil is spiritual evil. The cause of suffering is sin…God is the source of all life and joy. Therefore, when the human soul rebels against God, it loses its life and joy. Now a human being is body as well as soul. We are single creatures, not double: we are not even body and soul as much as we are embodied soul, or ensouled body. So the body must share in the soul's inevitable punishment – a punishment as natural and unavoidable as broken bones from jumping off a cliff or a sick stomach from eating rotten food rather than a punishment as artificial and external as a grade for a course or a slap on the hands for taking cookies.[5]

It is when we turn away from God that we lose life and joy; our soul is deprived of the most important two things that it thrives on. Therefore in its place evil resides as what ought to be there is absent, and something not of God, evil has taken its place.

Solution to Evil

Peter Kreeft explains the solution to the problem of evil.

> But even if you think the solution in thought is obscure and uncertain, the solution in practice is as strong as and clear as the sun: it is the Son. God's solution to the problem of evil is his Son Jesus Christ. The Father's love sent his Son to die for us to defeat the power of evil in human nature: that's the heart of the Christian story. We do not worship a deistic God, an absentee landlord who ignores his slum; we worship a garbageman God who came right down into our worst garbage to clean it up. How do we get God off the hook for allowing evil? God is not off the hook; God is the hook. That's the point of a crucifix.
> The Cross is God's part of the practical solution to evil. Our part, according to the same Gospel, is to repent, to believe, and to work with God in fighting evil by the power of love. [6]

Therefore when we turn back to God, it is by the power of love that we can conquer evil; that power of love flows from God, He is the source of love. The key is to ask God to forgive you, and then you will need to make a conscious decision to commit your life to the very cause of your existence. Then make some concrete steps in order to keep focus on God and to treat Him as someone important in your life.

Natural Evil

Natural evil is the term given to physical or material evil that occurs in the world, such as earthquakes, droughts, devastating floods, and other natural disasters. Theologians refer to natural evil as "ontic evil".
There are certain natural evils that relate to the creatures with souls. This includes pain, ageing, and fatigue. Louis Janssens explains natural evil relating to such creatures as:

> Any lack of perfection at which we aim, any lack of fulfillment which frustrates our natural urges and makes us suffer. It is essentially the natural consequence of our limitation. [7]

Therefore the limitation in itself is not evil, but when it causes creation suffering then it is; hence it is the intent that is a major contributor towards suffering.

Some of us may question: Why would God let natural evil happen? But Sacred Scripture gives us a wonderful answer relating to all creation being in disarray or imperfection as result of mankind's disobedience and not trusting, and hence not loving fully the Creator:

> In my estimation, all that we suffer in the present time is nothing in comparison with the glory which is destined to be disclosed for us, for the whole creation is waiting with eagerness for the children of God to be revealed. It was not for its own purposes that creation had frustration imposed on it, but for the purposes of him who imposed it – with the intention that the whole creation itself might be freed from its slavery to corruption and brought into the same glorious freedom as the children of God. We are well aware that the whole creation, until this time, has been groaning in labour pains. And not only that: we too, who have the first-fruits of the Spirit, even we are groaning inside ourselves, waiting with eagerness for our bodies to be set free.
> Romans: 8:18-24

Summary

We should not blame God for moral or natural evil. The former evil is the result of mankind's selfishness and his choice to be wicked or evil.

God showed us through His Son what it's like to suffer. To have a glimpse of this go to http://www.passion-movie.com/english/trailer.html and check out the trailer to the Jesus movie, due to be released in 2004. It indeed will be a movie to move the minds and hearts of many. The power of the Cross transcends time and this power is as powerful today – it is so powerful that it can free you from your offenses (e.g. mistrust or disobedience) against God. We have thrown His love back in His face. But He waits for us, longing for us to return. Jesus is the solution to the problem of evil. Our life on earth, and hence our suffering is like a drop of water in a vast ocean. So when we contemplate that we are being offered eternal life in heaven, and that scripture reveals there will be no more pain or suffering in heaven, and thus no more evil, then the choice is rather easy.

The following quote from Kreeft signifies the attitude that we should have in trusting our Creator. It really is a beautiful analogy:

A child on the tenth story of a burning building cannot see the firefighters with their safety net on the street. They call up, "Jump! We'll catch you. Trust us." The child objects, "But I can't see you." The firefighter replies, "That's all right. I can see you." We are like that child, evil is like the fire, our ignorance is like the smoke, God is like the firefighter, and Christ is the safety net. If there are situations like this where we must trust even fallible human beings with our lives, where we must trust what we hear, not what we see, then it is reasonable that we must trust the infallible, all-seeing God when we hear from his word but do not see from our reason or experience.[8]

It is us that are looking down, afraid to make a leap of faith, afraid to trust the Loving Creator. God is calling us to make the step, which to us seems like an eternity of distance. God is calling out to us, "I will catch you. I love you!" But our response is often, I don't believe you, you don't exist. If only we make that step, then God will catch us, and not only catch us but be our support. The biggest prize is on offer, eternal life. All we have to do for a few years on earth, until we die, (whether that be another 10, 50 or 80 years), is repent, be baptised (if we have not already done so) and follow God, which includes worshipping Him as part of a community (Church); it is through the Church that we are challenged, grow in our faith, and can help others.

Chapter 13 – Bibliography

1. Collins Pocket English Dictionary, London, 1986, 295
2. Johns A Hardon, SJ, Pocket Catholic Dictionary (Abridged edition of Modern Catholic Dictionary), Image Book, Doubleday, 1985, 136
3. http://www.vatican.va/edocs/ENG0216/_INDEX.HTM, section 12
4. Peter Kreeft, *Fundamentals of the Faith*, Ignatius Press, San Francisco, 1988, 55
5. Ibid, 55
6. Ibid, 56
7. Louis Janssens
8. Peter Kreeft, *Fundamentals of the Faith*, Ignatius Press, San Francisco, 1988, 57

CHAPTER 14

THE PHILOSOPHY OF GOD'S EXISTENCE

Like any judicial system it is satisfactory to prove a case beyond reasonable doubt. This doesn't mean that any particular evidence can be used on its own to convict someone, but that all the evidence must be taken as a whole. In this chapter I am seeking to do the same. Though philosophy can be used to rationalize the existence of God, it should be taken with the other evidence throughout this book. I believe that a Creator has left clues for us to find that He exists, and has done so in the case of philosophy.

Peter Kreeft in *Summa of the Summa*, in which he simplifies the Summa of St. Thomas Aquinas, gives us several examples of attempts to prove the existence of God:[1]

II. Cosmological
E. Design: Design can be caused only by an Intelligent Designer. Mindless nature cannot design itself or come about by chance.
F. The *Kalam* (Time) Argument: Time must have a beginning, a first moment (creation) to give rise to all other moments. (The "Big Bang" seems to confirm this: time had an absolute beginning fifteen to twenty billion years ago.) And the act of creation presupposes a Creator.

III. Psychological
A. from mind and truth
1. Augustine: Our minds are in contact with eternal, objective, and absolute truth superior to our minds (e.g. $2 + 2 = 4$), and the eternal is divine, not human.
2. Decartes: Our *idea* of a perfect being (God) could not have come from any imperfect source (cause), for the effect cannot be greater than the cause. Thus it must have come from God.
B. from will and good
2. Newman: Conscience speaks with absolute authority, which could come only from God.

C. from emotions and desire
1. C. S. Lewis: Innate desires correspond to real objects, and we have an innate desire (at least unconsciously) for God and Heaven.
2. Von Balthasar: Beauty reveals God. There is Mozart, therefore there must be God.
D. from experience
1. Existential Argument: If there is no God (and no immortality) life is ultimately meaningless.
3. Ordinary religious experience (prayer) meets God. (Prayer of the Skeptic: "God, if you exist, show me" – a real experiment.)
4. Love argument: If there is no God of Love, no Absolute that is love, then love is not absolute. Or, the eyes of love reveal the infinite value of the human person as the image of God.

It is pertinent here to revise the cosmological argument from the point of view of the Islamic theologian al-Ghazali. He defined it as:[2]

1. Whatever begins to exist has a cause.
2. The universe begins to exist.
3. Therefore, the universe has a cause.

St. Thomas Aquinas' 5 Ways

St. Thomas Aquinas, one of the brilliant minds of the Middle Ages, ironically had the nickname of the dumb ox by his peers. While a rather gentle and unassuming giant he became a Dominican monk, and even declined the opportunity to become a bishop. He unwound the intricacies of the Cosmological Argument which resulted in his acclaimed 5 key ways for illustrating the existence of God:[3]

1. Motion

The first and more manifest way is the argument from motion. It is certain and evident to our senses, that in the world some things are in motion. Now whatever is in motion is put in motion by another, for nothing can be in motion except it is in potentiality to that towards which it is in motion; whereas a thing moves inasmuch as it is in act. For motion is nothing else than the reduction of something from potentiality to actuality. But nothing can be reduced from potentiality to actuality, except by something in a state of actuality. Thus that which is actually hot, as fire, makes wood, which is potentially hot, to be actually hot, and thereby moves and changes it. Now it is not possible that the same thing should be at once in actuality and potentiality in the same respect, but only in different respects. For what is actually hot cannot simultaneously be potentially hot; but it is simultaneously potentially cold. It is therefore impossible that in the same respect and in the same way a thing should be both mover and moved, *i.e.,* that it should move itself. Therefore, whatever is in motion must be put in motion by another. If that by which it is put in motion be itself put in motion, then this also must needs be put in motion by another, and that by another again. But this cannot go on to infinity, because then there would be no first mover, and, consequently, no other mover; seeing that subsequent movers move only inasmuch as they are put in motion by the first mover; as the staff moves only because it is put in motion by the hand. Therefore it is necessary to arrive at a first mover, put in motion by no other; and this everyone understands to be God.

Aquinas is saying that with the Motion Argument there must be a first mover. He deals with causation in a very strict sense, and not simply relating to some factor we can control. When he speaks of cause he has in mind a clear-cut specific influence passed on from one substance to another, for example, the hot-plate is the cause of the pot getting hot. This is why we say something had to cause the Big Bang. This First Cause we call God. No one else caused God.

2. Efficient Cause

The second way is from the nature of the efficient cause. In the world of sense we find there is an order of efficient causes. There is no case known (neither is it, indeed, possible) in which a thing is found to be the efficient cause of itself; for so it would be prior to itself, which is impossible. Now in efficient causes it is not possible to go on to infinity, because in all efficient causes following in order, the first is the cause of the intermediate cause, and the intermediate is the cause of the ultimate cause, whether the intermediate cause be several, or one only. Now to take away the cause is to take away the effect. Therefore, if there be no first cause among efficient causes, there will be no ultimate, nor any intermediate cause. But if in efficient causes it is possible to go on to infinity, there will be no first efficient cause, neither will there be an ultimate effect, nor any intermediate efficient causes; all of which is plainly false. Therefore it is necessary to admit a first efficient cause, to which everyone gives the name of God.

Aquinas is stating that there has to be a First Cause, which means that no one caused God. If someone caused Him then He would not be the First Cause. Moreover, the First Cause must be All-Powerful to be just that, the First Cause.

3. Possibility and Necessity

The third way is taken from possibility and necessity, and runs thus. We find in nature things that are possible to be and not to be, since they are found to be generated, and to corrupt, and consequently they are possible to be and not to be. But it is impossible for these always to exist, for that which is possible not to be at some time is not. Therefore, if everything is possible not to be, then at one time there could have been nothing in existence. Now if this were true, even now there would be nothing in existence, because that which does not exist only begins to exist by something already existing. Therefore, if at one time nothing was in existence, it would have been impossible for anything to have begun to exist; and thus even now nothing would be in existence – which is absurd. Therefore, not all beings are merely possible, but there must exist something the existence of which is necessary.

But every necessary thing either has its necessity caused by another, or not. Now it is impossible to go on to infinity in necessary things which have their necessity caused by another, as has been already proved in regard to efficient causes. Therefore we cannot but postulate the existence of some being having of itself its own necessity, and not receiving it from another, but rather causing in others their necessity. This all men speak of as God.

This 3rd proof with the words, "Possible to be and not to be" is also related to the Contingent Being concept. A Contingent Being is something that depends on something else for its existence; this includes such things as:

- your computer
- your car
- the Rhine river
- the universe
- Planet Earth
- you

With Contingent beings there non-existence is possible. They can cease to exist in the future. For example, if you got so upset with your computer that you threw it off a cliff, and it smashed into thousands of pieces, with all the guts of computer strewn all over the rocks, you would have one big mess left, and no computer. Alternatively you might set fire to it, and thus you would not have a computer any more. Therefore the computer is dependent on a creator, and upon an intelligent being in order to keep it functioning; it is not the cause of its own existence.

The 3rd proof also relates to the concept of a Necessary Being. Aquinas says, "there must exist something the existence of which is necessary". Unlike the Contingent Being whose nonexistence is possible, the Necessary Being's non-existence is impossible. Furthermore the Necessary Being is not dependent on anything for its existence, is self-caused and thus eternal.

> To say that something is self-caused…means only that it exists, not contingently or in dependence upon something else, but by its own nature, which is only to say that it is a being which is such that it can neither come into being nor perish…If it makes sense to speak of anything as an *impossible* being, or something that by its very nature does not exist, then it is hard to see why the idea of a necessary being, or something that in its very nature exists, should not be just as comprehensible. [4]

> There seems, then, to be only one other possibility. The world (the sum total of all contingent beings) exists because it (like all contingent beings) depends upon a being other than itself. But in this case, the existence of the world must depend on the existence of a being that is *not* contingent. And if the only possible explanation for the existence of the world is noncontingent being, this explanation must be for a necessary being.[5]

Stephen Davis thus defends Aquinas, saying:

> His method was first to prove the existence of a Necessary Being (as well as the first mover and first cause of the first two Ways and the intelligent being who directs the behaviour of unintelligent things of the Fifth Way). He then did an inventory, so to speak, of all the beings he believed to exist on other grounds (including theological grounds). Finally, he asked, which of them could be the same being as the being or beings proved to exist in the Five Ways? The answer he found, naturally enough, was that only *God* could be a first mover, first cause, necessary being and Intelligent Designer…This was why he said, "and this all men speak of as God". Who else could a first mover be than God?[6]

St. Anselm speaks of a being that which, "nothing greater can be conceived":

> And so, Lord, do though, who dost give understanding to faith, give me, so far as thou knowest it to be profitable, to understand that thou art as we believe [Revelation, Faith and Reason]; and that thou art that which we believe. And, indeed, we believe that thou art a being than which nothing greater can be conceived.[7]

Therefore the First Cause is also the Necessary Being and is All-Powerful or Almighty as the First Cause and thus eternal.

4. Gradation to be found in things

> The fourth way is taken from the gradation to be found in things. Among beings there are some more and some less good, true, noble, and the like. But "more" and "less" are predicated of different things, according as they resemble in their different ways something which is the maximum, as a thing is said to be hotter according as it more nearly resembles that which is hottest; so that there is something which is truest, something best, something noblest, and, consequently, something which is uttermost being; for those things that are greatest in truth are greatest in being, as it is written in *Metaph.* ii. Now the maximum in any genus is the cause of all that genus; as fire, which is the maximum of heat, the cause of all hot things. Therefore there must also be something which is to all beings the cause of their being, goodness, and every other perfection; and this we call God.

Therefore God is truest, best, noblest and most loving. God loves you very much!

5. Governance of the world

> The fifth way is taken from the governance of the world. We see that things which lack intelligence, such as natural bodies, act for an end, and this is evident from their acting always, or nearly always, in the same way, so as to obtain the best result. Hence it is plan that not fortuitously, but designedly, do they achieve their End. Now whatever lacks intelligence cannot move towards an end, unless it be directed by some being endowed with knowledge and intelligence; as the arrow is shot to its mark by the archer. Therefore some intelligent being exists by whom all natural things are directed to their end; and this being we call God.

This Governance Argument reminds us of the Intelligent Design Theory, and how God has left his fingerprint on creation.

These Five Ways , Thomas Aquinas saw as pointing to God who lives in light inaccessible, until revealed to us in Revelation. It is important to note here that God has revealed himself to us through natural and Divine Revelation, which I will explain in more detail in the chapter, *Faith and Reason.*

The Summa Theologica can be found on the internet at: http://www.ccel.org/a/aquinas/summa/home.html; for his other writing, http://www.home.duq.edu/~bonin/thomasbibliography.html#summa; and for another Aquinas website including the 5 ways see http://www.aquinasonline.com/Topics/5ways.html.

Pascal's Wager

Blaise Pascal, was born in Clermont, France in 1623. He wrote what is termed the Wager, which I believe is for those who try to dismiss the concept of a Creator outright – a predetermined bias (the writings of Richard Dawkins show a certain contempt towards a Creator). For some people they need to stop and look at what the consequence of flippantly disregarding a Creator could be. Peter Kreeft & Ronald Tacelli explain it superbly:

> There is another, different kind of argument left. It has come to be known as Pascal's Wager. We mention it here and adapt it for our purposes, not because it is a proof for the existence of God, but because it can help us in our search for God in the absence of such proof.
>
> As originally proposed by Pascal, the Wager assumes that logical reasoning by itself cannot decide for or against the existence of God; there seem to be good reasons on both sides. Now since reason cannot decide for sure, and since the question is of such importance that we must decide somehow, then we must "wager" if we cannot prove. And so we are asked: Where are you going to place your bet?
>
> If you place it with God, you lose nothing, even if it turns out that God does not exist. But if you place it against God, and you are wrong and God does exist, you lose everything: God, eternity, heaven, infinite gain. "Let us assess the two cases: if you win, you win everything, if you lose, you lose nothing."

Suppose God does not exist and I believe in him. In that case, what awaits me after death is not eternal life but, most likely, eternal nonexistence. But now take the other diagonal: God, my Creator and the source of all good, does exist; but I do not believe in him. He offers me his love and his life, and I reject it. There are answers to my greatest questions, there is fulfillment of my deepest desires; but I decide to spurn it all. In that case, I lose (or at least seriously risk losing) everything.[8]

The authors inform us that though the "Wager can seem offensively venal and purely selfish", it can be reformulated to appeal to a higher moral motive: If there is a God of infinite goodness, and he justly deserves my allegiance and faith, I risk doing the greatest injustice by not acknowledging him."[9] Additionally they say that the Wager shouldn't coerce belief but rather should inspire the search for God and "to study and restudy the arguments that seek to show that there is Something – or Someone – who is the ultimate explanation of the universe and of my life."[10]

This last quote regarding Pascal's Wager and Pascal's explanation of the three groups should be taken as a generalization. When the authors say, "found God" I believe this would mean that they have truly found him, and love them with all their mind, heart, soul and strength; and truly love their neighbour – for example, Mother Teresa. Maybe we should also relate the italicized word below to contentment. The authors say:

Pascal says that there are three kinds of people: those who have sought God and found him, those who are seeking and have not yet found, and those who neither seek nor find. The first are reasonable and *happy*, the second are reasonable and unhappy, the third are both unreasonable and unhappy. If the Wager stimulates us at least to seek, then it will at least stimulate us to be reasonable. And if the promise Jesus makes is true, all who see will find (Mt 7:7-8), and thus will be *happy*.[11]

Experience

While Aquinas focused solely on scientific explanations for proving the existence of God, there is one area of evidence which I would like to bring to the readers attention; the evidence by experience. Some people discount religious evidence as superstition or imagination, but we need to look at all the evidence, before throwing out the baby with the bathwater.

If I could not find any confirmation of the Christian message in my own experience I would be less justified in accepting that message than I am in fact. To generalize the point, suppose that no one had ever experienced communion with God, had ever heard God speaking to him or her, had ever felt the strengthening influence of the Holy Spirit in a difficult situation. In that case Christian belief would be a less rational stance that is in fact.[12]

There are many truths that we learn by experience, i.e. by trial and error, such as what is too hot to touch. Also when growing up we increase our knowledge that most bad things we do have consequences – a case in point is that if we disobey our parents we will be punished. This experience of being punished usually makes us think twice before we repeat the same mistake, or it makes us explore alternative ways in which to escape getting caught (reason). Additionally, we learn how to grow in our relationships through experience. If you give your best friend or your lover only 5 minutes attention a week, you would soon learn that you couldn't sustain a relationship with such a lack of effort. Just reflect on how much time you give towards your relationship with God.

Similarly we learn through religious experience. There are different ways that we can feel the presence of God and Nash likens this to someone sensing a presence of someone else in a dark room:

Without seeing or hearing anything, someone in a dark room may become aware of another person's presence. Likewise, people testify, that they have become aware of God's presence or something like this, even though they had no specific sensation.[13]

Moreover, Nash reveals some of the different ways that we can feel God's presence:

We get glimpses, at least of God's will for us; we feel the Holy Spirit at work in our lives, guiding us, strengthening us, enabling us to love other people in a new way; we hear God speaking to us in the Bible, in preaching, or in the words and actions of our fellow Christians. Because of this we are more justified in our Christian beliefs than we would have been otherwise.[14]

There are many different ways that trigger a religious experience – such as:

- the birth of a newborn baby
- gazing in wonder at the universe
- prayer
- being given a second chance
- feeling loved
- loving others
- helping someone
- having your prayer answered beyond your expectations
- seeing a miracle
- staring death in the face
- a near death experience
- being brought to financial ruin
- death of a loved one
- sensing God's presence in the Eucharist
- reading Sacred Scripture
- contemplating the beauty of nature
- recognizing Intelligent Design within nature
- reading an inspiring book
- being touched by the Word of God – Sacred Scripture

This list is obviously not exhaustive but we can see that people are brought to a religious experience not just from what some would consider a point of weakness or using God as a 'crutch', such as financial ruin, but also includes times of joy. God can be found in all circumstances. This includes within testimonies, including those from my first two books show that we can indeed be brought closer to God through both good and bad times; but sadly some people only turn to God when the going gets tough, and then forget about Him when things are going smoothly. It's interesting to note that many people though brought to a belief in God when things are tough, often still to believe in Him when things are going well, which seems to defy the objection it is used only as a crutch.

A young soldier reflects on an experience he had on the existence of God. This soldier wrote the following prayer:

Look, God, I've never spoken to you before, but now I just want to say 'hello'. They told me you didn't exist, and like a fool I believed them. But last night I looked up at the sky from a shell hole. When I saw the beauty of the stars, and thought how big the universe is, I knew they were telling me a lie.
If wonder if you will shake hands with me when we meet? Somehow I feel you will understand all my failures. Strange how I had to come to this horrible place to get to know you. What was I doing before this?
There isn't much more to say, but I'm sure glad I got to know you today. I feel the zero hour will soon be here. This is going to be a horrible fight. Who knows but I may come to your house tonight. I'm crying! Fancy me crying! I never thought this could happen to me. I have to go now. Strange, since I met you, I'm no longer afraid to die.[15]

It is important to note that there have been many questionable claims made on the basis of experience. One has to sort out the valid experiential claims from the false, using the God given reason we have. However, the evidence from religious experience should not be discounted, but should be taken in conjunction with the other evidence in highly proving the existence of God. William Rowe advises us not to discard all such evidence:

If we reject the principle for all experiences (nonreligious and religious), we would be saying that *all* experiences should be judged guilty until proven innocent, a move that would entail skepticism with regard to a great deal of what we think we know about the world. On the other hand, Rowe admits, if we retain the principle of credulity with regard to nonreligious experience and reject it only with respect to religious experience, our move will appear arbitrary. So anyone like Rowe who wishes to counter the use of the principle of credulity in our argument for God's existence must tread carefully so as to avoid skepticism on the one hand and the appearance of a bigoted arbitrariness on the other.[16]

Summary

We can thus reason for the existence of God. The 5 ways of Thomas Aquinas reveal to us a Necessary and Loving Being - The First Cause. This Necessary Being is All-Powerful, and thus Almighty – this being we call God. He is truest, best, noblest, and pure love.

He reveals Himself through Intelligent Design, as well as through Religion, faith and reason and experience. God has left his fingerprint on creation. We can either wager for God or against his existence. Experience leads us closer to God. We should not discount someone's experience outright. There are so many treasures from the writings (thus experience) of the Church Fathers and the Saints; and the greatest experience is of Jesus and His apostles from Sacred Scripture.

It is important to remember that we live in a world that Divine Revelation explained has been redeemed, and in which the Holy Spirit is at work. The proofs of God, opened up to us through natural and Divine Revelation, help us in our quest to know and love the God of salvation.

But would should we do with the information from this chapter? This was not an intellectual exercise to merely help prove the existence of God, but more importantly, it is to show you another splendid aspect of God's nature, which is to be approached with openness, humility, reverence and conscious of our need to know this Necessary Being. This Necessary Being as I have pointed out earlier, has created us as unique individuals - His loving creation. Therefore this Necessary Being, God, is personal. We as personal beings reflect our Creator, the Eternal Loving God. Therefore God wants a personal relationship with you, as I reveal and expound upon in the chapter, *Personal God.*

Chapter 14 – Bibliography

1. Ed. Peter Kreeft, *Summa of the Summa*, Ignatius, San Francisco, 1990, 63-64
2. ed. William Dembski, *Mere Creation*, Science, Faith and Intelligent Design, InterVarsity Press, Downers Grove, IL, 1998, 333
3. See Ed. Peter Kreeft, *Summa of the Summa*, Ignatius, San Francisco, 1990, 65-69 (gives all 5 ways or proofs for the existence of God).
4. Richard Taylor, *Metaphysics*, 2d ed. (Englewood Cliffs, N.J: Prentice-Hall, 1974), 111
5. Ronald H Nash, *Faith & Reason: Searching for a Rational Faith,* Zondervan Publishing House, Michigan, 1988, 129
6. Stephen T. Davis, God, *Reason & Theistic Proofs*, WMB Eerdmans Publishing Company, Grand Rapids, Michigan, 1997,184
7. *Proslogion II*
8. Peter Kreeft & Ronald Tacelli, *Handbook of Christian Apologetics,* InterVarsity Press, Illinois, 1994, 86
9. Ibid
10. Ibid
11. Ibid
12. William P Alston, "Christian Experience and Christian Belief," in *Faith and*

Rationality, ed. A Plantinga & N Wolterstorff (Notre Dame, Ind.: University of Notre Dame Press, 1983), 103

13. Ronald H Nash, Faith & Reason: Searching for a Rational Faith, Zondervan Publishing House, Michigan, 1988, 145 – see Richard Swinburne, *The Existence of God* (Oxford: Clarendon Press, 1979), 250-251

14. William P Alston, "Christian Experience and Christian Belief," in *Faith and Rationality,* ed. A Plantinga & N Wolterstorff (Notre Dame, Ind.: University of Notre Dame Press, 1983), 103

15. Flor McCarthy (SDB), *New Sunday and Holy Day Liturgies Year B*, Dominican Publications, Dublin, 1999, 153

16. William Rowe, "Religious Experience and the Principle of Credulity," *International Journal for Philosophy of Religion* 13 (1982): 89

CHAPTER 15

MIRACLES TRANSCENDING NATURE

There are many reports of miracles in the Bible – actually they permeate throughout. But are they just a conglomeration of fables? Do they merely point to the creativity, and power of imagination? Is it true that there is no divine intervention, but only natural law? Throughout this chapter we will explore what miracles are, and whether in fact God could or would intervene in our cosmos, or even in our very lives.

We are faced with the fact that if God created the world, set the laws of nature in motion, then he could actually be made redundant if he hasn't already retired. Like the watchmaker analogy he could have set us ticking and then left us to our own devices, leaving the world to exist by setting the laws of nature in motion, and having no desire or even capability to intervene. Did God create the laws of nature, then us and leave us to our own devices, leaving us to fight to survive?

To the non-believer the concept of miracles sounds irrational, and for Christians it can be a struggle since there is not an obvious divine intervention in every occasion we ask for it.

In 1959 Julian Huxley, grandson of Thomas Henry Huxley, and one of the prominent speakers at the Darwinian Centennial, declared that supernatural religion was finished and that a new religion of evolutionary humanism with its basis in science would soon become the worldwide religion.

Macro-Evolution – A New Religion?

Was Huxley right? Has evolution become a new religion and made all other religions redundant? Though macro-evolution has crept into the fabric of society, and is proclaimed through science, education, and the media, it has also crept into some religions, devouring like a virus. It has proclaimed that we have not only come from apes, but all the way through the evolution chain to bacteria.

Macro-evolution has become a new religion. It has caused many to lose their faith as they have been told that evolution is not co-existent with a belief in God, and therefore they have lost their trust and love of God.

But though some members may disagree, many put their faith in the concept of macro-evolution, without studying it in-depth (by doing so we learn that there is a difference between micro and macro-evolution), God has ensured through the major religions that He will be loved as the Creator. It is important to note that all the major religions proclaim God as the Creator.

Free-Will

There is a better image to use than the watchmaker concept mentioned above. What about the concept of a loving parent? The Creator loves His creation. He has created us with a free will. John Polkinghorne explains it magnificently in *One World: The Interaction of Science and Theology:*

> The actual balance between chance and necessity, contingency and potentiality which we perceive seems to me to be consistent with the will of a patient and subtle Creator, content to achieve his purposes through the unfolding of process and accepting thereby a measure of the vulnerability and precariousness which always characterize the gift of freedom by love.[1]

This Creator of the universe respects our free will unconditionally – He may not want us to disobey him, but He allows us to – like a loving parent has to eventually let go of their control of their children. Like a loving parent God nudges us, but simultaneously respects our free will. It is only a nudge to say, "Hey I'm here. I love you!" But though God has to "let go" he never stops loving us, as we walk the path of life.

God is longing for us to search for Him, and his abundant love. God's love is unfailing – it is eternal. It is when we invite Him into our hearts, and ultimately our whole life, that He is able to intervene in our lives. But God never stops honouring our free will. Bit by bit we can allow him free reign in our hearts. The more we allow him and His love to transform us, the more we are fulfilled as we learn who we are meant to be.

It's like there is an anti-body type (perfect shape) hole in our heart. But though we may try to fill this hole with all sorts of things – some people take drugs, others abuse alcohol, and others abuse sex, to fill this chasm. But there is ultimately one perfect shape which will fill this chasm, and that is God's love. All the other love may temporarily plug parts of the chasm, but they are not a match.

> Late have I loved you, O Beauty so ancient and so new; late have I loved you! For behold you were within me, and I outside; and I sought you outside and in my ugliness fell upon those lovely things that you have made. You were with me and I was not with you.[2]

Now that I have focused on the need for God and His love, you can now discover one way that God intervenes in the lives of humanity – i.e. through miracles.

What is a Miracle?

These miracles are not what can be termed superficial. What I mean by a miracle is something that defies the laws of nature, for example, the instantaneous cure of someone ravaged by cancer.

The famous physicist Sir George Stokes said:

> It may be that the event which we call a miracle was brought on not by a suspension of the laws in ordinary operation, but by the super addition of something not ordinarily in operation.[3]

So miracles don't violate the normal laws of cause and effect, but merely transcend nature. For a definition of a miracle we simply refer to the Pocket Catholic Dictionary:

> A sensibly perceptible effect, surpassing at least the powers of visible nature, produced by God to witness to some truth or testify to someone's sanctity.[4]

Translated from the Latin, it also means to marvel or wonder. Therefore a miracle should lead us to marvel or wonder at God surpassing at least the powers of visible nature.

Jesus' Miracles

With Jesus' miracles it could be argued that the witnesses were not doctors, or professionals of medicine. But, these were miracles that were major, obvious: someone who could not see since birth was given the gift of sight; people with leprosy were cured; a hemorrhaging woman (imagine the sight of blood everywhere) was cured; Jesus actually raised someone from the dead. The writers of the New Testament new that these were miracles because they were so out of this world – they defied the rational, they were normally instantaneous; and they new that the miracles corroborated that Jesus was the Messiah.

Miracles Investigated Painstakingly By The Church

When it comes to miracles, the Catholic Church is one of the most stringent religious institutions. There is a strict criterion for something to be authenticated as a miracle. There are panels of doctors, including atheists, and agnostics, who examine and question the patient who believes they have been cured.

The Catholic Church has not been over-zealous to prove instances of the miraculous, but to the contrary, it has been very prudent to ensure that no stone is left unturned as to whether ulterior motives are involved, or a hoax has been perpetrated. The faithful are usually the ones that want a miracle declared, but they must wait a long time for the Church to investigate any such claims.

While the Church upholds particular miracles encouraging the faithful to believe, there is not the obligation to do so. But when one explores the reality of the miracle and the magnitude of the miracle then one can be left with awe that our Creator in fact transcends the laws of nature and molds them according to His loving purpose, like a potter would tweak his clay to get the beautiful outcome desired.

While thousands of miracles have been claimed at a famous pilgrimage site in Lourdes, France, over 5,000 reported healings have been recorded there and only 65 of these have been authenticated as miracles by the Church. These miracles were instantaneous healings, complete and they must last, therefore the person is rechecked yearly by doctors. In my previous book I wrote:

> Each year a certain number of declarations are made by formerly sick people who show testimony of their recovery. The "Bureau Medical de Notre Dame de Lourdes" has been given the task of proceeding with all the necessary examinations. It receives each year, more than 2,000 doctors of all nationalities, upon whose demand, whatever their beliefs, the office gives free access to all their records. Its works are supervised by an international medical committee.[5]

It must be noted that there have been many examples of other miracles, and that is the conversion of people visiting these pilgrimage cites; mostly the miracle includes examples of people who were bitter and couldn't forgive, then were not only able to forgive and trust Jesus, but were able to receive an incredible peace from Jesus. Many went to Lourdes and other pilgrimage sites begging God for a physical healing, but have returned with a spiritual healing which many state was better than a physical healing.

The Greatest Miracle

The incarnation, virgin birth, and Jesus overcoming death through His resurrection, are all wonderful miracles. I believe the greatest miracle that God has given us now, which has been with us since Jesus was on earth, is the Eucharist. I use the term miracle in relation to God transcending the law of nature so that the Eucharist becomes His body, soul and divinity.

Either Catholics, Orthodox and some Anglicans are mad, or we are following God's will in how we relate to the Eucharist. These major religions believe in the Real Presence of Christ in the Eucharist. Though many Anglicans believe in the Real Presence, it is still debatable whether they have the Apostolic Succession (see "Born to be Free" or www.kiwig.com for explanation of Apostolic Succession) and thus the God given authority to change the bread and wine into the Body and Blood of Christ.

The Eucharist is:

> The true Body and Blood of Jesus Christ, who is really and substantially present under the appearances of bread and wine, in order to offer himself in the sacrifice of the Mass and to be received as spiritual food in Holy Communion. It is called Eucharist, or "thanksgiving," because at its institution at the Last Supper Christ "gave thanks," and by this fact it is the supreme object and act of Christian gratitude to God.
>
> Although the same name is used, the Eucharist is any one or all three aspects of one mystery, namely the *Real Presence*, the *Sacrifice*, and *Communion*. As *Real Presence*, the Eucharist is Christ in his abiding action of High Priest, continuing to communicate the graces he merited on Calvary; and as *Communion*, it is Christ coming to enlighten and strengthen the believer by nourishing his soul for eternal life.[6]

Many of us have questioned why the appearance of the host, does not change, why our senses do not pick up any change. Matthias Scheeben, a 19th century theologian explains it succinctly:

> The greater, the more sublime, and the more divine Christianity is, the more inexhaustible, inscrutable, unfathomable, and mysterious its subject matter must be. If its teaching is worthy of the only-begotten Son of God, if the Son of God had to descend from the bosom of His Father to initiate us into this teaching, could we expect anything else than the revelation of the deepest mysteries locked up in God's heart? Could we expect anything else than disclosures concerning a higher, invisible world, about divine and heavenly things, which "eye hath not seen, nor ear heard," and which could not enter into the heart of any man? And if God has sent us His own Spirit to teach us all truth, the Spirit of His truth, who dwells in God and there searches the deep things of God, should this Spirit reveal nothing new, great, and wondrous, should He teach us no sublime secrets?[7]

Yes God has taught us many amazing secrets. He has chosen to reveal more of the depth of mystery (sacrament) of the Holy Eucharist through many Saints. The greatest Saints of the Church had a deep faith in the Real Presence of Christ in the Eucharist. It is from studying the writings of these Saints that we can be inspired by their love of Christ in the Eucharist, and this too can inspire us to make that leap of faith. Scheeban relates to us that the mysteries of the Church are essential to our faith:

> Far from repudiating Christianity or regarding it with suspicious eyes because of its mysteries, we ought to recognize its divine grandeur in these very mysteries. So essential to Christianity are its mysteries that in its character of truth revealed by the Son of God and the Holy Spirit it would stand convicted of intrinsic contradiction if it brought forward no mysteries. It's author would carry with Him a poor recommendation for His divinity if He taught us only such truths as in the last analysis we could have learned from a mere man, or could have perceived and adequately grasped by our own unaided powers.[8]

Therefore if we could only learn from mere man, we would not be able to encounter the sense of wonder, and the dawning of light as the truth begins to take root in us, and the sense of love and joy as it shines forth as we accept and encounter Christ's Real Presence in the Holy Eucharist.

Let's explore what the Early Christians, also known as the Early Church Fathers, had to say about the Eucharist:

St. Clement of Alexandria reveals the Eucharist as a wonderful mystery:

> The Word is everything to a child: both Father and Mother, both Instructor and Nurse. "Eat My Flesh," He says, "and drink My Blood [John 6:55]." The Lord supplies us with these intimate nutrients. He delivers over His Flesh, and pours out His Blood; and nothing is lacking for the growth of His children. O incredible mystery![9]

One of the earliest Christians to cover the concept of the Eucharist being the actual body and blood of Christ was St. Ignatius of Antioch, the third bishop of Antioch (after St. Evodius who was the immediate of successor of St. Peter, the apostle. Ignatius died about the year 110 A.D. In his letter to the Philadelphians he wrote:

> Take note of those who hold heterodox opinions on the grace of Jesus Christ which has come to us, and see how contrary their opinions are to the mind of God. For love they have no care, nor for the widow, nor for the orphan, nor for the distressed, nor for those in prison or freed from prison, nor for the hungry and thirsty. [Acts 10:41, Rom 1:3] They abstain from the Eucharist and from prayer, because they do not confess that the Eucharist is the Flesh of our Saviour Jesus Christ, Flesh which suffered for our sins and which the Father, in His goodness, raised up again.[10]

What is fascinating about this quote is that these people are devoid of love for those who Christ commanded us to love. Furthermore they do not recognize nor love Christ in the Eucharist.

It is clear that St. Ignatius is affirming that the Eucharist is the Flesh of Jesus Christ. There is no other reason that he would claim such a thing about a piece of bread. The evidence now becomes even stronger with the writings of other early Christians.

The writings of St. Ignatius reveal his belief in the power of the Eucharist, "I have no taste for corruptible food nor for the pleasures of this life. I desire the Bread of God [Matt 3:15], which is the Flesh of Jesus Christ, who was of the seed of David [Is 5:26, 11:12, 49:22, 62:10]; and for drink I desire His Blood, which is love incorruptible."[11]; and "Take care, then, to use one Eucharist, so that whatever you do, you do according to God: for there is one Flesh of our Lord Jesus

Christ, and one cup in the union of His Blood; one altar, as there is one bishop with the presbytery and my fellow servants, the deacons."[12]

Furthermore St. Justin the Martyr, who lived from about 100 AD until 165 AD (he was beheaded for his faith in Christ), reveals his belief and that of the Catholic Church at the time in the body being the real flesh of Christ. The following though written over 1800 years ago, sounds very much like what you would experience at a Catholic Mass today:

> Having concluded the prayers, we greet on another with a kiss [now a handshake for the sign of peace]. Then there is brought to the president [priest or bishop] of the brethren bread and a cup of water and of watered wine [Matt 25:39]; and taking them, he gives praise and glory to the Father of all, through the name of the Son and of the Holy Spirit; and he himself gives thanks at some length in order that these things may be deemed worthy.
>
> When the prayers and the thanksgiving are completed, all the people present call their assent, saying, "Amen!" *Amen* in the Hebrew language signifies *so be it*. After the president has given thanks, and all the people have shouted their assent, those whom we call deacons give to each one present to partake of the Eucharist bread and wine and water; and to those who are absent they carry away a portion [now days this is done as a ministry to the sick]
>
> We call this food *Eucharist*; and no one else is permitted to partake of it, except one who believes our teaching to be true and who has been washed in the washing which is for the remission of sins and for regeneration, and is thereby living as Christ has enjoined.[13]

Now Justin gets to the main point:

> For not as common bread nor common drink do we receive these; but since Jesus Christ our Savior was made incarnate by the word of God and had both flesh and blood for our salvation, so too, as we have been taught, the food which has been made into the Eucharist by the Eucharistic prayer set down by Him, and by the change of which our blood and flesh is nourished [food becomes part of our own body], is both the flesh and the blood of that incarnated Jesus.[14]

This is wonderful! We have testimony from one of the early Christians that the Eucharist is actually the body and blood of Jesus!

Sacrifice

Another aspect of the Eucharist is that of sacrifice. St. Irenaeus, (born approximately AD 140, became the second bishop of Lyons, succeeding St. Pothinus in about AD 178, and died about AD 202) explains:

> Again, giving counsel to His disciples to offer to God the first-fruits from among His creatures, not as if He needed them, but so that they themselves might be neither unfruitful nor ungrateful, He took among creation that which is bread, and gave thanks saying, "This is My Body. [Matt 26:26, Mark 14:22, Luke 22:19, 1 Cor 11:24]" The cup likewise, which is from among the creation to which we belong, He confessed to be His Blood.
> He taught the new sacrifice of the new covenant, of which Malachias, one of the twelve prophets, had signified beforehand: " 'You do not do My will,' says the Lord Almighty, 'and I will not accept a sacrifice at your hands. For from the rising of the sun to its setting My name is glorified among the gentiles, and in every place incense is offered to My name, and a pure sacrifice; for great is My name among the gentiles,' says the Lord Almighty [Mal 1:10-11]." By these words He makes it plain that the former people will cease to make offerings to God; but that in every place sacrifice will be offered to Him, and indeed, a pure one; for His name is glorified among the gentiles.[15]

Jesus does not die again, but the death and resurrection are sacramentally re-presented –"The sacrifice of Christ and the sacrifice of the Eucharist are one single sacrifice"[16] In fact, the power of the Cross transcends time, and thus qualifies as a miracle. The Pope says, "Whenever the Eucharist is celebrated at the tomb of Jesus in Jerusalem, there is an almost tangible return to his "hour", the hour of his Cross and glorification. Every priest who celebrates Holy Mass, together with the Christian community which takes part in it, is led back in spirit to that place and that hour."[17] Vatican Council II called it "the sacrifice of the Cross perpetuated down the ages."[18]

The Pope refers to the Council of Trent, a Church Council held from 1545 to 1563. "The Mass makes present the sacrifice of the Cross; it does not add to that sacrifice nor does it multiply it.[19] What is repeated is its memorial celebration, its "commemorative representation" (memorialis demonstration),[20] which makes Christ's one, definitive redemptive sacrifice always present in time."[21]

The Eucharist in the form of the Blood of Our Lord is the cup of salvation, while still remaining in the theme of transcending time:[22]

> The Church has received the Eucharist from Christ her Lord not as one gift – however precious – among so many others, but as the gift par excellence, for it is the gift of himself, of his person in his sacred humanity, as well as the gift of his saving work. Nor does it remain confined to the past, since "all that Christ is – all that he did and suffered for all men – participates in the divine eternity, and so transcends all times".[23]

He clearly states that the Eucharist sacrifice transcends time when he proclaims, "This sacrifice is so decisive for the salvation of the human race that Jesus Christ offered it and returned to the Father only after the he had left us a means of sharing in it as if we had been present there."[24]

He recalls the grace of redemption which embraces all of history, "In the paschal event and the Eucharist which makes it present throughout the centuries, there is a truly enormous "capacity" which embraces all of history as the recipient of the grace of redemption. This amazement should always fill the Church assembled for the celebration of the Eucharist. But in a special way it should fill the minister of the Eucharist."[25]

The next quote from the Pope is the most enlightening. Regarding the Eucharist as sacrifice he says:

> It unities heaven and earth. It embraces and permeates all creation. The Son of God became man in order to restore all creation. In one supreme act of praise, to the One who made it from nothing. He, the Eternal High Priest who by the blood of his Cross entered the eternal sanctuary, thus gives back to the Creator and Father all creation redeemed. He does so through the priestly ministry of the Church, to the glory of the Most Holy Trinity. Truly this is mysterium fidei which is accomplished in the Eucharist: the world which came forth from the hands of God the Creator now returns to him redeemed by Christ.[26]

Wow! The Eucharist as the body and blood of Christ unites heaven and earth. We are receiving what is also known as the body, blood, soul and divinity of Christ. We are being united with Christ. This leads us to the quote by St. Irenaeus in which he reveals the strong belief of the Eucharist having these senses of bread, but containing the divinity of Jesus:

For as the bread from the earth, receiving the invocation of God, is no longer common bread but the Eucharist, consisting of two elements, earthly and heavenly, so also our bodies, when they receive the Eucharist, are no longer corruptible but have the hope of resurrection into eternity.[27]

No wonder Vatican Council II called the Eucharistic Sacrifice "the source and summit of the Christian life"[28] Futhermore the Pope inspires us as he says, "Consequently the gaze of the Church is constantly turned to her Lord, present in the Sacrament of the Altar, in which she discovers the full manifestation of his boundless love."[29]

In conjunction with the Sacrifice we partake in the re-presentation of Christ's death and resurrection. Furthermore we receive the *Risen Christ* when we receive the Body and Blood of Christ.

Real Presence

God is omnipresent; therefore He is not limited to the Eucharist. However since Jesus said, "This is my body, this is my blood", it is a deep presence. I like to use an analogy of being in the room of your best friend. Even though you aren't talking there is a presence there, but when you are communicating, there is a deeper presence. And when you are laughing and smiling, then there is even a deeper presence. So in a way, we believe that God is laughing and smiling with us, through the Eucharist. Or to put it even more profoundly God is loving us, through the Eucharist, as we are united with Him.

The Pope says in *Ecclesia De Eucharistia* [30], "The sacramental re-presentation of Christ's sacrifice, crowned by the resurrection, in the Mass involves a most special presence which, in the words of Paul VI, "is called 'real' not as a way of excluding all other types of presence as if they were 'not real' , but because it is a presence in the fullest sense: a substantial presence whereby Christ , the God-Man, is wholly and entirely present.[31]

We can now explore the evidence from the Early Church Fathers and Sacred Scripture to the Real Presence of Christ in the Eucharist. St. Ephraim, a Syrian, was born about AD 306 and lived until AD 373. He was consecrated a deacon before AD 338 and never progressed to the priesthood. He gives the following inspirational testimony:

Our Lord Jesus took in His hands what in the beginning was only bread; and He blessed it, and signed it, and made it holy in the name of the Father and in the name of the Spirit; and He broke it and in His gracious kindness He distributed it to all His disciples one by one. He called the bread His living Body, and did Himself fill it with himself and the Spirit.

And extending His hand, He gave them the Bread which His right hand had made holy: "Take, all of you eat of this, which My word has made holy. Do not now regard as bread that which I have given you; but take, eat this Bread, and do not scatter the crumbs; for what I have called My Body, that it is indeed. One particle from its crumbs is able to sanctify thousands and thousands, and is sufficient to afford life to those who eat of it. Take, eat, entertaining no doubt of faith, because this is My Body, and whoever eats it in belief eats in it Fire and Spirit. But if any doubter eat of it, for him it will be only bread. And whoever eats in belief the Bread made holy in My name, if he be pure, he will be preserved in his purity; and if he be a sinner, he will be forgiven." But if anyone despise it or reject it or treat it with ignominy [shame], it may be taken as a certainty that he treats with ignominy the Son, who called it and actually made it to be His Body.[32]

Then at the last supper Jesus instigates the practice of the Eucharist:

Now as they were eating, Jesus took bread, and when he had said the blessing he broke it and gave it to the disciples. "Take it and eat," he said, "this is my body." Then he took a cup, and when he had given thanks he handed it to them saying, "Drink from this, all of you, for this is my blood, the blood of the covenant, poured out for many for the forgiveness of sins." Matthew 26:26-29

The following scripture, from the Gospel of Luke refers to the new covenant as the Body and Blood of our Lord in the Eucharist, "the cup is the new covenant" and so the Real Presence is the new covenant

Then he took break, and when he had given thanks, he broke it and gave it to them, saying, "This is my body given for you; do this in remembrance of me." He did the same with the cup after supper, and said, "This cup is the new covenant in my blood poured out for you."
Luke 22:19-20

As God's presence dwelled in the Ark of the Covenant during the Old Testament times (the Old Covenant}, since the Last Supper God's presence has dwelled through the consecration of bread and wine (the

New Covenant). During the Old Covenant only the High Priest could come into God's presence, while in the New Covenant the door was opened for all who chose to follow Christ, ("repent and be baptized") to receive the presence of Jesus. It is the closest intimacy with God that Christians can have on earth.

It is the very next verse that is very striking as it reveals the sacredness of the Eucharist. St. Paul says, "Therefore anyone who eats the bread or drinks the cup of the Lord unworthily is answerable for the body and blood of the Lord."[33]

Paul goes further in saying that we have to be very careful of our attitude towards the Body and Blood of the Lord. If the Body and Blood of the Lord were merely a symbol as claimed by some Christians, then Paul would not have written so strongly. He says, "Everyone is to examine himself and only then eat of the bread or drink from the cup; because a person who eats and drinks without recognizing the body is eating and drinking his own condemnation."[34]

As mentioned previously the blood of the covenant refers to the Eucharist and hence the Real Presence. Paul gives us a rather startling warning:

> Anyone who disregards the Law of Moses is ruthlessly *put to death on the word of two witnesses or three*; and you may be sure that anyone who tramples on the Son of God, and who treats *the blood of the covenant* which sanctified him as if it were not holy, and who insults the Spirit of grace, will be condemned to a far severer punishment.
> Hebrews 10:28-29

Paul links the blood of the covenant with the Spirit of grace. As mentioned regarding the belief of St. Cyril, we receive graces through receiving the Eucharist. It is so sad that many Christians have lost this sense of the Eucharist, and yet it is plainly in Sacred Scripture.

St. Cyril of Jerusalem was born in AD 315 and consecrated as bishop of Jerusalem in AD 348. The following from the *Mystagogic Catecheses* has been attributed either to St. Cyril or his successor, John of Jerusalem, though they could have been merely revised by John:

> Do not, therefore, regard the Bread and the Wine as simply that; for they are, according to the Master's declaration, the Body and Blood of Christ. Even though the senses suggest to you the other, let faith make you firm. Do not judge in this matter by taste, but –

be fully assured by your faith, not doubting that you have been deemed worthy of the Body and Blood of Christ.[35]

Though the taste does not change, we are to have faith and believe in it, precisely because Christ himself said it would be. Are we to call him a liar?

Jesus came to fulfill the law. Therefore it is not surprising that there are links between the Old Covenant and the New Covenant. Are we to deny that God's real presence dwelled in the Ark of the Covenant? Are we to deny that God's real presence was in the Holy of Holies in the Jewish Temple? The Holy of Holies was like one big tabernacle. Therefore if God's real presence could be there in a special way then could not God's presence be made manifest in what was once only a piece of bread?

As there are mysteries that God has revealed regarding religion, there have been mysteries that God has revealed regarding science. These include time, matter, entropy, the Big Bang, energy, and gravity. If we just take the immensity of the universe, we understand that we will not be able to explore it all. Since it is a mystery, the more we study it, we will never come to full knowledge of it. It is the same with the mysteries regarding religion. However reveals different depths of the Revelation that He has already given to His Church. He does this through the Church Councils and also through the Prophets and Saints. I would like to challenge you to start reading the writings of the Saints, and to enter into the depths of the mysteries.

The Trinity dwells in our hearts as a result of baptism. This is a mystery. But this is not a physical presence. As our hearts are a dwelling place for the presence of Jesus, so does the bread become a dwelling place for Jesus' presence once it is consecrated by a priest. Though neither have Jesus dwelling there physically. The words that the Church uses are, "real" and "substantive presence". She does not use the word physical – to do so is contrary to the Church.

Sadly it is mainly the Orthodox and Catholic Churches that hold such a profound reverence for the Eucharist. Though it must be admitted that many Catholics too have lost their reverence for the Eucharist, it is the Catholic and Orthodox Churches as a whole that believe in the Real Presence of Christ, and worships Jesus in the Eucharist. It is ironic that the healings that have occurred at such places as Lourdes as mentioned previously, happened when the people were blessed by the priest holding up the Eucharist and making the sign of the Cross with the body of the Lord, and also healings have occurred after a sick person has consumed the Eucharist.

Eternal Life

One of the greatest miracles that God has given us since the Last Supper is the Eucharist. This gift was given to all Christendom. First let's explore Sacred Scripture that reveals the Eternal Life offered through the Eucharist.

In the Gospel of John, Jesus reveals the concept of the Eucharist, with the miracle of the multiplication of loaves and in his discourse with the crowd the following day.

> "In all truth I tell you,
> you are looking for me
> not because you have seen the signs
> but because you had all the bread
> you wanted to eat.
> Do not work for food that goes bad,
> but work for food
> that endures for eternal life,
> which the Son of man will give you
> for on him the Father, God himself,
> has set his seal."   John 6:26-27

The crowd asked what they had to do to carry out God's work, and Jesus replied:

> "In all truth I tell you,
> everyone who believes has eternal life.
> I am the bread of life.
> Your fathers ate manna in the desert
> and they are dead;
> but this is the bread
> which comes down from heaven.
> so that a person may eat it and not die.
> I am the living bread
> which has come down from heaven.
> Anyone who eats this bread
> will live for ever;
> and the bread that I shall give
> is my flesh, for the life of the world."
> John 6:47-51

If we take into account what the Church Fathers had to say, this piece of Scripture should bring a new light to many:

In all truth I tell you,
If you do not eat
the flesh of the Son of man
and drink his blood,
you have no life in you.
Anyone who does eat my flesh
and drink my blood
has eternal life,
and I shall raise that person up
on the last day.
For my flesh is real food
and my blood is real drink.
Whoever eats my flesh
and drinks my blood
lives in me
and I live in that person.
As the living Father sent me
and I draw life from the Father,
so whoever eats me
will also draw life from me.
This is the bread
which has come down from heaven;
it is not like the bread our ancestors ate:
they are dead,
but anyone who eats this bread
will live for ever.   John 6:53-58

At this point, sadly, many of Jesus own followers said this was "intolerable language" and many of them left him. Jesus didn't call them back and say, "Hey I was only joking, I really meant it this way." Jesus new that they found this teaching tough, and throughout this discourse, he says repeatedly, "In truth I tell you" which is like us saying today, "Listen I have something important to tell you." He seems to try to drum it into them as it repeats the phrase, "eat my flesh and drink my blood". It is fascinating that this discourse follows on from the miracle of multiplication of the loaves, which itself is a pre-figuration of the Eucharist. Moreover Jesus does not reveal any other meaning to the twelve, his closest friends, as he does elsewhere. This is not a parable, but telling the disciples about the Eucharist.

In the Gospels Jesus reveals himself as the tree of life as well as the bread of life. In the book of Revelation Christians are invited to eat from the tree of life:

> "Let anyone who can hear, listen to what the Spirit is saying to the churches: those who prove victorious I will feed *from the tree of life* set *in* God's *paradise.*"
> Revelation 2:7

> "Blessed are those who will have washed their robes clean, so that they will have the right to feed on the tree of life and can come through the gates into the city." Revelation 22:14

St. Clement of Alexandria reveals as representing sharing in Christ's immortality. I believe this needs to be taken in conjunction other Sacred Scripture in which Jesus reveals what one must do to inherit eternal life (such as "repent, be baptized and believe in the Good News"). Clement says:

> The Blood of the Lord, indeed, is twofold. There is His corporeal Blood, by which we are redeemed from corruption; and His spiritual Blood, that with which we are anointed. That is to say, to drink the Blood of Jesus is to share in His immortality. The strength of the Word is the Spirit, just as the blood is the strength of the body. Similarly, as wine is blended with water, so is the Spirit with man [Clement believed that in receiving the Eucharist worthily we also receive an increase of the indwelling of the Holy Spirit]. The one, the Watered Wine, nourishes in faith, while the other, the Spirit, leads us on to immortality. The union of both, however, – of the drink and of the Word, – is called the Eucharist, a praiseworthy and excellent gift. Those who partake of it in faith are sanctified in body and in soul. By the will of the Father, the divine mixture, man, is mystically united to the Spirit and to the Word.[36]

Pope John Paul II refers back to his Apostolic Letter Dominicae Cenae (24 February 1980) pertaining to the Eucharist when he says, "Today I take up anew the thread of that argument, with even greater emotion and gratitude in my heart, echoing as it were the word of the Psalmist: "What shall I render to the Lord for all his bounty to me? I will lift up the cup of salvation and call on the name of the Lord" (Psalm 116:12-13)"[37]

Furthermore he gives us two fantastic insights into the eternal life aspect of the Eucharist. The first is when he quotes 1 Corinthians 11:26, "until you come in glory" and says[38], "The Eucharist is a straining towards the goal, a foretaste of the fullness of joy promised by Christ (cf. Jn 15:11); it is in some way the anticipation of heaven, the "pledge of future glory."[39]

The second is when he states so profoundly, that we are receiving eternal life now:[40]

> Those who feed on Christ in the Eucharist need not wait until the hereafter to receive eternal life: they already possess it on earth, as the first-fruits of a future fullness which will embrace man in his totality. For in the Eucharist we also receive the pledge of our bodily resurrection at the end of the world: "He who eats my flesh and drinks my blood has eternal life, and I will raise him up at the last day".
> (Jn 6:54)

If what the Catholic Church teaches is true, and the above is true, then all I can say is this is a glorious treasure, which is priceless, and sadly many people have ignored. No wonder the Pope says, "Here is the Church's treasure, the heart of the world, the pledge of the fulfillment for which each man and woman, even unconsciously yearns."[41]

Additionally the Eucharist is where the Church is most fully realised. It is where Christ and His sacrifice are made present now. Furthermore it is the summit towards which all the activity of the Church is directed and the source from which all its power flows.

Resurrection of the Body

Early in *God: Fact or Fiction?* I covered the concept of the resurrection of the body, and that our body and soul belong together. St. Irenaeus thus returns to the theme of the Resurrection of the Body as a result of receiving the Body and Blood of the Lord:

> In the same way that the wood of the vine planted in the ground bears fruit in due season; or as a grain of wheat, falling on the ground, decomposes and rises up in manifold increase through the Spirit of God who contains all things; and then , through the Wisdom of God, comes to the service of men, and receiving the Word of God,

becomes the Eucharist, which is the Body and Blood of Christ; so also our bodies, nourished by it, and deposited in the earth and decomposing therein, shall rise up in due season, the Word of God favoring them with resurrection in the glory of God the Father.[42]

We now move to the 3rd century to reveal the amazing writings of these early Christians. One such Christian, Tertullian the following sometime between AD 208 and AD 212. He reveals the belief that the body and imperishable soul belong together:

> No soul whatever is able to obtain salvation, unless it has believed while it was in the flesh. Indeed, the flesh is the hinge of salvation. In that regard, when the soul is deputed to something by God, it is the flesh which makes it able to carry out the commission which God has given it. The flesh, then, is washed, so that the soul may be made clean. The flesh is anointed, so that the soul may be dedicated to holiness. The flesh is signed, so that the soul too may be fortified. The flesh is shaded by the imposition of hands, so that the soul too may be illuminated by the Spirit. The flesh feeds on the Body and Blood of Christ, so that the soul too may fatten on God. They cannot, then, be separated in their reward, when they are united in their works.[43]

The Eucharistic Our Father Payer

St. Cyprian of Carthage, who was born to wealthy pagan parents, sometime between AD 200 and 210, converted to Christianity about AD 246 and was consecrated a priest soon afterwards. He was consecrated the Bishop of Carthage in either AD 248 or 249. He reveals a wonderful insight, tying in the Eucharist with the Our Father prayer:

> As the prayer continues, we ask and say, "Give us this day our daily bread [Matt 6:11]."... And we ask that this bread be given us daily, so that we who are in Christ and daily receive the Eucharist as the food of salvation, may not, by falling into some more previous sin and then in abstaining from communicating, be withheld from the heavenly Bread, and be separated from Christ's Body... He Himself warns us, saying, "Unless you eat the flesh of the Son of Man and drink His Blood, you shall not have life in you. [John 6:54]" Therefore do we ask that our Bread, which is Christ, be given to us daily, so that we who abide and live in Christ may not withdraw from His sanctification and from His body.[44]

Saint Thomas gives us an analogy comparing the food of nourishment with that of feeding the life of the soul. He says, "In the life of the soul, too, something is lost in us every day through venial sin which lessons the warmth of charity. But the Eucharist confers the virtue of charity, because it is the sacrament of love.[45]

With what we have learnt so far about the Eucharist, why would we not want to receive it more than just once a week?

Eucharist Brings Unity

As with any sharing of a meal there is a unity experienced, especially if everyone is able to participate. The Eucharist brings about a more powerful unity, though many different cultures we are one body:

> For that reason, my dear friends, have nothing to do with the worship of false gods. I am talking to you as sensible people; weight up for yourselves what I have to say. The blessing-cup, which we bless, is it not a sharing in the blood of Christ, and the loaf of bread which we break, is it not a sharing in the body of Christ? And as there is one loaf, so we, although there are many of us, are one single body, for we all share in the one loaf.
> 1 Corinthians 10:14-17

Other Christians are coming to appreciate the Real Presence of Christ in the Eucharist. Fr Groeschel and Fr Monti in *In the Presence of Our Lord* reveals such a case, when they say, "Despite this, there is the remarkable fact that the preeminent Lutheran theologian Yngve Brillioth, in his monumental work *Eucharistic Faith and Practice*, shows profound respect for Eucharistic devotion as practiced by Catholics past and present."[46]

One of the authors of the aforementioned book visited a shrine in honour of the Mother of Jesus, in England and says: "It is obvious that some members of the Anglican communion have managed to withstand the theological chaos and preserve Eucharistic devotion as it has come to flower with those referred to as "ritualists." Around 1990 I witnessed this myself at England's Shrine of Our Lady of Walsingham, where the Anglican Shrine leaves the Catholic completely in the shadows, sad to say, when it comes to Eucharistic devotion."[47]

Other Christians desire the unity to be found within the Eucharist as this following event shows the Pope was inspired by the heartfelt desire of Lutheran Bishops for true unity:[48]

In this respect I would like to mention one demonstration dictated by fraternal charity and marked by deep clarity of faith which made a profound impression on me. I am speaking of the Eucharistic celebrations at which I presided in Finland and Sweden during my journey to the Scandinavian and Nordic countries. At Communion time, the Lutheran Bishops approached the celebrant. They wished, by means of an agreed gesture, to demonstrate their desire for that time when we, Catholics and Lutherans, will be able to share the same Eucharist, and they wished to receive the celebrant's blessing. With love I blessed them. The same gesture, so rich in meaning, was repeated in Rome at the Mass at which I presided in Piazza Farnese, on the sixth centenary of the canonization of Saint Brigitta of Sweden, on 6 October 1991.

This deep desire for unity will be fulfilled as it is a yearning of God. There have been some rather sensational steps towards unity which sadly the secular media never pick up on. This includes the report by the *joint church commission, Anglican Roman Catholic International Commission,* entitled, "Gift of Authority" which is the fruit of a 30 year dialogue initiated by Archbishop Michael Ramsay and Pope Paul VI in 1968. For a commentary on the report see http://www.anglicancommunion.org/ecumenical/rc/authority/commtannerenglish.html. While the full report can be found at http://www.ewtn.com/library/Theology/Arcicgf3.htm.

To see some wonderful steps towards unity between the Anglican Church with other Churches see the resolutions of the Lambeth Conference 1998 http://www.aco.org/lambeth/4/sect4rpt.html.

Plus another earth-shattering development is the Joint Declaration on the Doctrine of Justification by the Lutheran and Catholic churches. This used to be such a major stumbling block between the churches, but now has been resolved with this joint declaration (see http://www.ewtn.com/library/CURIA/pccujnt4.htm)

Where to Now?

Now that we have explored the theory of the mystery of the Eucharist, it is important to apply what we have learnt. There is a saying that information without application is fascination, but when we apply the information we should get transformation. When Jesus said "Do this in memory of me" He didn't want us to merely just remember Him, but to receive Him as we have encountered through John 6. The Eucharist is a mystery of faith; we are required to have faith in order for full participation with the Sacrament and to gain the most from it. Therefore faith is fundamental - it is the prerequisite.

We are called to live the mystery of the Eucharist, to die to ourselves (becoming less selfish and more Christlike) and let the presence and essence of Christ in the Eucharist transform us. We are called to be a light to the nations, to be a witness of the loving nature of God.

Summary

Miracles are a suspension of natural laws. The question we are faced with concerning miracles is: Are they possible? For a contingency being, miracles would have to come as a result of the ability given to it. Miracles happen through prayer, especially when praying for someone who is terminally ill and they recover, for example, with the whole tumor disappearing without a trace – the natural laws are suspended.

In addition a miracle can happen as a result of the Necessary Being initiating the miracle. We have examples of this in Sacred Scripture. For example, St. Paul was blinded by God which caused His conversion to Christ [Acts 9:1-19]. Christianity is either the greatest miracle, or the greatest hoax ever! Either there are miracles that transcend nature, or these are just the wishful longing of billions of people throughout history. Furthermore either the Eucharist is really what I have written in here, or else it is just a piece of bread. But I believe the evidence from Sacred Scripture, and the Early Church Fathers is overwhelming; the Early Christians, including the successors of the Apostles believed that the bread and wine actually became the Body and Blood of Christ, and that His Real Presence was contained in the Eucharist. Additionally the scriptural evidence shows that Jesus meant that the bread and wine would become his Body and Blood and the Biblical Christians, such as St. Paul truly believed it. Most of all, the Eucharist gives us eternal life, if we but receive it worthily, and love the Lord also through loving others. Will you too believe in the Eucharist, or turn away from the Lord as shown by many of his followers when He commanded that we eat his body and drink his blood?

I wrote the following poem this year (2003). It reveals my love for Jesus in the Eucharist:

OH WHAT JOY!

I stand holding you in my hands
Expectation fills my heart
I receive your body
And your precious blood

Though the taste is natural
To my senses
What a sweet taste
Your deep presence is to my soul

Oh what joy fills my heart
I am uniting with my Jesus
What intimacy God has given me
I receive Him in
His Body, Soul and Divinity

Chapter 15 – Bibliography

1. John Polkinghorne, *One World: The interaction of Science and Theology*, Princeton University Press, Princeton, 1987, 69
2. [Saint Augustine]
3. International Standard Bible Encyclopedia, Grand Rapids: Eerdmans, 1939, 2036
4. John A Hardon, *Pocket Catholic Dictionary*, S.J., Image Books, New York, 1985, 262
5. Brendan Roberts, *Born to be Free*, Kiwi Graphix, Auckland, 1998, 132
6. Ibid, p118-199 as cited in Pocket Catholic Dictionary
7. Matthias Scheeban, The Mysteries of Christianity, 1961, 4) (see In the Presence of Our Lord)
8. Ibid
9. W.A Jurgens, *The Faith of the Early Fathers - Volume One*, The Liturgical Press, Collegeville, Minnesota, 1970, passage 408, p178
10. Ibid, passage 64, p25
11. Ibid, passage 54a, p22
12. Ibid, passage 56, p22
13. Ibid, passage 128, p55
14. Ibid, passage 128, p55
15. Ibid, passage 232, p95
16. Catechsim of the Catholic Church, 1367
17. http://www.vatican.va/edocs/ENG0821/_INDEX.HTM, Ecclesia De Eucharistia, passage 4
18. Cf. Second Vatican Ecumenical Council, Constitution Sacrosanctum Concilium, 47: "...our Saviour instituted the Eucharistic Sacrifice of his body and blood, in order to perpetuate the sacrifice of the Cross throughout time, until he should return".
19. Cf. Ecumenical Council of Trent, Session XXII, Doctrina de ss. Missaw Sacrificio, Chapter 2: DS 1743: "It is one and the same victim here offering himself by the ministry of his priests, who then offered himself on the Cross; it is only the manner of offering that is different".
20. Pius XII, Encyclical Letter Mediator Dei (20 November 1947): AAS 39 (1947), 548
21. http://www.vatican.va/edocs/ENG0821/_INDEX.HTM, Ecclesia De Eucharistia, passage 12

22. http://www.vatican.va/edocs/ENG0821/_INDEX.HTM, Ecclesia De Eucharistia, passage 11

23. Catechsim of the Catholic Church, 1085

24. http://www.vatican.va/edocs/ENG0821/_INDEX.HTM, Ecclesia De Eucharistia, passage 11

25. http://www.vatican.va/edocs/ENG0821/_INDEX.HTM, Ecclesia DeEucharistia, passage 5

26. http://www.vatican.va/edocs/ENG0821/_INDEX.HTM, Ecclesia De Eucharistia, passage 8

27. W.A Jurgens, *The Faith of the Early Fathers - Volume One*, The Liturgical Press, Collegeville, Minnesota, 1970, passage 234, p95

28. Second Vatican Council, Dogmatic Constitution on the Church Lumen Gentium, 11

29. http://www.vatican.va/edocs/ENG0821/_INDEX.HTM, Ecclesia De Eucharistia, passage 1

30. http://www.vatican.va/edocs/ENG0821/_INDEX.HTM, Ecclesia De Eucharistia, passage 15

31. Encyclical Letter Mysterium Fidei (3 September 1965): AAS 57 (1965), 764

32. W.A Jurgens, *The Faith of the Early Fathers - Volume One*, The Liturgical Press, Collegeville, Minnesota, 1970, passage 707, p311

33. 1 Corinthians 11:27

34. 1 Corinthians 11:28

35. W.A Jurgens, *The Faith of the Early Fathers - Volume One*, The Liturgical Press, Collegeville, Minnesota, 1970, passage 846, p361

36. Ibid, passage 410, p 179

37. http://www.vatican.va/edocs/ENG0821/_INDEX.HTM, Ecclesia De Eucharistia, passage 9

38. http://www.vatican.va/edocs/ENG0821/_INDEX.HTM, Ecclesia De Eucharistia, passage 18

39. Solemnity of the Body and Blood of Christ, Second Vespers, Antiphon to the Magnificat

40. http://www.vatican.va/edocs/ENG0821/_INDEX.HTM, Ecclesia De Eucharistia, passage 18

41. http://www.vatican.va/edocs/ENG0821/_INDEX.HTM, Ecclesia De Eucharistia, passage 59

42. W.A Jurgens, *The Faith of the Early Fathers - Volume One*, The Liturgical Press, Collegeville, Minnesota, 1970, passage, 249, p99

43. Ibid, passage 362, 149

44. Ibid passage 559, 223

45. *Summa Theologica*, Pt. III, Q.79, Art. 4

46. Father Benedict J Groeschel, CFR & James Monti, *In the Presence of Our Lord,* The History, Theology, and Psychology of Eucharistic Devotion, Our Sunday Visitor Publishing Division, Huntington, Indiana, 1997, 60, as cited in *Eucharistic Faith and Practice* by Yngve Brilioth

47. Ibid, 60

48. Pope John Paul II, May We Be One, Item 72, - http://www.vatican.va/edocs/ENG0221/_INDEX.HTM

CHAPTER 16

DOES SECULAR EVIDENCE CONFIRM JESUS' EXISTENCE?

Isn't the Bible composed of statements and structured claims by either the Jews or, in particular the Christians who uphold an obscure Jew, who pretended to be God's Son, and left no impression upon humanity except for the Christians? Is there really even a single word that has been mentioned of such a character by at least one historian, especially a non-Christian, from the early 1st century? Or are they just bogus claims by a group of Christians with a spectacular imagination.

These are honest questions that have faced countless people throughout the centuries. Witnesses within any time-period are so valuable as their testimonies strengthen any case. It is the same with Sacred Scripture, and Christianity. How strong is the evidence? Are there any witnesses that have attested to Jesus being a historical figure who actually walked and breathed on earth? Do these eyewitnesses attest to Jesus performing any wonders or miracles? Does this evidence itself corroborate the Bible, or is it just a lot of fables, a big hoax? You will be very surprised what this chapter reveals, as I uncover the answers to these questions and take you on a journey back to the time of some fascinating historical characters.

A brilliant book which confronts these questions and more is *The Case For Christ* by Lee Strobel. The author embraces this challenge from a fascinating angle; he considered himself an atheist, with the bible a product of wishful thinking, mere hallucinations, ancient mythology and primitive superstition. Upon the conversion of his wife to Christianity, he was surprised and fascinated with the striking transformation of her character – the building of integrity, personal confidence, and joy. Therefore he decided to put his 20+ years of journalistic experience to a new vigorous all-out investigation into the facts surrounding the case for Christianity. His research led him through a two year journey which would transform him from only giving the biblical evidence a cursory look, and tossed in the 'to do one day' pile, to in fact being astounded beyond his wildest dreams.

His conversion occurred as a result of the thousands of man hours poured into delving into the depths of the historicity of Christianity; starting as a skeptic, he scrutinized the evidence from specific experts, plowing through enormous resources. In fact his scrupulous investigation would in fact lead to a decision which would change his life forever!

In *The Case for Christ*, he interviewed many experts in such diverse subjects as: eyewitness testimony, documentary, corroboratory, rebuttal, scientific, psychological, circumstantial and fingerprint evidence.

The book is compelling reading and will open up your eyes to his stunning and inspiring research and for some will lead you to opening up your mind and heart to the truth. It would be interesting to hear from anyone, especially journalists who find this chapter very helpful.

But before we explore some of the enthralling evidence I will quote a pertinent analogy from Strobel:

> If you were selected for a jury in a real trial, you would be asked to affirm up front that you haven't formed any preconceptions about the case. You would be required to vow that you would be open-minded and fair, drawing your conclusions based on the weight of the facts and not on your whims or prejudices. You would be urged to thoughtfully consider the credibility of the witnesses, carefully sift the testimony, and rigorously subject the evidence to your common sense and logic. I'm asking you to do the same.[1]

I hope you will enter into this section of the book with an open mind, as I'm sure you have, regarding the purely scientific aspects that I've covered. Hey, you must have since you haven't ripped this book to shreds or burnt it, lol.

So let's look at some of the evidence which Strobel extrapolates as we look at the case of the existence of Jesus and claims whether he was the Son of God and whether he should be the most acclaimed individual in history. This could lead to the most startling discovery in your life, and possibly the most momentous decision you will ever make. So if you have any preconceptions, then check yourself, and tell yourself you will enter this chapter with an open mind and heart.

Edwin Yamauchi, Professor at Miami University, Oxford, Ohio has quite an impressive academic prowess. This includes the delivery of 71 papers before learned societies and lecturing at more than 100 seminaries; and the publishing of 80 articles in 37 scholarly journals. He, believes that from non-biblical historical sources alone, the following could be ascertained re the life of Jesus:[2]

- He was a Jewish teacher
- Many people believed he performed healings and exorcisms
- Some people confessed he was the Messiah
- He was rejected by the Jewish leaders
- He was crucified under Pontius Pilate during the reign of Tiberius
- Despite Jesus shameful death, his followers, who believed he had risen, spread beyond Palestine so that there were multitudes of them in Rome in AD. 64
- All kinds of people from the cities and countryside – men and women, slave and free – worshipped him as God.

Jewish Historian

A Jewish historian and Pharisee (Jewish priest), named Josephus recorded the history of his people from 70 to 100 A.D. In his comprehensive writing, *Antiquities*, he states:

> Now, there was about this time, Jesus, a wise man, if it be lawful to call him a man, for he was a doer of wonderful works, a teacher of such men as receive the truth with pleasure. He drew over to him both many of the Jews and many of the gentiles. He was the Christ and when Pilate, at the suggestion of the principal men amongst us, had condemned him to the cross, those that loved him at the first did not forsake him. For he appeared alive again the third day, as the divine prophets had foretold these and ten thousand other wonderful things concerning him; and the tribe of Christians, so named from him, are not extinct to this day.[3]

Before you get too excited over this passage, it must be noted that scholars, both Jewish and Christian now believe that interpolations have been in inserted into the text, probably by Christians, after Josephus wrote the above. But there are believed to be only three such interpolations. These are what Josephus, a Pharisee (Pharisees believed in the resurrection, but the Sadducees didn't) would not have written:

- "if it be lawful to call him a man" – implies he was more than a man
- "He was the Christ" – Josephus would not have viewed him as the Messiah; and in the earlier quote by Josephus he said that Jesus was *called* the Christ."
- "For he appeared alive again the third day" – this would be a declaration of belief in the resurrection.

Therefore we can reliably ascertain that Jesus was the doer of wonderful works, a teacher of men, and drew to him many Jews and Gentiles. Furthermore, Pilate had condemned him to the Cross, and the tribe of Christians still existed at the time that this historical record was written.

Roman Historians

We now encounter the testimony of a Roman historian, Tacitus, who wrote in AD 115:

> Nero fastened the guilt and inflicted the most exquisite tortures on a class hated for their abominations, called Christians by the populace. Christus, from whom the name had its origin, suffered the extreme penalty during the reign of Tiberius at the hands of one of our procurators, Pontius Pilate, and a most mischievous superstition, thus checked for the moment, again broke out not only in Judea, the first source of the evil, but even in Rome... Accordingly, an arrest was first made of all who pleaded guilty: then, upon their information, an immense multitude was convicted, not so much of the crime of firing the city, as of hatred against mankind.[4]

It is very significant that Tacitus witnessed to the fact that an "immense multitude" obviously believed in this "mischievous superstition". Yamauchi highlights the incredible spread of the religion:

> How can you explain the spread of religion based on the worship of a man who had suffered the most ignominious death possible? Of course, the Christian answer is that he was resurrected. Others have to come up with some alternative theory if they don't believe that. But none of the alternative views, to my mind, are very persuasive.[5]

Another Roman, Pliny the Young, who became governor of Bithynia in northwestern Turkey, reveals himself as a persecutor of Christians through letters to his friend, Emperor Trajan, and thus corroborates more of the testimony we've received from the Church; Sacred Scripture; and the Early Church Fathers who also quote most of the Gospels:

> I have asked them if they are Christians, and if they admit it, I repeat the question a second and third time, with a warning of the punishment awaiting them. If they persist, I order them to be led away for execution; for, whatever the nature of their admission, I am convinced that their stubbornness and unshakable obstinacy ought not to go unpunished...

They also declared that the sum total of their guilt or error amounted to no more than this: they had met regularly before dawn on a fixed day to chant verses alternately amongst themselves in honour of Christ as if to a god, and also to bind themselves by oath, not for any criminal purpose, but to abstain from theft, robbery and adultery…
This made me decide it was all the more necessary to extract the truth by torture from two slave-women, whom they called deaconesses. I found nothing but a degenerate sort of cult carried to extravagant lengths.[6]

It is obvious Pliny chose what he thought was the weakest victims to torture. But the question remains, "Why would anyone be so stubborn, or have such unshakable faith if it was all a hoax? Why would someone be willing to give up their life, or in fact be willing to suffer terrible torture and humiliation, for something they really didn't believe in? Could it be, that they believed because they were witnesses, even first and secondhand witnesses to the fact that a man called Jesus, claimed to be the son of God, performed "wonders" in which many of the 'outcasts' were cured, and transformed religion into one which was personal, and full of hope.

Josephus also refers to the high priest, Ananias seizing the advantage of the death of the Roman governor Festus – also mentioned in the New Testament – to ensure that James, the brother of Jesus is killed, by stoning.[7]

But Josephus and Tactitus are not the only non-Christians to testify to the existence of Jesus; in fact there are many more. The writings of the early historians, outside Sacred Scripture testify that Jesus performed wonders, or 'wonderful works' as recorded by Josephus. As they were not believers they did not support Jesus, rather some referred to his wonders to sorcery, while his supporters called them miracles.

Pliny the Younger, Emperor of Bythynia in northwestern Turkey, reveals the attitude of the early Christians:

They were in the habit of meeting on a certain fixed day before it was light, when they sang an anthem to Christ as God, and bound themselves by a solemn oath not to commit any wicked deed, but to abstain from all fraud, theft and adultery, never to break their word, or deny a trust when called upon to honor it; after which it was their custom to separate, and then meet again to partake of food, but ordinary and innocent kind.[8]

Evidence Re Pontius Pilate

Evidence to the fact that Pontius Pilate, the governor reported to have presided over the trial of Jesus, was a real historical person, was discovered in Caesarea Maritama in 1961:

An Italian archaeologist named Antonio Frova uncovered a fragment of a plaque that was used as a section of steps leading to the Caesarea Theatre. The inscription, written in Latin, contained the phrase, "Pontius Pilatus, Prefect of Judea has dedicated to the people of Caesarea a temple in honour of Tiberius." This temple is dedicated to the Emperor Tiberius who reigned from 14-37 A.D. This fits well chronologically with the New Testament which records that Pilot ruled as procurator from 26-36.[9]

The Roman, Tacitus, in 115 A.D recorded Nero's persecution of the Christians, and confirms the existence of Pontius Pilate:

Christus, from whom the name had its origin, suffered the extreme penalty during the reign of Tiberius at the hands of one of our procurators, Pontius Pilatus, and a most mischievous superstition, thus checked for the moment, again broke out not only in Judea, … but even in Rome.[10]

The website www.probe.org/docs/arch-nt.html states that, incredibly, there are over 39 extra-biblical sources, excluding the Early Church Fathers, who attest to over one hundred facts regarding the life and teaching of Jesus.

This wonderful website also reveals that archaeology actually supports the accuracy of the Gospels in so far as confirming many cities that were mentioned in Sacred Scripture. Also as you will read in the chapter on archaeology it has been revealed how Jesus would have been nailed to the Cross. Below is an example of the archaeology confirming descriptions painstakingly recorded in Sacred Scripture.

Forty feet underground, archaeologists discovered a pool with five porticoes, and the description of the surrounding area matches [Saint] John's description.[11]

In the Gospel of John we read, "After this there was a Jewish festival, and Jesus went up to Jerusalem. Now in Jerusalem next to the Sheep Pool there is a pool called Bethesda in Hebrew, which has five porticos; and under these were crowds of sick people, blind, lame, paralysed."[12]

Evidence Re Global Earthquake and Darkness at 3pm

Another fascinating revelation is the phenomena that happened after Jesus died, which the gospels attest to, and the historian, Thallus confirms. Though none of his original text remains, he is quoted by Julius Africanus in *Chronography*, regarding the crucifixion of Christ:

> On the whole world, there pressed a most fearful darkness, and the rocks were rent by an earthquake, and many places in Judea and other districts were thrown down. [13]

Thallus refers to this darkness, "as appears to me without reason, an eclipse of the sun."[14]

Scholar, Paul Maier, refers to the darkness and earthquakes in a footnote in his book *Pontius Pilate*:

> This phenomenon, evidently, was visible in Rome, Athens [Greece], and other Mediterranean cities. According to Tertullian… it was a "cosmic" or "world event." Phlegon, a Greek author from Caria writing in a chronology soon after 137 A.D., reported that in the fourth year of the 202nd Olympiad (i.e. 33 A.D) there was "the greatest eclipse of the sun" and that "it became night in the sixth hour of the day [i.e. noon] so that stars even appeared in the heavens. There was a great earthquake in Bithynia, and many things were overturned in Nicea." [15]

In the Gospels of Luke and Matthew the above is confirmed:

> It was now about the sixth hour and the sun's light failed, so that darkness came over the whole land until the ninth hour [3pm].
> Luke 23:44

> From the sixth hour there was darkness over all the land until the 9th hour. Matthew 27:45

> And suddenly, the veil of the Sanctuary was torn in two from top to bottom, the earth quaked, the rocks were split, the tombs opened and the bodies of many holy people rose from the dead, and these, after his resurrection, came out of the tombs, entered the holy city and appeared to a number of people. Matthew 27:51-53

Apostolic/Church Fathers

The "Apostolic Fathers" or "Church Fathers", date from the Apostles to about AD 749. The Pocket Catholic Dictionary defines the term as:

Saintly writers of the early centuries whom the Church recognizes as her special witnesses of the faith. Antiquity, orthodoxy, sanctity, and approval by the Church are their four main prerogatives." [16]

Of these writers St. Ignatius of Antioch, a Catholic bishop and the third bishop of Antioch (St. Peter, the apostle, was the first) is one of the most important, especially in his early period in history after Christ (Ignatius was martyred in AD 117). St. Ignatius emphasised the humanity of Jesus, as well as the historicity of Jesus walking the earth; in The Letter to The Trallians (AD. 110) he says:

> Turn a deaf ear, then, when anyone speaks to you apart from Jesus Christ, who was of the family of David and of Mary, who was truly born, who ate and drank, was truly persecuted under Pontius Pilate, was truly crucified and died in the sight of those in heaven and on earth and in the underworld, who also was truly raised from the dead when His Father raised Him up. And in the same manner His Father will raise us up in Christ Jesus, if we believe in Him without whom we have no hope. [17]

Here is written historic evidence of Jesus and his persecution and death at the hands of Pontius Pilate, followed by his resurrection.

Evidence re the death of Jesus

The Koran claims that Jesus pretended to be dead on the Cross (Surah IV:157). But the evidence from the Bible is that the lance thrust into Jesus' side would have pierced his right lung, the sack around the heart, and the heart itself. Not only were the soldiers futures at risk, but their very lives were too, because if any crucified prisoner survived, they themselves would be put to death, for not fulfilling their duty. Therefore it was in more than their best interests to ensure that Jesus was dead, it was vital. There was no doubt in the minds of the executioners, the professionals, that Jesus was in fact dead. Pilate also wanted the reassurance that Jesus was dead, so that the matter could be put to rest without having to worry that Jews would hassle him once again. Not to mention the fact that Pilate would have been in serious trouble from his superior, if a condemned crucified prisoner survived. So Pilate asked for the confirmation that Jesus was dead before releasing his body for burial:

> Pilate, astonished that he should have died so soon, summoned the centurion and enquired if he had been dead for some time. Having been assured of this by the centurion, he granted the corpse

to Joseph who bought a shroud, took Jesus down from the cross, wrapped him in the shroud and laid him in a tomb which had been hewn out of the rock. Mark 15:44-46

In an article in the Journal of the American Medical Society it is explained that the evidence is overwhelming that Jesus would have died:

> Clearly, the weight of historical and medical evidence indicates that Jesus was dead before the wound to his side was inflicted and supports the traditional view that the spear, thrust between his right ribs, probably perforated not only the right lung, but also the pericardium and heart and thereby ensured his death. Accordingly, interpretations based on the assumptions that Jesus did not die on the cross appear to be at odds with modern medical knowledge.[18]

Summary

There is overwhelming evidence outside of Sacred Scripture of the existence of Jesus and Christianity; and that Jesus was a historical figure, performed wonders and was crucified. Even the Roman authorities said that Christianity was a peaceful religion, and that Christians were law abiding. We are obviously faced with the realization, and fact that it is very likely that Christ was who He and the writers of Sacred Scripture said acclaimed and that Christianity is truly the fulfillment of the Jewish religion, as already covered in the previous chapter (Jesus said the cup was the new covenant) and the 'doorway' to heaven.

Tacitus, the Roman historian, reveals that the spread of religion, based on the worship of a man who suffered a most ignominious death possible, was due to him being resurrected is the only plausible option among alternative views.

The stubbornness of the victims tortured occurred as a result of their faith. Many of them would have been the first-hand witnesses to the life, death and resurrection of Jesus. And yet they chose to give up their lives rather than denounce Jesus.

It's fascinating that we have confirmation through historians of the earthquake, and darkness mentioned in the gospels. The evidence is building concerning the reliability of Sacred Scripture. The next chapter will reveal even more.

Though such a religious book as the Koran says that Jesus pretended to be dead on the Cross the historical and medical evidence reveals that Jesus was in fact dead! When we take the corroborative evidence of Sacred Scripture revealing that Pilate ensured that Jesus was dead and that the Roman soldiers' lives depended on it, the evidence is overwhelming. Jesus died! The following chapter will also reveal what evidence there is to the resurrection of Jesus. This chapter does not give evidence of spiritual truths, such as whether Jesus was the Son of God, whether he ascended into heaven, therefore in the following chapter we explore the spiritual truths that were revealed through Sacred Scripture.

Chapter 16– Bibliography

1. Lee Strobel, *The Case for Christ*, Zondervan, Grand Rapids, Michigan, 1998, 18
2. Ibid, 115
3. Josephus, Book 18, Chap 3:3 – taken from www.probe.org/docs/arch-nt.html, 3/10/2002
4. Tacitus, *Annals* 15.44.
5. Lee Strobel, *The Case for Christ*, Zondervan, Grand Rapids, Michigan, 1998, 108
6. Ibid, 109
7. Ibid, 102
8. http://www.probe.org/docs/arch-nt.html 3/10/2002
9. Ibid
10. Julius Africanus, *Chronography*, 18:1 www.probe.org/docs/arch-nt.html, 3/10/2002
11. http://www.probe.org/docs/arch-nt.html 3/10/2002
12. John 5:1-4
13. Julius Africanus, *Chronography*, 18;1 www.probe.org/docs/arch-nt.html, 3/10/2002
14. Ibid
15. Paul L. Maier, *Pontius Pilate* (Wheaton, Ill.: Tyndale House, 1968), 366, citing a fragment from Phlegon, *Olympiades he Chronika* 13, ed. Otto Keller, *Rerum Naturalium Scriptores Graeci Minores,* 1 (Leipzig: Teurber, 1877), 101. Translation by Maier.
16. John A Hardon, Pocket Catholic Dictionary, S.J., Image Books, New York, 1985, 146
17. Ignatius, *Trallians* 9
18. William D. Edwards, M.D., et al. "On the Physical Death of Jesus Christ, *Journal of the American Medical Association,* 255:11, March 21, 1986, 1463

For further articles by Edwin Yamauchi see:

http://www.leaderu.com/everystudent/easter/articles/yama.html (Was Easter a myth?)

http://www.irr.org/yamauchi.html (The Life, Death and Teaching of JesusCompared with Other Great Religious Figures)

CHAPTER 17

SCRIPTURAL EVIDENCE

We covered in the preceding chapter evidence to the existence of Jesus as a historical figure who not only walked this earth but performed "wonders" as well. Now we will explore the evidence of Jesus from scriptural sources, including the witnesses and likely dates for the composition of their evidence.

Authors of the Gospels

We return to the acclaimed author, Lee Strobel, to reveal the evidence he uncovered. In order to glean this evidence, he interviewed Dr. Craig Blomberg, renowned scholar and author of *The Historical Reliability of the Gospels*. Blomberg confesses that though strictly speaking the gospels (the biographies of Jesus in the New Testament), are anonymous, there is evidence from the early Church and many scholars who swear that the authors are:

- Matthew, the tax collector, and disciple and author of the first gospel
- Luke, Paul's "beloved physician", the author of both the gospel of Luke and Acts of the Apostles.
- John, the beloved disciple, wrote the gospel of John and the book of Revelation.

Blomberg asserts that it is most unlikely that anyone had the motivation to lie in claiming the above as the authors of the New Testament. Considering that Mark and Luke were not even disciples, it is astounding, since anyone staging a hoax, would have used such names for the Gospels as either the inner circle of Jesus group, the disciples, and even his favourite disciple whom he called Peter, translated as rock ("And I say to you, you are Peter, and upon this rock I will build my church, and the gates of the netherworld shall not prevail against it..." Matt 16:18-19) or even of his dear Mother. In fact, much later (after A.D 200 when fanciful apocryphal gospels were written, Philip, Peter, Mary and James were the well-known names to be chosen as authors. However these writings were not accepted by the Catholic Church to be part of Sacred Scripture.

St. Irenaeus at about AD 180 wrote the following, revealing who the individual gospel writers relied on as eyewitnesses:

> Matthew published his own gospel among the Hebrews in their own tongue, when Peter and Paul were preaching the gospel in Rome and founding the church there. After their departure, Mark, the disciple and interpreter of Peter, himself handed down to us in writing the substance of Peter's preaching. Luke, the follower of Paul, set down in a book the Gospel preached by his teacher. Then John, the disciple of the Lord, who also leaned on his breast, himself produced his Gospel while he was living at Ephesus in Asia. [1]

Strobel explains that if the gospels were written by the authors using a journalistic-type discourse, including Luke the historian then we can be assured that they have recorded history based on either direct or indirect eyewitness testimony. Therefore either the writers witnessed the actual events they have recorded, or they interviewed those that were the direct witnesses.

The gospel writers used a particular genre as the people of 'ancient' cultures did not record all the details of someone's life but focused on aspects which they particularly wanted to preserve, so that the followers of Jesus could learn from the historical experiences. So the main emphasis in the gospels are Jesus birth, presentation in the temple, public ministry, instigation of the Eucharist, and his death and resurrection; and the therefore these are the main aspects that the Christian Churches emphasise.

The four gospels have parts that overlap each other, with almost every major theme being paralleled in each gospel. Though this has been severely critiqued it is important to note that scholars would not grant them authenticity because if all the gospels were identical they would be called copies. As mentioned previously it is worthwhile to note that Matthew relied on Peter as a fellow eyewitness. Strobel says that, "Although Matthew had his own recollections as a disciple, his quest for accuracy prompted him to rely on some material directly from Peter in Jesus' inner circle."[2]

Dating of the Gospels

Blomberg asserts that the standard scholarly beliefs concerning the dating of the particular gospels are Mark in the AD 70's, Matthew and Luke in the 80's, and John in the 90's. Therefore in relation to the authenticity concerning a historically written account these should be claimed as authentic; the accepted biographies of Alexander the Great astonishingly enough were written more than four hundred years after Alexander's death and are accepted as authentic. Jesus died about 30 A.D (the date is disputed and could be 33 A.D) so a written record 40, 50 or 60 years after a historic figure's death, should be held in at least the same, if not more regard than a record written 400 years afterwards.

Authenticity of the Gospels

> Not only keeping in mind the above, but the astonishing fact that there have been recovered over 5,600 copies of the gospels in Greek, 8,000-10,000 Latin Vulgate, 8,000 in Ethiopic, Slavic and Armenian. This gives a grand total of about 24,000 manuscripts.[7]

This is astonishing! There are so many manuscripts, and they date back to the early part of the 2nd century. Bruce Metzger, Ph. D., scholar and author or editor of over 50 books, mainly on the New Testament, believes that compared to other well known works of antiquity they stack up extremely well.

Yamauchi explains the historical uniqueness of the biographies of Jesus Christ:

> "When people begin religious movements, it's often not until many generations later that people record things about them." Yamauchi said. "But the fact is that we have better historical documentation for Jesus than for the founder of any other ancient religion."[8]

Wow! That's exciting! The New Testament, especially St. Paul's writings and the gospels are better historically, than for example, the scriptures of Buddha, who lived in the sixth century B.C. These scriptures were not put into writing until after the Christian era, and the first biography of Buddha was written in the first century A.D. In comparison, Muhammad lived from AD 570 to 632. In the Koran, his biography was not written until A.D 767 – more than a full century after his death.

Son of Man

In three of the gospels Jesus refers to himself as the "Son of Man". While some claim that this only refers to Jesus humanity, the Old Testament confirms the title and refers to something much more powerful than just Jesus' humanity; in fact it is quite startling – it was a claim to Jesus divinity – to being the Son of God. In the book of Daniel is written:

> In my vision at night I looked, and there before me was one like the son of man, coming with the clouds of heaven. He approached the Ancient of Days [God] and was led into his presence. He was given authority, glory and sovereign power; all peoples, nations, and men of every language worshipped him. His dominion is an everlasting dominion that will not pass away, and his kingdom is one that will never be destroyed. Daniel 7:13-14 (New American Bible)

Therefore we can see from the book of Daniel, written way before Jesus arrived on the scene, that the Son of Man has a special authority, glory and sovereign power, and that he was worshipped. This is obviously referring to the divinity of Jesus.

The interesting point to note here is that Jews would have known that Jesus was claiming to be the Son of God as they would have known the book of Daniel off-by-heart.

The most frequently used title of Christ in the New Testament, which occurred over 82 times was a messianic title (Daniel 7:2-14), Son of Man. This title refers both to the humanity and, to a degree even more so, to the divinity and messiahship of Christ. A clear distinction is made in Matthew 26:64:

> Jesus said to him in reply, "You have said so. But I tell you:
> From now on you will see 'the son of Man
> seated at the right hand of the Power'
> and coming on the clouds of heaven.'" (New American Bible)

Ironically, though some claim that Jesus never said he was the Son of God, he never stopped his followers from addressing him as such. But before we look at that let's see an example where Jesus claimed to be the Son of Man:

> Jesus heard they had ejected him, and when he found him he said to him, "Do you believe in the Son of Man?" "Sir," the man replied, "tell me who he is so that I may believe in him." Jesus said, "You

have seen him; he is speaking to you." The man said, "Lord I
believe," and worshipped him.
John 9:35-38

Son of God

Now let's look at instances where Jesus' followers claimed Jesus
was the Son of God. The first example is when Peter walks on water
towards Jesus and then when he noticed the force of the wind he
became afraid and began to sink:

> "Lord," he cried, 'save me!" Jesus put out his hand at once and
> held him. "You have so little faith," he said, "why did you doubt?"
> And as they got into the boat the wind dropped. The men in the
> boat bowed down before him and said, "Truly, you are the Son of
> God."   Matthew 14:30-33

For the men to bow down before God means they performed an act
of worship. Their action of worship precedes their statement in the
belief that Jesus was the Son of God.

In the gospel of Luke the disciples again worship Jesus, this time
when Jesus has just ascended into Heaven:

> Now as he blessed them, he withdrew from them and was carried
> up to heaven. They worshipped him and then went back to
> Jerusalem fully of joy; and they were continually in the Temple
> praising God. Luke 24:51-53

Another example whereby one of Jesus' followers claimed he was
the Son of God was the result of questioning them on what others
believed about the Son of Man, and then he asked them whom the
disciples believed he was – therefore confirming He was the Son of
Man. Interestingly Peter spoke up for the disciples and proclaimed,
"You are the Christ, the Son of the living God." Matthew 16:16

In each example where someone claims that Jesus is the Son of God,
he does not rebuke or correct them. In the case where Jesus is on trial
and questioned whether he is the Son of God, he does not deny the
claim to save his own skin:

> But Jesus was silent. And the High Priest said to him, "I put you
> on oath by the Living God to tell us if you are the Christ, the Son

of God." Jesus answered him, "It is you who say it. But, I tell you that from this time onward you will see the *Son of man seated at the right hand of the Power and coming on the clouds of heaven. [see Psalm 110:1 and Daniel 7:13]*
Matthew 26:63-64

It should be noted here that Jesus was put on oath and he answered in the way which clearly shows he believed he was the Son of God, and the Christ, the one to redeem Israel.

It's enlightening that Jesus did not correct or stop him from worshipping Him. Therefore Jesus viewed himself as the Son of Man, and viewed himself as equal to God, and therefore God.

At the beginning of his Gospel, Matthew clearly asserts Jesus is the Son of God:

Now all this took place to fulfill what the Lord had spoken through the prophet:

Look! the virgin is with child
 and they will give birth to a son
 whom they will call Immanuel [Isaiah 7:14]
 a name which means 'God-is-with-us'.
Matthew 1:23
[see also Mark 1:24; 5:7; Luke 4:34; 8:28; John 2:4]

In the Gospel of Matthew (Matt 27:43) while Jesus is being crucified He is taunted to admit that he is the Son of God, "He has put his trust in God; now let God rescue him if he wants him. For he did say, "I am God's son."" [see Psalm 69:21]

What is as fascinating is that upon Jesus' death, a Gentile defends Jesus' claim to be the Son of God:

"And suddenly, the veil of the Sanctuary was torn in two from top to bottom, the earth quaked, the rocks were split, the tombs opened and the bodies of many holy people rose from the dead, and these, after his resurrection, came out of the tombs, entered the holy city and appeared to a number of people. The centurion, together with the others guarding Jesus, had seen the earthquake and all that was taking place, and they were terrified and said, "In truth this man was son of God."
Matthew 27:51-54

Earliest Writings of the New Testament

St. Paul's writings have been declared to be the earliest in the New Testament. Paul was a Jew, and after being blinded by an intense light attributed to God, he was consequently cured of that blindness by a Christian's prayer and thus he became a believer in Jesus. Paul's letters attest to his worshipping Jesus as God, which was no small thing for him, as previously he had been a ferocious supporter of the persecutors of Christians, and so had detested Jesus and His followers. Central to Paul's letters are Jesus' death and resurrection, and the future resurrection of Christians who persevere, including the resurrection of our very bodies. When Christ rose he had a resurrected body, and Paul attests that we upon the glory of the next world will also have a resurrected physical body. As have covered in the chapter *Evil: Does it Exist?*, our soul and body belongs together, hence we too will conquer death:

> What I am saying, brothers, is that mere human nature cannot inherit the kingdom of God: what is perishable cannot inherit what is imperishable. Now I am going to tell you a mystery: we are not all going to fall asleep, but we are all going to be changed, instantly, in the twinkling of an eye, when the last trumpet sounds. The trumpet is going to sound, and then the dead will be raised imperishable, and we shall be changed, because this perishable nature of ours must put on imperishability, this mortal nature must put on immortality.
> And after this perishable nature has put on imperishability and this mortal nature has put on immortality, then will the words of scripture come true: *Death is swallowed up in victory. Death, where is your victory? Death, where is your sting?* The sting of death is sin, and the power of sin comes from the Law. Thank God, then, for giving us the victory through Jesus Christ our Lord.
> 1 Corinthians 15:50-57

Jesus conquered death and so will we. Eternal life awaits us, if we respond to Christ's call. What is intrinsically tied to the Death and Resurrection of Jesus is His ascension; if Jesus did not ascend into Heaven, but had merely died later, then His Resurrection would not have held such importance. We can relate Jesus' ascension to that of several people in the Old Testament ascending into heaven, for example, Elijah:

Now as they walked on, talking as they went, a chariot of fire appeared and horses of fire coming between the two of them; and Elijah went up to heaven in the whirlwind. 2 Kings 2:11

The interesting comparison with Elijah is that Jesus was able to ascend without any assistance such as a fiery chariot or a whirlwind, since He was the Son of God:

And so the Lord Jesus, after he had spoken to them, was taken up into heaven, there at the right hand of God he took his place, while they, going out, preached everywhere, the Lord working with them and confirming the word by the signs that accompanied it. (Mark 16:19-20)

As St. Paul's writings are the earliest in the New Testament, let's explore the earliest creed so that we can discover what the earliest Christians believed. Scholars believe this creed to be written within 2 – 8 years after the death and resurrection of Jesus.

The tradition I handed on to you in the first place, a tradition which I had myself received, was that Christ died for our sins, in accordance with the scriptures, and that he was buried; and that on the third day, he was raised to life, in accordance with the scriptures; and that he appeared to Cephas [Rock/Peter]; and later to the Twelve; and next he appeared to more than five hundred of the brothers at the same time, most of whom are still with us, though some have fallen asleep; then he appeared to James, and then to all the apostles.
1 Corinthians 15:3-7

This record by Paul, is a creed (a statement of religious belief). The tradition was handed onto Paul that, "Christ died for our sins, in accordance with the scriptures, and that he was buried, and that on the third day, he was raised to life, in accordance with the scriptures..." This tradition was a creed that was believed and promulgated before Paul. Therefore if Paul wrote this from 2 – 8 years after the death and the resurrection of Jesus, then this creed was being promulgated anywhere from 0 – 7 years prior to Paul's utilizing it; we have a historic creed which links the forgiveness of sins, with the death and resurrection of Jesus. Lee Strobel brings forward the latest date that the creed could be written; he links the letter of Paul to be within 2 years of Jesus Resurrection, therefore the creed would have been promulgated 0 –2 years before Paul.[6]

While the late F.F. Bruce, author and eminent professor at the University of Manchester, England asserted, "There is no body of ancient literature in the world which enjoys such a wealth of good textual attestation as the New Testament."[9]

Sir Frederic Kenyon, former director of the British Museum, also confidently asserts that, "In no other case is the interval of time between the composition of the book and the date of the earliest manuscripts [copies] so short as that in the New Testament."[10]

I've heard people refer to the implausibility of Sacred Scripture in relation to the gospels being written a number of years after Jesus death, and so it was a revelation that Strobel was able to uncover some fascinating facts from Blomberg. As the Jews were an oral culture, scrolls and papyrus were rare, computers and recorders didn't exist. With the recalling of the life of Jesus the early speakers would have been corrected by the disciples or the direct witnesses if they omitted vital details in their recollection. Therefore for the gospel writers to all confirm that Jesus worked miracles is remarkable, and is obviously an essential aspect which the writers wanted to portray.

Blomberg recounted to Strobel:

> "I'm saying that it's likely that a lot of similarities and differences among the synoptics can be explained by assuming that the disciples and other early Christians had committed to memory a lot of what Jesus said and did, but they felt free to recount this information in various forms, always preserving the significance of Jesus' original teaching and deeds." [11]

Blomberg implores us to consider the way the gospels have been written as implicit evidence: He tells us that they are written in a sober, responsible way, with accurate incidental details, with obvious care and precision; omitting any outlandish flourishes or any "blatant mythologising" found in many ancient writings. Therefore the gospel writers intended to record what actually occurred.

Falsifying Facts in the Gospels?

It is also conspicuous that there are several precedents for the gospel writers to have omitted certain details from their writings. This includes portraying Peter as a bumbling fool; even denying the existence of Jesus three times; the disciples as bickering over petty arguments; most of them ran away and hid like scared rats when Jesus was arrested and crucified; and even one disciple was a thief and betrayed Jesus. Blomberg underscores the motive of writing with so much detail and honesty:

> "So had they left some of this out, that in and of itself wouldn't necessarily have been seen as falsifying the story.
> But here's the point: if they didn't feel free to leave out stuff when it would have been convenient and helpful to do so, is it really plausible to believe that they outright added and fabricated material with no historical basis?"[12]

It is imperative to note that the books of Sacred Scripture, were individual documents (scrolls) or letters. One of the Church Fathers, St. Athanasius (A.D 295 - 373) reveals which books of the New Testament were considered as Sacred Scripture (see The Thirty-Ninth Festal Letter) - 27 New Testament writings. But it was not simply St Athanasius who made this decision. Such a significant decision needed the authority of a Church council. The 'canon' of scripture was decided by the Council of Hippo in 393, and also the Council of Carthage in 397. The question was again revisited by Pope Innocent 1 (405), and the Council of Trent in 1546 which responded to the various claims and attacks of Luther and the Protestant Reformation. (The printing press was invented in 1436 and only about 5% of the population could read at that time – it was an oral culture.) It was at the Council of Trent that the 'canon' (or what was to be included in the Old Testament) was officially defined by the Catholic Church. For the Catholic Church the 'canon' of scripture consists of 46 books in the Old Testament and 27 Books of the New Testament, 73 Books in all.

Corroborating Evidence of the Gospel

Corroborative evidence supports the notion that Jesus did in fact rise from the dead. At the arrest of Jesus and following his death, his disciples were terrified; they feared that they too would be arrested, beaten and put to death. Therefore if they were so afraid, why would they claim that Jesus had risen, and draw attention to themselves? Why would they publicly testify that they had seen Jesus alive following his death and resurrection? This would surely make them vulnerable to the Jewish and Roman authorities, or worse to the religious fanatics. Why would they encounter beatings, and imprisonment and probably death, and yet still continue with their testimony? Why would they ultimately give up their very lives to continue this testimony? In addition, why did the Jewish authorities never manage to produce a body, when in fact the tomb was guarded? Jesus followers knew and saw Him after His resurrection. This inspired them with hope, and they knew in fact only God could resurrect – to resurrect is to give life. No one but God could have done this. He obviously had God the Father's seal of approval. Therefore everything Jesus said, testifying to be the Son of God, and being sent by the Father was true. He was the Messiah.

But not only having hope, the followers of Jesus now had a special authority in which they could preach with. In order for 5,000 Jews to be converted at one time, there would have been a special authority with the words proclaimed; Peter preached with conviction, and resorted to his testimony of seeing Jesus, and that Jesus was crucified, which many of the Jews present would have been witnesses to, and that He rose again, and some of the Jews present may have seen him following His resurrection. Therefore that, along with the power of God, could only bring conviction. This was no meager thing for Jews to convert to Christianity which held many new teachings. For many it was abhorrent that their fellow Jews would believe in a fulfillment of the divinely inspired Jewish Scriptures; to them it would seem as if Jesus supplanted their beliefs with teaching of His own. The followers of Jesus, the Christians would have known they would be making a huge sacrifice, including being ostracized by one's family; giving up the deeply held belief that there is only Yahweh, and having that belief transformed into the Trinity (see Chapter on *Personal God* for definition).

John Morton, in *Man Science and God*, refers to Dr. A.R.C Leaney's in a lecture series entitled, "Selwyn Lectures" in 1996 on the topic of "The Christ of the Synoptic Gospels".

> He is firm in the view that the Gospels contain a great amount of material that is altogether credible, which it is hard to think anyone would invent, like the statements describing Jesus as man of Nazareth, his taking a house as a mission centre at Capernaum, and so on. Its point was to show that Jesus, a man about whom other and wonderful things might be narrated, was a man well known in a local time and place. Most of his contemporaries rejected him, not because he was an imposter making claims he could not perform, but because he had done great deeds and yet they knew him as an ordinary man. This was a 'stumbling block' to them. In Dr. Leaney's assessment, the plain historical material in St. Mark's Gospel fastens Jesus to history as firmly as he was nailed to the cross. [13]

It was a major stumbling block for the ordinary folk; Jesus wasn't an earthly king as they expected that the Messiah would overthrow the Romans. Therefore when Jesus was crucified it was truly remarkable that his followers risked torture, often welcomed death, and that Christianity flourished so rapidly. A major question facing us concerning the motives behind the Christian faith at its beginnings is: If this was a hoax, why were the founders willing to be tortured, and die for this 'hoax'?

Old Testament Prophecies Of The Messiah

The Old Testament books are the writings of the Jews written over many centuries prior to Christ, and were inherited by the Church, the new Israel. There is overwhelming evidence in the writings of the Jews, which not only relate to a Messiah, but also to a suffering messiah, which in fact relate directly to Jesus. In fact these ancient prophecies have never related to, or been claimed to relate to anyone else in history. First, let me quote one of the most acute scriptures that refer to the Messiah:

Who would believe what we have heard?
To whom has the arm of the Lord been revealed?
He grew up like a sapling before him,
like a shoot from the parched earth;
There was in him no stately bearing
to make us look at him,
nor appearance that would attract us to him.
He was spurned and avoided by men,
a man of suffering, accustomed to infirmity,
One of those from whom men hide their faces,
spurned, and we held him in no esteem.

Yet it was our infirmities that he bore,
Our sufferings that he endured,
While we thought of him as stricken,
as one smitten by God and afflicted.
But he was pierced for our offenses,
crushed for our sins,
Upon him was the chastisement that makes us whole,
by his stripes we were healed.
We had all gone astray like sheep,
each following his own way;

But the Lord laid upon him
the guilt of us all.

Though he was harshly treated, he submitted
and opened not his mouth;
Like a lamb led to the slaughter
or a sheep before the shearers,
he was silent and opened not his mouth.
Oppressed and condemned, he was taken away,
And who would have thought any more of his destiny?
When he was cut off from the land of the living,
and smitten for the sin of his people,
A grave was assigned him among the wicked
and a burial place with evildoers,
Though he had done no wrong
Nor spoken any falsehood
[But the Lord was pleased to crush him in infirmity.]

If he gives his life as an offering for sin,
he shall see his descendants in a long life,
and the will of the Lord shall be accomplished through him.
Because of his affliction he shall see the light in fullness of days;
Through his suffering, my servant shall justify many,
and their guilt he shall bear.
Therefore I will give him his portion among the great,
and he shall divide the spoils with the mighty,
Because he surrendered himself to death
and was counted among the wicked;
And he shall take away the sins of many,
and win pardon for their offenses.
Isaiah 53:1-12 (New American Bible)

cross references:
v2 – John 19:1-5
v3 – 1 Peter 2:3-8, Luke 23:27-31, 19:41
v4 – 11 Cor 5:18-21, 1 Peter 2:24
v4-12 – 2 Cor 5:18-21, 1 Pet 2:24
v5 – John 19:1, 1 Pet 2:24
v7 – Matt 26:63, 27:12-14, Act 8:35
v8 – John 18:28, 2 Cor 5:21 (?)
v9 – Matthew 27:57-60
v10 – Acts 2:23, 3:18
v12 – Luke 23:34, Mark 15:27-28

This scripture gives a startling portrayal of the Messiah. He was to carry "our infirmities"... "pierced for our offences, crushed for our sins." Therefore to carry our infirmities means Jesus took upon himself our sins and suffered as a consequence. The Lord (God the Father) "laid upon him the guilt of us all."; and "smitten for the sin of his people" (this implies a kingship). "If he gives life as an offering for sin." The final sentence reveals that Jesus had the power to take away (forgive) sins and that his sacrifice was to overcome sin, "and he shall take away the sins of many, and win pardon for their offenses."

Jesus' lineage was from the line of King David, and the following prophecy points to a descendant of David being blessed with the spirit of grace and prayer, but it also points to remorse over treating someone very cruelly. In hindsight we know that is a prophecy relating to the Messiah, and thus to Jesus:

> But over the house of David and the inhabitants of Jerusalem I shall pour out a spirit of grace and prayer, and they will look to me. They will mourn for the one whom they have pierced as though for an only child, and weep for him as people weep for a first-born child. Zechariah 12:10-11

This is similar to Isaiah 52:13-53, 12. It was fulfilled in John 19:33 when Jesus was pierced in the side:

> When they came to Jesus, they saw he was already dead, and so instead of breaking his legs [confirms Psalm 34:20] one of the soldiers pierced his side with a lance; and immediately there came out blood and water. This is the evidence of one who saw it – true evidence, and he knows that what he says is true – and he gives it so that you may believe as well. John 19:33-35

The words of Psalm 22 have an erie ring to them, as they are the words Jesus cried out to God while on the Cross, suffering excruciating pain.

> My God, my God, why have you forsaken me?
> The words of my groaning do nothing to save me,
> My God, I call by day but you do not answer,
> At night, but I find no respite.
> Psalm 22:1-2

It is interesting to note that Jesus would have been crying out in prayer to God the Father, during both day and night, as night descended prematurely, possibly via an eclipse. In the Gospels we see this prophecy come to fruition:

> From the sixth hour there was darkness over all the land until the ninth hour. And about the ninth hour, Jesus cried out in a loud voice, "*Eli, eli, lama sabachthani?*" that is, '*My God, my God, why have you forsaken me?*'
> Matthew 27:45-46 [see also Mark 15:34]

Another section in Psalm 22 also has a strange resonance as here it would imply Jesus saying he is a worm, and less than human. Jesus would have felt like he was at the pit of despair, the lowest anyone could go, because he had miraculously taken all our sins upon him as mentioned above. Therefore Jesus took upon Himself our evil. And because of that He felt totally abandoned by God.

> But I am a worm, less than human,
> scorn of mankind, contempt of the people;
> all who see me jeer at me,
> they sneer and wag their heads,
> He trusted himself to Yahweh, let Yahweh set him free!
> Let him deliver him, as he took such delight in him.'
> Psalm 22:6-8

Once again there is a fulfillment of the prophecy in the Gospels:

> The passers-by jeered at him; they shook their heads and said, 'So you would destroy the Temple and in three days rebuild it! Then save yourself if you are God's son and come down from the cross!' The chief priests with the scribes and elders mocked him in the same way, with the words, 'He saved others; he cannot save himself. He is the king of Israel; let him come down from the cross now, and we will believe in him. He has put his trust in God; now let God rescue him if he wants him. For he did say, "I am God's son."' Even the bandits who were crucified with him taunted him in the same way.
> Matthew 27:39-44 [see also Mark 15:29-32]

The next part of this psalm that I'd like to highlight is the section which describes the victim (therefore Jesus), as he faces his accusers and possible destruction:

Many bulls are encircling me,
wild bulls of Bashan closing in on me.
Lions ravening and roaring
open their jaws at me.
My strength is trickling away,
my bones are all disjointed,
my heart has turned to wax,
melting inside me.
My mouth is dry as earthenware,
my tongue sticks to my jaw.
You lay me down in the dust of death.

A pack of dogs surrounds me,
a gang of villains closing in on me
as if to hack off my hands and my feet.
I can count every one of my bones,
While they look on and gloat;
they divide my garments among them
and cast lots for my clothing.
Psalm 22:12-19

In John 19:24 it explicitly states that Jesus clothes are gambled for with the casting of lots. "So they said to one another, "Let's not tear it, but cast lots for it to see whose it will be," in order that the passage of scripture might be fulfilled..."

Some skeptics claim that Jesus manipulated events to fulfill the prophecies. Passover was a time for the Jews to remember Israel's deliverance from the terrible persecution and slavery of Egypt. During this time it was a tradition for the Roman Procurator to release a prisoner. Ironically the Jews chose Barabbas, a brigand, a criminal, over that of someone who performed wonders such as healing the sick.

In addition, how could Jesus manipulate the Sanhedrin to offer Judas thirty pieces of silver and that Judas would throw the money in the temple and betray Jesus? This confirmed the Scripture in the Old Testament:

I then said to them, "If you see fit, give me my wages; if not, never mind." So they weighed out my wages: thirty shekels of silver. Yahweh said to me, "Throw it to the smelter, this princely sum at which they have valued me!" Taking the thirty shekels of silver, I threw them into the Temple of Yahweh, for the smelter.
Zechariah 11:12-13

The Smelter quoted above is the same as a Potter, and so it is remarkable to see what the New Testament says in relation to the betrayer of Jesus:

> When he found that Jesus had been condemned, then Judas, his betrayer, was filled with remorse and took the thirty silver pieces back to the chief priests and elders saying, "I have sinned. I have betrayed innocent blood." They replied, "What is that to us? That is your concern." And flinging down the silver pieces in the sanctuary he made off, and went and hanged himself. The chief priests picked up the silver pieces and said, "It is against the Law to put this into the treasury; it is blood-money." So they discussed the matter and with it bought the potter's field as a graveyard for foreigners, and this is why the field is still called the Field of Blood. The word spoken through the prophet Jeremiah was then fulfilled: And they took the thirty silver pieces, the sum at which the precious One was priced by the children of Israel, and they gave them for the potter's field, just as the Lord had directed me. [Zechariah 11:12-13]

It's remarkable that both scriptures show that the betrayer refused his reward, that he threw the money (30 pieces/shekels of silver) in the temple and that a Potter would receive the blood money. Another question we are faced with is, how could Jesus arrange the method of his death?

> The chief priests and the elders, however, had persuaded the crowd to demand the release of Barabbas and the execution of Jesus. So, when the governor spoke and asked them, "Which of the two do you want me to release for you?" they said, "Barrabas." Pilate said to them, "But in that case, what am I to do with Jesus who is called Christ?" They all said, "Let him be crucified!"
> Matthew 27:20-22

How could Jesus arrange that soldiers would gamble for his clothing and not tear his garment into pieces?

> When the soldiers had finished crucifying Jesus they took his clothing and divided into four shares, one for each soldier. His undergarment was seamless, woven in one piece from neck to hem; so they said to one another, "Instead of tearing it, let's throw dice to decide who is to have it." In this way the words of Scripture were fulfilled: They divide my garments among them
> And cast lots for my clothes [Psalm 22:18]

How could Jesus manipulate the fact that He has been the only one to fulfill the Messianic prophecies of the Old Testament?

These are serious and honest questions. This overwhelming evidence alone should lead us to the conclusion that Jesus was the Messiah. When the disciples of John came to Jesus and questioned him as John wanted to know whether He was the Messiah, Jesus said:

> Then he gave the messengers their answer, "Go back and tell John what you have seen and heard: the blind see again, the lame walk, those suffering from virulent skin-diseases are cleansed, and the deaf hear, the dead are raised to life, the good news is proclaimed to the poor; and blessed is anyone who does not find me a cause of falling."
> Luke 7:22

What is interesting here is that John already knew that Jesus was the Messiah, (see Luke 3:1-18) as he baptized Jesus in the river Jordan, but he still doubted later on. The answer that Jesus gave confirmed what the prophet Isaiah wrote:

> "Then the eyes of the blind will be opened,
> the ear of the deaf unsealed,
> then the lame will leap like a deer" Isaiah 35:5-6

In addition it confirms the scripture of Isaiah 61:1-3 that Jesus read out in the synagogue, and claimed he fulfilled it:

> "He came to Nazara, where he had been brought up, and went into the synagogue on the Sabbath day as he usually did. He stood up to read, and they handed him the scroll of the prophet Isaiah. Unrolling the scroll he found the place where it is written:

> "The spirit of Lord Yahweh is on me
> for he has anointed me
> to bring the good news to the afflicted.
> He has sent me
> to proclaim liberty to captives,
> sight to the blind,
> to let the oppressed go free,
> to proclaim a year of favour
> from the Lord."

He then rolled up the scroll, gave it back to the assistant and sat down. And all eyes in the synagogue were fixed on him. Then he began to speak to them, "This text is being fulfilled today even while you are listening." And he won the approval of all, and they were astonished by the gracious words that came from his lips."
Luke 4:16-22

Jesus' miracles are a sign indicating the coming of the kingdom of God. They are a foretaste of what the kingdom is going to be like.

There is much evidence pointing to Jesus being the Messiah. The following reasons put to us by Strobel may seem rather haunting as it could make us face the strong possibility that Jesus was the Messiah, God become man.

"And what about his relationship – if we can call it that - with the Roman authorities? We have to ask why they crucified him. If he had merely been an innocuous sage telling nice little parables, how did he end up on a cross especially at a Passover season, when no Jew wants any Jew to be executed? There had to be a reason why the sign above his head said, "This is the king of the Jews."…Either Jesus had made that verbal claim or someone clearly thought he did".[14]

Evidence re the Resurrection of Jesus

In Jesus' resurrected state, he appeared to more than 500 of His followers. This was on several different occasions, over a forty-day period. During this time he communicated with them, ate with them, let them touch Him, and cooked breakfast for them. Is this what an illusion would do?

But the fact that both the Old Testament and Jesus Himself predicted His resurrection, makes this miracle even more significant.

They were on the road, going up to Jerusalem; Jesus was walking on ahead of them; they were in a daze, and those who followed were apprehensive. Once more taking the twelve aside he began to tell them what was going to happen to him, "Now we are going up to Jerusalem, and the Son of man is about to be handed over to the chief priests and the scribes. They will condemn him to death and will hand him over to the gentiles, who will mock him and spit at him and scourge him and put him to death; and after three days he will rise again.
Mark 10:32-34

Jesus not only predicted it, but it is mentioned clearly in the Old Testament as well. First let's explore the Scriptures which predicted that the Messiah would overcome death (Sheol is another word for death):

So my heart rejoices, my soul delights,
My body too will rest secure,
For you will not abandon me to Sheol,
You cannot allow your faithful servant to see the abyss.
Psalm 16:9-10

Yahweh, you have lifted me out of Sheol,
From among those who sink into oblivion you have given me life.
Psalm 30:3

But my soul God will ransom
From the clutches of Sheol, and will snatch me up.
Psalm 49:15

I shall not die, I shall live
To recount the great deeds of Yahweh.
Though Yahweh punished me sternly,
He has not abandoned me to death. Psalm 118:17

The People of the Old Testament did not know the meaning of these scripture passages, but it was following the death and resurrection of Jesus that the Catholic Church revealed their meaning. It is important to note that Yahweh punishing Jesus was because Jesus took upon himself the sins of the world.

A former atheist, Wolfhart Pannenburg, now a famous scriptural scholar, examined the evidence for the Resurrection. At the conclusion of his investigation he declared:

The resurrection of Jesus acquires such decisive meaning, not merely because someone has been raised from the dead, but because it is Jesus of Nazareth, whose execution was instigated by the Jews because He had blasphemed against God. If this Man was raised from the dead, then that plainly means that the God whom He supposedly blasphemed has committed Himself to Him.[15]

The same theme is displayed in an article in *Time* magazine regarding a Jewish rabbi who recognised the Resurrection of Jesus:

Pinchas Lapide's Logic escapes me. He believes it is a possibility that Jesus was resurrected by God. At the same time he does not accept Jesus as the Messiah. But Jesus said that He was the Messiah. Why would God resurrect a liar? [16]

Indeed, if God did resurrect Jesus, and Jesus claimed to be the Messiah, equal with God, then God did not resurrect a blasphemer, but in fact God resurrected the Messiah, the chosen one, Prince of Peace, God's very own Son. Therefore Sacred Scripture is the very word of God – the living Word by which we all should study and follow, with the guidance of God's Church. If Jesus was a liar, and a blasphemer he would not be the Son of God. Therefore God did not resurrect a liar!

There were many witnesses to the fact that Jesus rose from the dead – including a crowd of 500 hundred men (women and children would have been additional to this number). That's so incredible, that so many people simultaneously witnessed Jesus walking the earth after he had risen from the dead. The evidence to the resurrection of Jesus is comprehensive.

Hallucinations

Some denounce the scriptural accounts of the resurrection of Jesus as hallucinations by Jesus' loved ones, hallucinating that he had risen. Gary Habermas, Ph.D. D.D, psy, and author of over seven books concentrating on the resurrection of Jesus, rebuts this:

> Hallucinations are individual occurrences. By their very nature only one person can see a given hallucination at a time. They certainly aren't something which can be seen by a group of people. Neither is it possible that one person could somehow induce an hallucination in somebody else. Since an hallucination exists only in this subjective, personal sense, it is obvious that others cannot witness it. [17]

It was impossible for there to have been mass hallucinations as there are many instances of Jesus appearing after his resurrection, and this includes to over 500 people in one instance (see 1 Cor 15:6) and consequently Jesus ate with his disciples (Luke 24:44-49).

Jesus appeared to two women, "Mary of Magdala, and the other Mary" (see Matt 28: 1-7). It is remarkable that Matthew would write this as being a Jew and a male, if he had fabricated it, he would have put someone seemingly of 'more' importance then a couple of women – socially and religiously they were viewed as less important than men. So culturally it would have been repugnant that Jesus would appear to women first.

> And suddenly, coming to meet them, was Jesus. "Greetings," he said. And the women came up to him and, clasping his feet, they did him homage. Then Jesus said to them, "Do not be afraid; go and tell my brothers that they must leave for Galilee; there they will see me." Matthew 28:9-10

Jesus was resurrected, and the following passage shows that he could be touched. It is vital to note that if Jesus had not in fact died, and merely became unconscious he would not have been able to walk unaided! And He would definitely not ask his followers to touch the wounds of the crucifixion, which he asked Thomas to do (John 20:24-29) – that would have been excruciating agony!

> They set out that instant and returned to Jerusalem. There they found the Eleven assembled together with their companions, who said to them, "The Lord has indeed risen and has appeared to Simon. Then they told their story of what had happened on the road and how they had recognized him at the breaking of bread. They were still talking about all this when he himself stood among them and said to them, "Peace be with you!" In a state of alarm and fright, they thought they were seeing a ghost. But he said, "Why are you so agitated, and why are these doubts stirring in your hearts? See by my hands and my feet that it is I myself. Touch me and see for yourselves; a ghost has no flesh and bones as you can see I have." And as he said this he showed them his hands and his feet. Their joy was so great that they still could not believe it, as they were dumbfounded; so he said to them, "Have you anything here to eat?" And they offered him a piece of grilled fish, which he took and ate before their eyes. Luke 24:33-43

Summary

No other historical figure has ever had all the Old Testament prophecies concerning the Messiah attributed to them – only Jesus Christ has. The evidence is compelling. Isaiah 53, in itself, is a descriptive scripture of the crucifixion scene, before the method of crucifixion was even invented. Moreover, it's remarkable that even the amount with which Christ would be betrayed with, was prophesied. The gospels provide powerful evidence for the life, wonders (miracles), death and resurrection of Jesus, the Messiah, the Son of God. St. Paul provides us with the grounds of an early creed of the Church which testifies to the death and resurrection of Jesus. The followers of Jesus embraced beatings, and even death (many were cruelly tortured and executed) for no material gain. They explicitly believed that Jesus was the Son of God, the Messiah, and that he died and rose again for the forgiveness of sins. The disciples eventually (yeah they were a bit slow) viewed Jesus as the Son of God; Peter was the first of the disciples to proclaim this. If Jesus had not risen from the dead the Jews would have laughed at Peter or Paul when they claimed that Jesus had been seen risen from the dead. In addition after Jesus saved Peter from possibly drowning and calmed the wind His disciples worshipped him (Matthew 14) and also at the ascension they worshiped Jesus (Luke 24:50-53) The evidence is before you. You can either accept it, or reject it; Jesus was who he and others claimed to be. The choice is yours – you can ignore or accept the evidence.

Chapter 17 – Bibliography

1. Irenaeus, Adversus haereses 3.3.
2. Lee Strobel, *The Case for Christ*, Zondervan, Grand Rapids, Michigan, 1998, 33-34
3. Edited by: Raymond E Brown, S.S., Joseph A Fitzmyer, S.J., Roland E Murphy, O.Carm, New Jerome Biblical Commentary, Geoffrey Chapman, 1992)
4. The New Jerusalem Bible, Pocket Edition, Darton Longman + Todd, 1990, 1448
5. John A Hardon, Pocket Catholic Dictionary, S.J., Image Books, New York, 1985
6. Refer Lee Strobel, *The Case for Christ*, Zondervan, Grand Rapids, Michigan, 1998, 44
7. Lee Strobel, *The Case for Christ*, Zondervan, Grand Rapids, Michigan, 1998, 81
8. Ibid, 114
9. F.F Bruce, *The Books and the Parchments* (Old Tappan, NJ Revell, 1963) 178, cited in Josh McDowell, *Evidence That Demands a Verdict* (1972; reprint, San Bernadino, Calif: Here's Life, 1986), 42
10. Frederic Kenyon, *Handbook to the Textual Criticism of the New Testament* (New York: Macmillan, 1912), 5, cited in Ross Clifford, *The Case for the Empty Tomb* (Claremont, Calif.: Albatross 1991), 33.
11. Lee Strobel, *The Case for Christ*, Zondervan, Grand Rapids, Michigan, 1998, 55

12. Ibid, 64
13. John Morton, Man Science and God, Collins, Auckland, 1972, 217
14. Lee Strobel, *The Case for Christ*, Zondervan, Grand Rapids, Michigan, 1998, 180
15. Wolfhart Pannenburg, cited by William Lane Craig in *The Son Rises* (Chicago: Moody Press, 1984) 141
16. *Time*, June 4, 1979
17. Gary Habermas and J.P Moreland, *Immortality: The Other Side of Death*, Nashville: Nelson, 1992, 60

CHAPTER 18

PERSONAL GOD

Who is God? What is God? With these questions we ponder our very existence. You may have the perception that God is an "out there" God who is looking down from above, watching, waiting for you to step out of line and then wham you'll be done for dinner! Or maybe you think God is still "out there" but that like a watch he has set the cosmos ticking and he's bored with little, you and me, and that he gets a kick out of seeing humanity suffer and kill each other.

Power of God

Only a God with incredible power could not only create the universe, but sustain it. But this word "power" is limiting, as we have misconceptions due to the abuse of it. But contemplate that fact, the Creator of the universe, created it for us mere mortals that we could enjoy it, and explore it. Without God sustaining the universe, life would not be sustainable on earth, as you have read regarding the fine-tuning of the universe in the chapter, *The Wonder of the Universe.*

God is also moral as He created the moral law. Part of what He knows is the difference between right and wrong. Not only is God moral, but He is good; God created good. Not only is God good, but He is love. God created love, and God is Love. Whatever creates something that is true, e.g. love, must be that in essence (a cause can't give what it hasn't got). Therefore God is moral, good, and love.

I could use this line of reasoning to go into all the characteristics of God, but this gives you an idea. You can think of the other good characteristics such as mercy, peace, truth, etc and relate these to God.

But the bad characteristics such as those encompassing evil are not of God. As mentioned in the chapter on evil, evil is the "absence of what ought to be there". Evil is not part of God. Therefore God is not the opposite of love.

Who Caused God?

This is a question many ponder? OK, so if God caused the Big Bang, then who caused God? But when we ask this question we use a filter, which blocks the truth, and blinds us to the answer. It is only when we say that everything needs a cause, that we ask this question. But when we ask this question in relation to something that has not had a beginning (Necessary Being) then the answer is God did not have a beginning.

To simplify it even more we can say that man is the pinnacle of God's creation. We are lead to this as result of man being the only one to reason between right and wrong, and especially that man is the only one with an eternal soul which we have discovered through Divine Revelation. Furthermore, we think abstractly, ponder our very existence, and are highly creative (able to change our environment and traverse not only our habitat, but the oceans, the skies, and the universe. It is through Jesus that we realize how great God's love truly is for mankind. God chose to send his beloved son to die so that we could be free from the power of sin (moral evil) and death (we conquer death as Jesus did), and that we could return to the love God freely offers us. We could also reflect on how immense and fine-tuned for life our Universe is, as already covered in *God: Fact or Fiction?*, and that this awesome wonderful universe is a gift from the Creator for us. We can gaze in wonder at its beauty, power and immensity, and often this wonder leads us to God. This gift of creation, is a reflection of God's love for us. Moreover, Sacred Scripture reveals mankind as extra-special; God created all but mankind *ex nihilo*. Mankind was created with other creation as his base or structure. Hence man was built upon existing creation. Plus as you will read in this chapter God told man to be the stewards of creation.

Because God is the Alpha and the Omega. The beginning, in which He was the Necessary Being, the First Cause – He set everything in our universe into motion and is outside time, space, matter and energy. Whatever created before time existed, must have lived forever, and so is eternal, and therefore if this Creator lived forever, then this Creator is all powerful. So there was nothing greater than this Creator as He is all powerful. There could only be the one powerful God who created out of love, is eternal and all powerful. Also God is the Omega, He is the end, in so much as He will be there at the 'end' and we have the opportunity to be there too. So in some respects we are the Omega as well, as we have the opportunity to live eternally. Therefore God is eternal, eternal love!

Personal God

In all truth, a term to incorporate the characteristics of God is a *Personal God* and He has created this world as a gift; and a loving one at that – what an amazing gift for mankind – the entire universe! This gift includes the cosmos with all the laws of nature that were there for humanity to discover. God is not an "out there" God but He created the cosmos and loves His creation:

> In the beginning God created heaven and earth. Now the earth was a formless void, there was darkness over the deep, with a divine wind sweeping over the waters.
>
> God said, "Let there be light," and there was light. God saw that light was good, and God divided light from darkness. God called light 'day', and darkness he called, 'night'. Evening came and morning came: the first day.
>
> God said, "Let there be a vault through the middle of the waters to divide the waters in two." And so it was. God the made the vault, and it divided the waters under the vault from the waters above the vault. God called the vault 'heaven'. Evening came and morning came: the second day.
>
> God said, "Let the waters under heaven come together into a single mass, and let dry land appear." And so it was. God called the dry land 'earth' and the mass of the waters 'seas', and God saw that it was good.
>
> God said, "Let the earth produce vegetation: seed-bearing plants, and fruit trees on earth, bearing fruit with their seed inside, each corresponding to its own species." And so it was. The earth produced vegetation: the various kinds of seed-bearing plants and the fruit trees with seed inside, each corresponding to its own species. God saw that it was good. Evening came and morning came: the third day.
>
> God said, "Let there be lights in the vault of heaven to divide day from night, and let them indicate festivals, days and years. Let them be lights in the vault of heaven to shine on the earth." And so it was. God made the two great lights: the greater light to govern the day, the smaller light to govern the night, and the stars. God set them in the vault of heaven to shine on the earth, to govern the day and the night and to divide light from darkness. God saw that it was good. Evening came and morning came: the fourth day.
>
> God said, "Let the waters be alive with a swarm of living creatures, and let birds wing their way above the earth across the vault of heaven." And so it was. God created great sea-monsters and all

the creatures that glide and teem in the waters in their own species, and winged birds in their own species. God saw that it was good. God blessed them, saying, "Be fruitful, multiply, and fill the waters of the seas; and let the birds multiply on land." Evening came and morning came: the fifth day.

God said, "Let the earth produce every kind of living creature in its own species: cattle, creeping things and wild animals of all kinds." And so it was. God made wild animals in their own species, and cattle in theirs, and every creature that crawls along the earth in its own species. God saw that it was good.

God said, "Let us make man in our own image, in the likeness of ourselves, and let them be masters of the fish of the sea, the birds of heaven, the cattle, all the wild animals and all the creatures that creep along the ground."

God created man in the image of himself,
In the image of God he created him,
male and female he created them.

God blessed them, saying to them, "Be fruitful, multiply, fill the earth and subdue it. Be masters of the fish of the sea, the birds of heaven and all the living creatures that move on earth." God also said, "Look, to you I give all the seed-bearing plants everywhere on the surface of the earth, and all the trees with seed-bearing fruit; this will be your food. And to all the wild animals, all the birds of heaven and all the living creatures that creep along the ground, I give all the foliage of the plants as their food." And so it was. God saw all he had made, and indeed it was very good. Evening came and morning came: the sixth day.
Genesis 1:1-31

The first three words of the Bible, "In the Beginning" reveals the truth that God created out of nothing (ex nihilo) and the Big Bang reveals that God created out of nothing as to create from where there was no space, time, matter or energy, and hence nothing, then God would have had the ability and desire to create – from nothing.

You were created in the image of God. Verse 26 says, "Let us make man in our own image." This can only relate to the Trinity as angels can not create. So the Trinity created you, and you are the greatest of God's creation – created in the image of the Trinity. God is the Creator of the universe, and you are the pinnacle of His creation. God is the loving Creator. He knows you by name:

Yahweh, you examine me and know me,
you know when I sit, when I rise,
you understand my thoughts from afar.
You watch when I walk or lie down,
You know every detail of my conduct.

A word is not yet on my tongue
before you, Yahweh, know all about it.
You fence me in, behind and in front,
you have laid your hand upon me.
Such amazing knowledge is beyond me,
a height to which I cannot attain.

Where shall I go to escape your spirit?
Where shall I flee from your presence?
If I scale the heavens you are there,
if I lie flat in Sheol, there you are.

If I speed away on the wings of the dawn,
if I dwell beyond the ocean,
even there your hand will be guiding me,
your right hand holding me fast.

Psalm 139

Mankind was given a choice to either love, obey and trust God or to trust the word of Satan. Unfortunately their lack of utilizing reason resulted in trusting the word of Satan:

Now, the snake was the most subtle of all the wild animals that Yahweh God had made. It asked the woman, "Did God really say you were not to eat from any of the trees in the garden?" The woman answered the snake, "We may eat the fruit of the trees in the garden. But of the fruit of the tree in the middle of the garden God said, "You must not eat it, nor touch it, under pain of death."" Then the snake said to the woman, "No! You will not die! God knows in fact that the day you eat it your eyes will be opened and you will be like gods, knowing good from evil." The woman saw that the tree was good to eat and pleasing to the eye, and that it was enticing for the wisdom that it could give. So she took some of its fruit and ate it. She also gave some to her husband who was with her, and he ate it.
Genesis 3:1-6

When they were standing before God and God questioned whether they had eaten from the forbidden tree, the man accused the woman as being the instigator and the woman accused the snake. While Satan was the tempter, it was mankind that believed the lie, and thus did not trust God, and so did not truly love the Creator of life. This is classified as the Fall of Humanity. Because of mankind's disobedience there would be repercussions. One of the repercussions was that Original Sin would be passed onto the offspring of each generation. Romans 5:12 says, "Well then; it was through one man that sin *came into the world*, (Wisdom 2:24) and through sin death, and thus death has spread through the whole human race because everyone has sinned." But the answer is through Jesus Christ as v 17 tells us, "It was by one man's offence that death came to reign over all, but how much greater the reign in life of those who receive the fullness of grace and the gift of saving justice, through the one man, Jesus Christ." Paul then tells us in Romans 6:3 that it is through baptism that we are redeemed, "You cannot have forgotten that all of us, when we were baptized into Christ Jesus, were baptized into his death. So by our baptism into his death we were buried with him, so that as Christ was raised from the dead by the Father's glorious power, we too should begin living a new life…so that the self which belonged to sin should be destroyed and we should be freed from the slavery of sin."

As you read in the chapter, *Evil: Does it exist?* Satan wants to spoil the party that God wants us to enjoy. God wants us to have heaven on earth now. That is the reality. God's master plan to restore right relationship with him, a personal relationship, not bound on fear, was by sending his only son to become one of us – God became man.

The following parable has such an ironic ring to it, as mankind treated God's only Son this way:

> "Listen to another parable. There was a man, a landowner, who planted a vineyard; he fenced it round, dug a winepress in it and built a tower; then he leased it to tenants and went abroad. When vintage time drew near he sent his servants to the tenants to collect his produce. But the tenants seized his servants, thrashed one, killed another and stoned a third. Next he sent some more servants, this time a larger number, and the dealt with them in the same way. Finally he sent his son to them thinking, "They will respect my son." But when the tenants saw the son, they said to each other, "This is the heir. Come on, let us kill him and take over his

inheritance." So they seized him and threw him out of the vineyard and killed him...
Matt 21:33-43

Trinity

God sent his messengers so his Creation, his children, would turn back to him; but we discover that each messenger in Sacred Scripture was severely mistreated and some killed. But the messengers were only a small part of the master plan. The master plan was that God the Father planned to send his only Son [the Incarnation – God becoming man] to take upon the sins of the world by dying for humanity and thus opening the doors to a personal relationship with Him, His Son and the Holy Spirit (the Trinity). The Trinity is known as three persons but one God – you have God the Father, Jesus the Son, and the love between the two – the Holy Spirit. What is so awesome is that the Holy Spirit is love, and we are given the Trinity at our baptism. God is so intimate! We have been given so many gifts – life itself, the universe, the Eucharist, and the Trinity. Ian McKenzie in *The Dynamism of Space* explains:

> The Trinity is all sufficient and acts solely in that sufficiency. The role of the angels is not that of active mediators in the work of creation; they are ministers and servants, whose function is to understand the creative intent of the Triune God for all creation in its respective orders (including themselves) and to gather up all adoration, praise and thanksgiving for the wonders they behold. They are witnesses to the love and grace and order of the Trinity in creating immediately in the first twinkling of light all that is. In this way, light, illumination, grace and love and order are beheld and gathered up in the one instant angelic proclamation of creation before God.

> The profundity of the doctrine of the incarnation is that this Infinite and Eternal, the Author of all that is created and on whom all creation depends, without forsaking, changing, compromising, diluting or denying what he is in himself, takes our being and integrates it to his Existence. This is not a quantitative union between a greater and a lesser, whereby the greater swallows up the lesser and the lesser is lost in its essential being and nature in the greater. It is a union of two existences utterly distinct in their respective qualities.[1]

In *Son of God*, taken from BBC One series, Tilby shares in the book of the same title, that if Jesus was truly the Son of God then his coming to earth was very personal, and very significant:

> However, the stories about Jesus' infancy and boyhood, sparse though they are, may have contributed something in the long term to the way in which Christian culture came to value childhood. It is still an astonishing and moving claim that the Son of God could be born in a humble stable and cry and feed like any other baby. Not only does it make God seem more approachable, but it gives a dignity to the beginning of human life that has not been present in all cultures.[2]

Wow! The Son of God became one of us for our salvation – for love! He did so to give humanity dignity and reveal Himself – a God of love!

The Incarnation

The incarnation is the term given for God the Father sending his Son, Jesus Christ to become one of us, and yet retaining his divine nature at the same time. Yes, this is another mystery in which God has chosen to reveal himself. Just imagine what the incarnation is really like. It's like you becoming an ant, and yet retaining your human nature, to save the ant race from eternal destruction. The difference is that you didn't create ants, and so you have no immense love for them. The fact is that God created you and gave you an imperishable soul. Therefore He loves you! Yes his heart is burning with love for you! He longs for you to turn back and love Him in return. Wow! How radically profound and mysterious the incarnation really is! Many have written entire books on this subject alone, but I can only touch briefly upon it.

The definition of incarnation as given by the Pocket Catholic Dictionary is as follows:

> The union of the divine nature of the Son of God with human nature in the person of Jesus Christ. The Son of God assumed our flesh, body, and soul, and dwelled among us like one of us in order to redeem us. His divine nature was substantially united to our human nature. Formerly the Feast of the Annunciation was called the Feast of the Incarnation. In the Eastern Churches the mystery is commemorated by a special feast on December 26.

(etym. Latin *incarnatio*; from *in-*, in + caro, flesh: *incarnare,* to make flesh.)[3]

The Incarnation was God's free gift – his one and only Son. And yet God knew that this free gift would come at a cost. It was God the Father's plan for Jesus to be sacrificed in order to save us from eternal destruction.

Death of Christ

Mankind had disobeyed God and so had to suffer as a consequence, but with the death and resurrection of Jesus, death was conquered. Yes Jesus conquered death, leaving the path open for us also to conquer death; however we must follow Jesus in order to do so. If we want to love the Father, we must love the Son and the Holy Spirit.

Ian Mackenzie tells us what cost God the Father in giving us His only Son:

> This chaos is the groaning and travailing of all creation. But if all this, and indeed human failings, are taken into account in the light of what has been said about the mode of God creating through incarnation, we can see that God has taken stock of the cost of creation, and borne the vulnerability of its freedom by involving his very Being and taking that cost and pain upon himself in the Word made flesh.[4]

> This means that the place we have for ourselves and which we make for ourselves, and the place which all the other orders of creation have and make, is the freedom he gives to us and to the natural forces, to be what we are in ourselves as he intended us to be. But this freedom comes in terms of the cost to God which he has taken to himself in the Word made flesh, that order may come out of chaos, that all things may be upheld in their courses despite waywardness, that all things may work together for good.
> This can only be sought and known in the fact that God is not without his Word, through Whom he has given place for us, in Whom he has made all things to consist, and in Whom all things have their beginning and their fulfillment.[5]

Resurrection of Christ

If Jesus, the Son of God, merely died, then the greatest event of history ever recalled would have remained a mere story. But, Jesus, the Son of God, did not merely die, but He rose from the dead. Jesus conquered the power of death! The Son of God did what no one had every accomplished in their own power, He rose from the dead (the Gospels recall Jesus raising people from the dead). Humanity was given a foretaste of the fact that we too will conquer death when upon Jesus death the graves of many were opened as Matthew 27:51-53 tell us, "And suddenly, the veil of the Sanctuary [of the Temple] was torn in two from top to bottom, the earth quaked, the rocks were split, the tombs opened and the bodies of many holy people rose from the dead, and these, after his resurrection, came out of the tombs, entered the holy city and appeared to a number of people." You will recall that non-Christian historians have confirmed the earthquake and darkness.

The power of Jesus death and resurrection is in the fact that He rose from the dead – the first to do so – Christians too will conquer death.

The Mediator of God

God became man as free gift to us:

> To understand Jesus as the effective mediator of God, we must never forget – along with his true Godhead – his perfect and vulnerable humanity. God took manhood upon him without any stint or withholding. He became like us in everything: in the capacity to be hurt, to feel sorrow and even despair, and to know temptation, except alone that he was without sin....In the fullness of his sacrifice, he can utter the cry of dereliction in which the Son of God, bearing the sins of a whole humanity, experiences in his own nature the uttermost abandonment possible to human despair.[6]

> However vitiated our lives may be by sin and self-will, we have the image of God so stamped on our nature as to make it in principle possible that he should visit us... Love must be revealed through the meaning and service of a particular human life.[7]

This is so awesome! The image of God is stamped on our very nature. This is how we can come to discover God – through science (natural revelation), faith and reason, experience and Divine Revelation.

Love Has Three Legs

Like a three legged stool/chair, there are three legs to love. Each is essential for our whole wellbeing. The first leg is the first commandment; "Love the Lord your God with all your heart, mind and soul." The second leg was God fulfilling the first when Jesus said, "Love your neighbour…" and the third, is when Jesus said, "…as you love yourself." Without any one these then we will not be whole – you will topple over!

God created you because he loves you. It is in our very being to love God. He has given a part of us, our very soul, in order for us to communicate and love Him. For those who have chosen to love God, these quotes from Teilhard de Chardin are so beautiful:

> Do you, Lord Jesus, 'in whom all things subsist', show yourself to those who love you as the higher Soul and the physical centre of your creation? Are you not well aware that for us this is a question of life or death? As for me, if I could not believe that your real Presence animates and makes tractable and enkindles even the very least of the energies which invade me or brush past me, would I not die of cold? [8]

> Myriads of worlds following their appointed course through vastness of space exist because He would have it so. But that self-willed souls should be won to love Him, and thus make love and not self the centre of their being – that costs what is represented by Gethsemane and the Cross. The world as a vale of soul-making is full of darkness and tragedy into which God himself must enter. [9]

> For God has endowed each personality with a freedom he will neither bend nor constrain. Though he has 'laid the foundations of the earth and put wisdom to the inward parts and understanding to the heart' he will not by his peremptory [authoritative] power compel a single human will to obedience. This is the value that creation must entail to God, showing us at once the depth of his love and immensity of his sorrow in our fall. [10]

Furthermore, God created you to be in right relationship with everyone – so you must love your neighbour, and to be trustworthy stewards of the creation that God has bestowed on us. God created beauty for you to enjoy. Next time you see a beautiful sunrise/sunset, or hold a newborn baby in your arms ponder on that fact. God is a Personal God. He longs to share His creation, His beauty, and His love with you.

God created you to love yourself. It is through loving God that we can truly love ourselves. If we can truly say, "Thank you God for creating me as me, rather than saying, "I wish I had a model's legs, or butt, or nose." We must accept ourselves, and say thanks God. God loves you for who you are – He views His creation, you, as very good.

God has created you in a partnership. There is one significant part which you must contribute to. We have to want God to share in our life, as He has created us with an eternal soul, and we want to fill it with everything but God, but we will only be truly fulfilled when we let God in. No one wants to be impotent, but we are impotent spiritually, and in fully knowing God, if we don't let Him into our hearts, if we don't make him an important part in our lives. We have to want God to guide our lives.

Jesus death and resurrection were crucial to us having the opportunity to receive eternal life:

> But without his victory over death, we could have no particle of assurance that the love he showed was capable of ultimate triumph.[11]

The soul and body are complimentary:

> God calls even the flesh to the resurrection and promises it eternal life. To announce the good news of salvation to man was in effect to announce it to the flesh. For what is a man if not a reasonable being composed of soul and body? Shall we say that the soul in itself is the man? No, it is the soul of the man. And the body alone – is that the man? By no means; we should rather say that it is the body of the man. Since, then, neither soul alone nor body alone are man, but the thing called man arises out of their union, when God called man to the resurrection and the life, he called no mere part of man, but the whole man, body and soul together in one.[12]

As we have read in the previous chapter on "Evil: does it exist?" there is a battle between good and evil. Reflecting on the above statement I question how there could be a morally neutral Creator. How could someone create something and then forget about it and not intervene when His creation is crying out for help? Stephen Weinberg challenges the concept of a God of love with a god of suffering, "the God of birds and trees would have to be also the God of birth defects and cancer (remember, this is physical evil). As we have read in one of the previous chapters, man choosing to defy God and reject His love, has caused consequences. We must now face the repercussions. I know that from various experiences of suffering I wouldn't be who I am today. Good can come from suffering, e.g. our character is formed and strengthened by conquering suffering. We can tend to be like spoilt children when we have not experienced suffering, and therefore not able to identify or really relate to those who do suffer. I don't have all the answers; but I do know that God is a God of love, and that suffering will cease after our existence on earth, for those who chose to follow Him. We know from Sacred Scripture that God has the ultimate victory, and that there will be no more tears, or suffering.

> The centrality of man in creation is understood theologically in the light of Christology. It is not a question of seeing the centrality of humanity on the basis of humanity considered in relation to other created orders, and interpreted within that great dimension alone. Rather, it is the assertion that humanity occupies a central and significant role in creation because of its special relation to the Creator. For the existence of humanity is directly related, without compromising its created nature, to the existence of God, without compromising the divine nature.[13]

Know Yourself

Humanity can only know itself by first knowing God, and consequently you can only truly know yourself by knowing God. God created us to be fulfilled, and we can only be fulfilled by truly knowing ourselves and God:

> The role of humanity in creation is further seen in that relation, in that its knowledge of creation can only be properly gained in the light of its knowledge of God.[14]

As John Calvin, the founder of the Calvinists, pointed out, we must first contemplate God and from that spring we may truly gain self-knowledge of ourselves:

> ...it is evident that man never attains to a true self-knowledge until he has previously contemplated the face of God, and come down after such contemplation to look at himself.[15]

Therefore you have intrinsic value. You have it from the past, from the present (ongoing) and from the future. Additionally you can obtain self-knowledge from spending time with God in prayer, and by sharing His love. You are also valuable from what you can contribute. You can do this so many ways. One practical way you could do this now, would be to pray for someone, or think of someone who doesn't get many visitors or phone calls, and let them know someone cares by just seeing how they are. This simple gesture is a form of sharing God's love with others. A simple gesture of a smile normally doesn't take much effort, but it's power is amazing. So go on share a smile with someone.

You could also encourage someone by telling them how much they mean to you – when did you last tell someone in your family that you love them? I hope it wasn't on your wedding day! These actions are valuable – so valuable for their contribution to sharing God's love, and bringing joy and love to someone else's heart. You don't have to be a Christian to share the love of God - because God is love! So many people think that only Christians can share God's love. I think it helps as we can draw from the source of love – the Father, Son and Holy Spirit. However, don't wait until you feel you are Christian to do so. Your attitude of self-giving does matter. It matters now – it touches the heart of God!

A personal religion has the task of creating the kingdom of God on earth *now*, as we discover from the prayer revealed by Jesus.

> "Our Father in Heaven, your kingdom come, your will be done,
> on earth, as it is in Heaven."

As we have discovered earlier in *God: Fact or Fiction?* it was always God's intention for His kingdom to reign on earth. That was what the Garden of Eden was about – a kingdom of love and peace. It is only our disobedience and God respecting our free will that there is not real love and peace existing over the whole earth and all the sinners (including me) being consigned to oblivion. As there is still evil in the world, God does not reign yet except in the hearts of those who truly love and obey Him. But from Sacred Scripture (in the book of Revelation) you can read and know that God will reign, and that there will be true love and peace on earth when Satan is defeated forever.

Believe it or not, we are all searching. We are searching for truth, and for love. God is love (1 John 4:16) and it is in God that we find true fulfillment. Sure we have a taste of this love through such things as a true friendship or through the sacrament of marriage which is blessed by God, but God is the source of love, and when we seek to follow God then we are truly fulfilled. You can seek and experience God's love by: reading his word, Sacred Scripture; prayer; seeking to grow as part of a community (join a Church, return to Church, or attend a Church prayer group); through Holy Communion which is offered in several churches (in the Catholic and Orthodox churches it is taught that we are united with God through Holy Communion as it is His Real Presence and the greatest source of God's love – as explained in the chapter, *Miracles Transcending Nature* and Born to be Free:

> In its initial and primary meaning the term 'Body of Christ' is limited, in this context, to the consecrated species of Bread and Wine. But... the host is comparable to a blazing fire whose flames spread out like rays all round it. [16]

In other religions you may get a taste of the truth and love of God, but it is within Christianity that you find more truth, as you would have discovered in earlier from the chapter, *Truth: Subjective or Objective?* While it is in the Churches that offer Holy Communion with the Real Presence of Christ, you will find the best source of truth and love.

There are also many ways we can express God's love, whether it is through a simple smile, praying for someone, or helping someone in need.

> Christian love is incomprehensible to those who have not experienced it. That the infinite and the intangible can be lovable, or that the human heart can beat with genuine charity for a fellow-being, seems impossible to many people I know – in fact almost monstrous. But whether it be founded on an illusion or not, how can we doubt that such a sentiment exists, and even in great intensity? We have only to note crudely the results it produces unceasingly all round us. Is it not a positive fact that thousands of mystics, for twenty centuries, have drawn from its flame a passionate fervour that outstrips by far in brightness and purity the urge and devotion of any human love? Is it not also a fact that, having once experienced it, further thousands of men and women are daily renouncing every other ambition and every other joy save that of abandoning themselves to it and labouring within it more and more completely. [17]

Another aspect of the personal God being transposed to humans is the ability of humour. How can science explain why the structuring of words can extrapolate a response of laughter? Yet depending on our character, personality, morality and culture, we will either laugh or not laugh at a particular joke.

> When we say that the place of creation participates in the Place of God – that is that our created existence is established in God's Existence with Christ – all questions and statements concerning the presence of God – 'Where is God?'; 'God is everywhere' – become banal and superficial. In so asking and stating, we have turned the issue upside down. The question should be 'where do we participate in God?' and the answer "Everywhere and at all times in Christ".

> In the centre, so glaring as to be disconcerting, is the uncompromising affirmation of a personal God: God as providence, directing the universe with loving, watchful care; and God the revealer, communicating himself to man on the level and through the ways of intelligence.[18]

God created us for eternity! He didn't just say, "Hey I'll create Simone and play with her until I get bored, and then obliterate her with a lightning bolt and watch her atoms explode!

God created you to live and enjoy eternity – He gave you an imperishable, thus an eternal soul. Like the concept of the eternally expanding universe, you will exist forever. God created Heaven so that after you die, you have the choice to live there forever. Alternatively you could choose the place where there would be no love! Just imagine it, to be somewhere where no one can love. It would be Hell! Atheist Jean-Paul Satre noted in his play *No Exit*, that the gates of hell are locked from the inside by man's free choice. I would like to add to that analogy that Satan has written on the gates, "Push", like sadly, the inhabitants have pushed God away. But only if they did not believe Satan, the Father of Lies, then they could pull the doors and be free. Only if they had pulled God to them, and trust and loved Him then they would not have to be there.

I acknowledge there could be inadequacies in this analogy, that is of having the ability to escape Hell, only those who have rejected God, and followed Satan, will have chosen to be there. As for Christians we say like Jesus did on the Cross, "Thy will be done", while for those who have rejected God, Jesus will reluctantly and sadly say, "thy will be done" to his child who has chosen not to follow him.

In *Crossing the Threshold of Hope* Pope John Paul II explains whether it is God who rejects an individual as a consequence of one's turning their back on God or whether man does the rejecting:

> ...resurrection of the body is to be preceded by a *judgment* passed upon the works of charity, fulfilled or neglected. As a result of this *judgment*, the just are destined to eternal life. There is a destination to eternal damnation as well, which consists in the ultimate rejection of God, the ultimate break of the communion with the Father and the Son and the Holy Spirit. *Here, it is not so much God who rejects man, but man who rejects God.*[19]

The above is not so straight forward. While Hell will be for those who chose it, by not choosing God, we must not forget no one can say for certainty that anyone is there. Some fundamentalist Christians unfortunately say, "All Catholics are going to hell.", which their misguided judging goes against Sacred Scripture which they hold so dear. With such a statement they forget a fundamental part of God's nature, that is God's mercy. I covered this briefly at the start of this chapter, in the section "Who is God? What is God?" What about the prayers of loved ones? As I have covered in "Born to be Free", my earlier book, there is an important aspect of praying for the dead [St. Cyril of Jerusalem says, "...if a king were to banish certain persons who had offended him, and those intervening for them were to plait a crown and offer it to him on behalf of the ones who where being punished, would he not grant a remission of their penalties? In the same way we too offer prayers to Him for those who have fallen asleep, though they be sinners. We do not plait a crown, but offer up Christ {probably meaning the Eucharist} who has been sacrificed for our sins; and we thereby propitiate the benevolent God for them as well as for ourselves.[20]], and it is in Sacred Scripture, but only in those books that have not been removed from Bibles (they differ only regarding the Old Testament) such as the book of Wisdom, which is a beautiful part of God's word. If we implore God's mercy, like the scripture of the widow persistently begging the judge, then He will hear us. Recognizing a sincere and truly repentant heart He will be a lenient judge. Returning briefly to the aspect of God's mercy, I love the analogy that a drop of water is like all our sins, the sins of all mankind, compared to the ocean which represents God's love and mercy for us.

As for those cases in which God is lenient, they will spend more 'time' or will need more purifying – we call this purgatory. The Church Father

Tertullian says, "In short, if we understand that prison of which the Gospel speaks [Luke 16:22 ff] to be Hades, and if we interpret the last farthing [Matt 5:25-26] to be the light offense which is to be expiated there before the resurrection, no one will doubt that the soul undergoes some punishment in Hades, without prejudice to the fullness of the resurrection, after which recompense will be made through the flesh also."[21] Therefore they will be purified before they access Heaven.

Heart burning with love

It's fascinating that a relationship with our Loving God is so similar to that of falling in love with someone here on earth for the first time. Your heart literally burns with fire, and you are eager, almost desperate to know more and more about this person. And you feed your mind on thoughts of that person. It is as if God has let us have love for someone of the opposite sex, and yet at the same time yearns for us to love Him. Wow! What an unselfish God, to create us like this! Millions of Christians go through the experience of their heart burning with love for God when they discover that they can have a personal relationship with their Loving God, and then seek to build that friendship, and build their love of Him. What is also amazing is that the love burning heart matures, and instead of a love ingrained in feelings, we love from experience, knowledge (reason) and faith, revealed by the Creator Himself. Our love is therefore much deeper.

St. Catherine of Genoa said:

> O that I could tell you what the heart feels, how it burns and is consumed inwardly! Only I find no words to express it. I can but say, might one little drop of what I feel fall into Hell, Hell would be transformed into a Paradise. [22]

> 'Almighty' as applied to God does not mean power as we know it in this created dimension extended to its absolute. What we ultimately know of power is naked force. That is carelessly extended to interpret the term 'Almighty', with disastrous consequences for an understanding of the acts of God and the mode of his working. It inevitably leads to the question 'Why does God not do such and such?, or 'Why does God permit this and that?' Rather, the term 'Almighty' implies that all force in this created dimension, however awesome, is contained and controlled by the power of God which does not express itself in the same way as this force.[23]

Angels

> In some instances, for example the appearances in the Abraham saga in
> *Genesis*, the angelic presences are more or less manifestations of God
> himself. They do not speak of themselves; they bear no witness as to
> their existences; their sole function is to witness to God and proclaim his
> activity. They are servants of God, doing his bidding. That there is a
> pleroma of angelic beings in the biblical narratives merely emphasises
> the variety and richness of the works of God towards creation.[24]

Therefore Angels represent God and always bring messages from Him
and are like signposts pointing the way towards Him. We too have a choice
– we can be roadblocks of God's love or alternatively signposts pointing the
way towards a healthy relationship with the Saviour of the human race.

Prayer

Prayer is the means in which we can communicate with God via our
soul. That is, without our soul God would not be able to 'hear' us. It is
through the soul that God can in fact communicate with us. This could be
through such means as diverse as 'hearing a voice, seeing a vision, thinking
of some pertinent scripture which comes to us out of the blue, or someone
says something that inspires or challenges us.

Prayer, simply speaking, is communication, for example, talking. God
seeks to communicate with you. It needs to permeate one's life. It is our
gas to keep on going on the journey of life. It develops our trust in the
Loving Creator, and it develops our knowledge and love of our wonderful
Saviour! Prayer is our life source, and like blood is crucial to our survival,
or communication with our loved ones is essential to any relationship, as
a devoted Christian, prayer is essential to our relationship with God.
Without prayer we are essentially cutting ourselves off from God's
intervention in our lives, and telling our Creator that we don't need him
in our lives, except maybe for one or two hours on Sunday.

Mother Teresa viewed prayer as something essential to her work for the
poor. The good works, did not come first and then prayer, but prayer
came first, and from that love of God came the service of others and her
great love for them. In fact, God's love emanated from Mother Teresa, as
she sought to top that love up with prayer.

For someone who practices a religion, for example, Christian, Muslim,
Jewish, they can't just act like God exists and believe in God and go and
worship Him for just one or two hours of the week, and then for the rest act

like He doesn't exist. Sadly this does happen, and apparently, a lot. But this is not being true to ourselves, let alone to God. God is longing to communicate with you; he is longing for you to spend time with him.

St. Augustine's commentator, Bishop Ullathorne wrote the following about God communicating with us:

> Let it be understood that we cannot turn to God unless we first enter into ourselves. God is everywhere but not everywhere to us; and there is one point in the universe where God communicates with us and that is the centre of our own soul. There he waits for us, there he meets us. To seek him we enter into our own interior.[25]

> It is not that works are primary and prayer helps them. Prayer is primary and works test it.[26]

God has created everything as Scripture reveals:

> He is the image of the invisible God,
> the firstborn of all creation.
> For in him were created all things
> in heaven and on earth,
> the visible and the invisible,
> whether thrones or dominions or
> principalities or powers;
> all things were created through
> him and for him.
> He is before all things
> And in him all things hold together.
> Colossians 1:15-17

God has also given the world the Communion of Saints, or put simply our spiritual family – the extension of the Church into heaven, that we can communicate with. Unfortunately it is only the Orthodox Church, Catholic Church, and a wing of the Anglican Church that believes in the Communion of Saints. God has given us them for us to seek their prayers (their communicating with God), just like we might ask, or be grateful for someone praying for us. As I covered in *Born to be Free* Saints are those people that the Church has confirmed are not only already in heaven, but that their lives of exemplary devotion to God and witness for God should be emulated – they are similar to, but heaps more than your favourite star/hero.

There are many types or styles of prayer. These include such methods as the Ignatius method in which you visualise yourself as being a character in

Sacred Scripture and you visualise, smell and hear what is happening. This is great for a prayer group event and for many people who practice this on their own can discover Sacred Scripture opened up in an even more vivid, challenging and exciting way.

There is also the Rosary which is observed by Catholics, and even by some Muslims, as the pilgrimage sight in Medjugorje has been visited by Catholics, Muslims and people of many different faiths. On October 16 2002 Pope John Paul II in an encyclical letter suggested the addition of another "Mystery" to the Rosary, the Mystery of Light or Luminous Mysteries.

A very important creed, the Nicene Creed was issued in A.D 325 by the Council of Nicaea (a council of the Catholic Church) which is in essence a prayer, sums up so much of the Christian faith, and is proclaimed by many Christian denominations:

> We believe in one God
> The Father Almighty
> Who made both heaven and earth
> All that is seen and unseen
> Light from Light
> True God from True God
> One being with the Father
> From him all things were made
> For us, and our Salvation
> He came down from Heaven
> By the Power of the Holy Spirit
> He became incarnate
> And was made man
> He was conceived by the power of the Holy Spirit
> Born of the Virgin Mary
> Suffered under Pontius Pilate
> Died and was buried
> On the third day
> He rose again
> He ascended into Heaven
> And is seated at the right hand of the Father.
> He will come again
> To judge the living
> And the dead
> And his kingdom will have no end

We believe in the Holy Spirit
The Lord the giver of Life
Who proceeds from the Father and the Son
We believe in the Holy Catholic Church
The Communion of Saints
The Forgiveness of Sins
The resurrection of the body
And life everlasting.
Amen.

The theme of freedom permeated my first two books, and so it is pertinent to raise it here. It is through a relationship with our Loving Creator, His Son who suffered for us, and the giver of life and love of the trinity, the Holy Spirit, that we are able to embrace that freedom – prayer in fact sets us free. You were called to be free, so take the steps to embrace that freedom.

God calls everyone to know Him. He is calling us to pray, and so it is up to us to respond. We may answer, "No, go away", or "Later God, I've got no time" or "My favorite TV Program is on now" or "Yes, Lord I can give you some time, give me the graces to pray, stay with me, lead me, and teach me to pray."

The greatest prayer of all time, taught to us by the Son of God, Jesus is the Our Father, which is a wonderful prayer to our Loving Father:

Our Father in Heaven
may your name be held holy,
your kingdom come,
your will be done,
on earth as in heaven.
Give us today our daily bread.
And forgive us our debts,
as we have forgiven those
who are in debt to us.
And do not put us to the test,
But save us from the Evil One.
Matthew 6:9-13

Answer to Prayer

Why is it that we believe that God only rarely answers our personal prayers? The fact is that God is a loving God and He always answers your prayers. But fortunately, and seemingly unfortunate for you at the time, God doesn't always answer the prayer the way we want Him to. God answers prayers which we can summarize as, "Yes", "No" or "Wait". So when He doesn't say yes to a prayer which we have really desired a "Yes" for we can tend to think that God has not answered our prayer – as if God has in fact ignored us. But God loves you and he knows you through and through:

> You created my inmost self,
> knit me together in my mother's womb.
> For so many marvels I thank you;
> A wonder am I, and all your works are wonders.
>
> You knew me through and through,
> my being held no secrets from you,
> when I was being formed in secret,
> textured in the depths of the earth.
>
> Your eyes could see my embryo.
> In your book all my days were inscribed,
> every one that was fixed is there.
> Psalm 139:13-16

Yes God loves you and knows the best for you. Therefore the answer from God, your Creator, is in fact the best answer for you, even if the answer hurts so much. So next time you say a prayer, thank God that He loves you; thank Him for creating you and this glorious and awesome universe that we live in; and thank Him that He will answer your every prayer.

Summary

> I suggest that the whole event of incarnation, crucifixion, resurrection and ascension, is the interaction of the Being of God, as he creates, with what he has created. It is the cost to his Being, which, in overflowing love in creating an entity distinct from himself in its freedom to be the creation it is yet dependent upon him for its necessary upholding in existence, he himself bears.[23]

God loves you so much. The magnificence of His love is really beyond our comprehension. The closest we can come is that Jesus' incarnation, crucifixion, resurrection and ascension was just for you. In addition to these wonderful mysteries, Jesus is going to create a new heaven and a new earth (Rev 21:1-4), in which there will be no more suffering. God is creating this for you cause He loves you so much!

The following hymn sums up this chapter beautifully:

How Great Thou Art

O Lord my God
When I in awesome wonder
Consider all the works thy hands have made
I see the stars
I hear the mighty thunder
Your power throughout the universe displayed

Chorus
Then sings my soul
My Saviour God to thee
How great thou art
How great thou art (Repeat)

When through the woods and forest glades I wander
And hear the birds sing sweetly in the trees;
When I look down from lofty mountain grandeur
And hear the brook
And feel the gentle breeze;

And when I think
That God his Son not sparing
Sent him to die,
I scarce can take it in
That on the Cross,
My burden gladly bearing
He bled and died to take away my sin

When Christ shall come
With shouts of acclamation
And take me home
What joy shall fill my heart
Then I shall bow in humble adoration
And there proclaim
My God how great thou art!

Chapter 18 – Bibliography

1. Iain Mackenzie, *The Dynamism of Space*, The Canterbury Press, Norwich, 1995, 177
2. Angela Tilby, *Son of God*, Hodder and Stoughton, London, 2001, 31
3. John A Hardon, *Pocket Catholic Dictionary*, S.J., Image Books, New York, 1985
4. Iain Mackenzie, *The Dynamism of Space*, The Canterbury Press, Norwich, 1995, p 137-138
5. Ibid, 138
6. John Morton, *Man Science and God*, Collins, Auckland, 1972, p158
7. Ibid, 159
8. Teilhard de Chardin, *The Phenomenon of Man* p.295
9. Ibid, 289
10. Teilhard de Chardin, *Hymn of the Universe* p 25
11. John Morton, *Man Science and God*, Collins, Auckland, 1972, p221
12. E.L Mascall, *Christian Theology and Natural Science,* Longmans, Green, London, 1956, *p* 208 ff.
13. Iain Mackenzie, *The Dynamism of Space*, The Canterbury Press, Norwich, 1995, p 103
14. Ibid
15. John Calvin: Institute of the Christian Religion 1:1:2
16. [email brendanr@ihug.co.nz if you need this reference]
17. William Temple, 'Creation and Redemption', University Sermon, 1925, *Cambridge Review*
18. John Morton, *Man Science and God*, Collins, Auckland, 1972, p158
19. Pope John Paul II, *Crossing the Threshold of Hope*, p 72
20. W.A Jurgens, *The Faith of the Early Fathers - Volume One*, The Liturgical Press, Collegeville, Minnesota, 1970, passage 853, p363
21. Ibid, passage 352, p145
22. no reference given
23. Iain Mackenzie, *The Dynamism of Space*, The Canterbury Press, Norwich, 1995, 80
24. Ibid, 160
25. W.B Ullathorne, Groundwork of the Christian Virtues, p.74
26. see William Temple, *Readings in St. John's Gospel* (Macmillan London, 1945), pp302-6
27. Iain Mackenzie, *The Dynamism of Space*, The Canterbury Press, Norwich, 1995, 142

CHAPTER 19

IS GOD DEAD?

Many claim a victory – "God is dead!" As I asked in the introduction to *God: Fact or Fiction?* all those aeons ago, to many it seems a reality. As far back as the 1960s, the following statement from Friedrich Nietzsche became the catch cry for the "God is dead" movement:[1]

> "Where is God gone?" he called out. "I mean to tell you! *We have killed him* – you and I! We are all murderers! ...Do we not hear the noise of the grave diggers who are burying God? ...God is dead! God remains dead!"

What an ironic ring that statement has in the shadow of the 60's, when nuclear war was a looming reality, when war with Russia was virtually a given. But in fact, the walls of communism have crumbled and Russia is not a threat anymore. With the speed in which communism crumbled, with little bloodshed in the process of the walls falling (sadly millions and millions were murdered in the name of communism), can we truly say God is dead?

In fact many of us claim or act like God is dead. We are trying to traverse the journey of life alone. When in fact our God, our Creator, wants us to take Him with us, not leave him on some far distant shore, or just access Him when we need Him.

In this chapter we will explore the evidence to why God is in fact not dead. You will discover in essence for yourself, whether God has been killed, or whether in fact, Nietzsche's statement is flawed, and that God is very much alive. But if the latter is the case, can we in fact ignore it? If the evidence is overwhelming, can we sit silently, ignoring God?

Some of us may claim that God is dead. Some could even claim that you are dead. But we know that is only perception and not truth. How could God be dead? If he is beyond time, and eternal then how could the First Cause just die? No, if God is not bound by time, space, or our universe, then he is not dead. In fact he is the Living God!

Be Not Afraid

Most of the time when the angels appeared to humans their first words were, "Do not be afraid." Therefore the pertinent heading for this chapter is the same. I admonish you to not be afraid, but to trust in the loving Creator, who made all things, seen and unseen, who according to Psalm 139 knows you so intimately.

There are many who believe that they have screwed up so much that God couldn't possibly love or forgive them. Well Sacred Scripture has many examples of people who screwed up big time, but the key is that God forgave those who came back to His loving arms.

Now King David really screwed up big time! [whoops excuse the pun there, lol] He really blew it! He let his pants do the thinking and not his brain. Not only did he have an affair with someone else's wife, but he had the husband killed. [2 Samuel 11:2-12:15] Woah! Yes that's pretty bad, and most of us wouldn't forgive someone who did that. But God is so much greater than us. His mercy is endless, if we but turn to Him truly seeking it. Yes God forgave David but there were repercussions that he had to suffer because of the hurt he had caused to others due to his sin.

St. Peter, who at times was a bumbling idiot, put his foot in his mouth several times. Jesus rebuked him strongly once, calling him Satan. But this would not compare to the event in which most of the disciples had deserted Jesus upon His arrest. Peter denied three times, that he even knew Jesus or was His disciple. [John 13:36-38 and 18:15-27]

The Prodigal Son is a beautiful parable in which a son leaves his Father and squanders His inheritance, but his Father waits longingly for him to return. When he returns the Father embraces him and holds a party for him, ordering his prized calf to be killed for the occasion. The Father represents God the Father, and he waits longingly for you.

As mentioned in Sacred Scripture and *Does Secular Evidence Confirm the Existence of Jesus?* chapter that this could be the most important, decision you could ever make. You have journeyed through this book, on a wonderful exploration of science, and religion. You have discovered the overwhelming scientific, psychological, and corroboratory evidence that there is a Creator. This evidence has covered such diverse areas as the Big Bang, to DNA, astronomy, paleontology and biblical and non-biblical evidence. You have also explored such concepts within religion such as evil, the nature of God, God being a loving and personal God, and prayer. The chapter on prayer will probably have shown you that God is calling you to follow him, He is calling you to a partnership. But first you must make a momentous decision. If you are a Non-Christian, or a lapsed Christian this indeed would prove to be the most vital decision of your life. (If you are already a Christian then you can make a recommitment if you feel God wants you to.) This momentous decision involves a decision, possibly an eternal one. Will you chose to follow God by letting him into your life? By seeking to join a Church and live as part of a family of God? If the answer is yes, then ask God for forgiveness, for your sins, and ask Him to help you to follow Him. If you were baptised Catholic or Orthodox then call your nearest priest and let him know that you would like to see him for the sacrament of Reconciliation.

So God is not dead but is the eternal living God. Not only is God not dead, but the Church is the living Church, and his word is the living word, and sacred Tradition (Revelation by God which has been handed on) is living Tradition.

Do not be afraid that God will call you to do more than you will be able to handle. God will give you the all graces that you will need:

"but he has answered me, "My grace is enough for you: for power is at full strength in weakness." 2 Cor 12:9

The key is to respond to God, and each time we overcome temptation we become stronger, as we respond to the grace that God has given us.

Do not be afraid, following your Loving Creator now is preparing you for eternity. The greatest reward you could ever receive will be waiting for you – eternal life.

Chapter 19 – Bibliography

1. Friedrich Nietzsche, *Joyful Wisdom*, trans. By Thomas Common (New York: Frederick Unger Publishing Co., 1960), section 125, pp. 167-168

CHAPTER 20

CONCLUSION

God in the Dock

If God was on trial – man vs God case No 1 – and the evidence produced in this book and elsewhere were brought before the judges. Guess who would win?

There is too much compelling evidence in the Cosmos for it to be by chance. Contrary to popular belief the evidence is there to prove beyond reasonable doubt that a Creator exists, one that is loving, and created you because He loves you – you were created in His image.

Intelligent Design is evident in living cells; within species; within nature; within our solar system; there is order within the universe. If we just focus on the species aspect, and in particular humans, we see an incredible creativity, intellect that has discovered the laws of the universe, and abstract thought. Humans are the only species that according to evolutionists that purely by chance have been able to speak articulately, create their own spoken and written languages, and discover and create codes. Scientifically man is the only species to advance so much – algebra, and move onto more in-depth equations, such as physics (the discovery of relativity); chemistry (which has led to anti-dotes for poisons and cures for diseases). With the discovery of the elements of the cell humans have now explored biochemistry and genetics. The sciences of archeology and paleontology have helped us learn from the past. Furthermore, the science of astronomy has led to the exploration of the universe and shown us the wonder of God's creation. Humans are the only species with the desire to ponder their own existence and ask: Why? We are the only species to want to solve the problems of nature, such as diseases; the only species to advance so much technologically; the only species to explore the Universe; and the only species to reveal scientific answers to the universe.

There are several defects in the theory of macro-evolution which I have covered extensively. In itself the Intelligent Design theory with the information richness and specified complexity within the cell and especially proteins and DNA refute the materialistic view of Natural Selection. The mindlike qualities of Natural Selection, scrutinizing and selecting, point towards a mind, and thus we are pointed towards a Creator. Either Natural Selection is one of the greatest hoaxes perpetrated in the name of science or it reflects Intelligent Design, and thus our Creator.

There have been many marvelous discoveries in science, and science has helped humanity to live longer, and explore the depths of the universe – though admittedly we still have a long way to go to be able to explore the fartherest outposts, the other galaxies of the universe. Science has also opened our eyes to the wonders of nature as we discovered how genes are able to be transmitted through the generations, and that some mutations lay dormant for a long time.

Science alone does not give us all the answers to life, to knowledge. The quest for knowledge must be explored through religion and science. These two, give us the wholeness, and make us complete. You can not throw the baby out with the bath water. This saying means if you try to get rid of the problem without an alternative solution then you are seeking trouble. If you throw away science, you are left with just various religious parties quibbling over scientific meanings – including the age of the universe – and more importantly you would not have the quality of life that we in the western world have (which incidentally, has it's positives and negatives) – Science has brought marvelous cures for diseases, and life saving operations can now be performed which never could be in the past.

Alternatively, you can not throw away religion and keep science. Without religion, then some scientists would seek to stretch the moral limits of science. We are already seeing this with various people trying to clone humans. Isn't it amazing how history repeats itself. Hitler would have loved to have the ability to clone. He would have cloned blue eyed blond men, and these would have been his army – an army that could be replaced at breakneck speed.

Without religion there are no moral constraints. But more importantly there is no hope. As we discovered through the writing of Richard Dawkins, there is no real meaning or purpose.

So Science and Religion compliment each other. God intended us to use our brains to discover the intricacies of His creation. He gave us brains in order to create; and thus the ability to be creative is a God given gift.

While we speak of individual judgment in assessing Scripture and history, we must not forget the Church's role. Theology is ultimately

– we have maintained – a function of the Church as the body of Christ. The theologian is a believing member of that body to whom this special activity has been entrusted. The Church is moreover the believing company of Christians across all ages; so that no theology can be entirely contemporary, but must take account of the interpretation genius of Christian men and women of other times.[1]

But why did God give humans such a gift? God did not have to give us the gift of such creativity. Why didn't he bestow this gift on the other creatures in the animal kingdom? It is because his plan was for us to be superior to other creatures - though sometimes I think some of us are dumber than dumber! While animals can be superior in sight, and maybe brain power, we are superior in our creativity, can think abstractly, and do not rely so much on instinct. In fact as Divine Revelation has explained we are created in the image of the Trinity.

Yes a whale has a huge brain compared to ours, but a whale can not escape it's environment - a whale can not survive on land, fly, or explore the universe. A whale is limited to what it was created to be. Sure it still has a whale of a time, as it seeks to be what God created it to be.

We are the crown of God's creation. We are the only species to be created with an eternal soul, and the only species to reason - to reason between right and wrong, between good and evil. This is something to ponder, and thank God for. You are the only species that has an imperishable soul. You are the only species that can reason between good and evil. It's not just the ability to choose between good and evil, other creatures can do that. But it is the gift to reason why you have made such a choice.

While Science can improve and enhance our lives, the abuse of science, (e.g. abortion, euthanasia) can in fact destroy our lives. While religion can improve and enhance our lives, the abuse of religion (from within or without) can also destroy our lives and destroy our countries – nations have been ravaged especially by people choosing to turn away from the loving Creator. The main social upheavals are caused because people choose not to follow the Creator, or they have a twisted, or erroneous view of their God – e.g. so called religious terrorists such as al-Qaeda and the IRA.

But when we seek and discover God's tremendous love for the crown of His creation, you and me, then we discover the purpose for life, and purpose which embraces everyone around us – the purpose to love God and to love others.

At this point I want to again quote Robert Jastrow regarding the scientist who has disregarded God:

> For the scientist who has lived by his faith in the power of reason, the story ends like a bad dream. He has scaled the mountains of ignorance; he is about to conquer the highest peak; as he pulls himself over the final rock, he is greeted by a band of theologians who have been sitting there for centuries.[2]

With the embracing of science and religion we can indeed discover the wonders that I have touched upon to a limited degree. If we really delved into the all the areas of science and the traces of evidence God has left us, then many more books could be written. I hope you have enjoyed this book as much, if not more, than I have, in researching and writing it. Trust in God, and above all talk to Him. It is through this dialogue (remember, prayer is a dialogue) that you will discover truly who you are and to an extent who God is. Please be assured that all of you who read this book are in my prayers. May our wonderful, loving Creator bless you and reveal more of His truth of who He is as you seek it – God is indeed *fact* and not fiction.

God bless.

Brendan Roberts

Chapter 20 – Bibliography

1. John Morton, Man Science and God, Collins, Auckland, 1972, p214
2. Robert Jastrow, *God and the Astronomers* (New York: Warner Books, 1978) 105-106

Author's Note

If you are reading this version of *God: Fact or Fiction?* then it will be the self-published one. I'm endeavouring to get international publishers – including publishing my writing into many different languages. If you have any contacts, or wish to contribute financially, then we can make this happen. It's a difficult process trying to break into the inner publishing circle of existing authors. But I know it will be happen with perseverance. So a prayer or two would be wonderful!

Additionally before I finished this book I received some wonderful encouragement from someone who read my draft manuscript; he believed very strongly that it would also suit high school and university students (unfortunately the USA publishers I have approached have not seen it's true potential). So please, make sure it gets into your local school, (or you could sponsor a class/school for them to get *God: Fact or Fiction?*) university, school libraries, and your local public library too. It would be wonderful for schools to purchase as a study resource.

This was such an exciting book to research for, and write. The book has certainly evolved into what I hope was an amazing journey of discovery for you.

Moreover, since I am now a full-time author, and have dispensed with Personal Assistant duties, except on a temporary or contractual basis, I am available for international public speaking. Even before this book was finished I was interviewed on a Christian Radio Station here in New Zealand. I also look forward to being invited to give public presentations on the subjects contained in this book, whether it be for a prayer group, or for an international conference. For the latter I will create a Power Point presentation to help the audience take in the wonderful facts of science, religion and the origin of life covered.

Please contact me regarding the above or to give feedback:
C/- 9 Elm Place
Tikipunga
Whangarei
New Zealand
email:brendanr@ihug.co.nz or mekiwi_@hotmail.com
(note my email is my first name as spelt on the cover of this book followed by the first initial of my surname.)

Index

Anglican Communion/Church 30, 134, 182, 197, 198, 256
    Changed it's stance on contraception 134
Anglican Roman Catholic International Commission 197
Augustine 10, 56, 147, 165, 256
Archaeology 117, 124-125, 128-129, 207

Behe, Michael 4, 17, 49, 51, 61-64, 69-70, 72-76, 85
Big Bang 5, 6, 8-11, 54, 102-106, 113, 115, 149, 161, 179, 187, 199,
    223, 255, 258
Blomberg 213, 216, 221-222
Brain (human) 77, 99, 267
Broom, Neil 27, 71-72, 77, 81

Cell 10, 23, 33, 37, 53, 58, 60-67, 69-79, 91, 265
Chance 6, 17, 22,-23, 27- 28, 31-33, 35, 37- 38, 41, 49, 55, 57, 65,
    66, 69-71, 79, 83, 89, 91, 98, 135, 152, 165, 179, 265
Christian 10, 23, 27-28, 30, 53, 55-56, 58, 105, 127, 134, 139, 145,
    147, 162, 173, 178, 182-187, 189, 190, 193, 195-197, 199, 202, 204-
    205, 207, 210, 214-215, 219-220, 223-224, 244, 250- 252, 254-
    255, 257, 264, 267
    Fundamentalist 253
Code 31, 50, 64, 67, 68, 72, 75, 139, 265
Code DNA 68, 91
Colson, Charles and Pearcey, Nancy 8, 9, 32, 65
Contingency 31, 49, 58, 71, 179
Contingency Being 54, 198
Contingent Being 87, 168, 169
Creationists 55, 56
    Old Earth Creationists 56
    Young Earth Creationists 55, 59
Creator 8-9, 11- 14, 20, 22, 27,-28, 53-
    58, 60, 64, 71, 79, 80, 89, 92, 100, 101, 104, 105, 108, 113-
    115, 129, 132, 137, 141, 146, 149, 156, 159, 161, 163, 165, 169,
    171-172, 179, 181, 187, 237-238, 240, 242, 248-249, 254-255, 258-
    259, 262-267
Crucifixion 125-126, 128, 208, 234, 259

Darwin, Charles 14,-23, 25-26, 28, 30, 32- 33, 35-38, 79, 95, 99
Davies, Paul 11, 54, 103
Dawkins, Richard 36, 43, 88-90, 171, 266
Dembski, William 43, 44, 46
Design 3, 6, 17, 20, 25-27, 30-32, 34, 37-38, 50-51, 54-55, 57, 66,
    68, 70-72, 76, 79, 87, 89, 105, 112-114, 165, 170

Divine Revelation 129, 136, 145, 152-154, 171, 176, 246, 267
DNA 10, 31, 42, 47, 50, 53, 58, 60, 63-69, 71,72, 75, 79- 80, 85, 87-
      88, 90-91, 112, 263, 266

Eucharist 156, 174, 182-191, 193-197,199, 214, 243, 253
      Body, Soul & Divinity 182,187,199
Evil 158-164, 205, 227, 237, 241, 248, 250, 267
      Moral Evil 158, 238
      Natural/Physical/Ontic Evil 158, 161-162, 163,248
Evolution 2, 8, 14, 16-17, 19-23, 27-28, 31-33, 35-36, 38, 41-42,44-
      47, 49,54-58, 75-77, 82-84, 88, 90-92, 96-100, 113, 178, 265
      Micro-Evolution 28, 58, 79, 113
      Macro-Evolution 1, 3, 14, 17, 19-20, 27-28, 30, 32, 38, 47, 51,
      54, 58,75,77, 79, 82-84, 86, 89-91, 96, 98-100, 178-179, 265
Expansion rate of the universe 103, 106, 112
Experience 24, 50, 135, 137, 139, 140, 143,155, 156, 164, 166, 172-
      176, 184, 246, 250, 254

Faith 48, 57, 135, 139, 141-142, 145-150, 154-155, 164, 170, 172,
      178, 183-184, 188, 190, 194, 197-198, 206, 211, 217, 224, 254, 257
Faith and reason 149, 154, 156, 175, 246
Fossils 15, 16, 19, 21, 43, 44, 46, 49, 94, 95, 97, 98
Free Will 31, 135, 136, 137, 179, 250

Historians 126, 205-206,211,246
      Josephus 204, 206
      Tacitus 212, 214, 217
Hoyle 32,66, 112

Information 37, 50, 53, 60-62, 64-67, 69, 72, 75, 77-80, 91, 176, 198,
      205, 221, 265
Intelligent Design 2, 38, 49-50, 51-55, 58, 60, 64, 70-72, 74-76, 78-80,
      87,89,92, 94, 105,114, 153, 156, 165,169,171, 174-175, 265-266
Intent 36-38, 71, 89, 158, 163, 243
Irreducible Complexity 49, 51, 54, 58, 61, 68, 71, 73-74, 76, 79, 91,
      101, 105-106, 110, 149

Jesus 25, 126-127, 142-144, 147-148, 152-154, 160, 163, 172, 176, 180-
      182,184-193, 197-199, 202-204, 206-211, 213-224, 226-235, 238, 244-
      246, 248, 258, 263
Kreeft, Peter 161, 162, 163, 165, 171

Love 23, 35, 54,56, 101, 105, 115, 137, 139, 144, 149, 150-151, 153-
      154, 158-160, 162-163,166,170, 172-173, 175-176, 179-180, 183-
      184, 196-197,199, 204, 233, 237-238, 241, 243-255, 258-259, 263,
      265-267

Materialism 33-36, 38

Messiah 144, 154, 180, 204, 216, 223-225, 230-233, 235

Metzger, Bruce 215

Miller, Stanley 83, 84, 85, 87, 92

Miracle 25, 148, 153, 174, 178, 180-182, 191, 193, 198-199, 202, 221, 231, 235

Mother Teresa 172, 255

Mystery 15, 77, 148, 152, 154-156, 160, 182-183, 187, 190-191, 198, 219, 244, 257, 259

Natural Revelation 90, 152, 153, 246

Natural Selection 14-23, 25-28, 35-38, 43, 46-47, 49, 54, 71, 84, 88, 91, 97, 149, 266

Newton, Isaac 49, 108

Non-Christian 114, 202, 206, 246, 264

Ontological Argument 140

Origin Of Life 1, 2, 6, 28, 70, 115

Orthodox Church 135, 182, 191, 251, 256, 264

Personal God 247, 251-252, 264

Pontius Pilate 204, 205, 207, 208, 209, 257

Pope Innocent I 222

Pope John Paul II 145- 146, 150, 154- 156, 160, 186- 188, 194-195, 197, 252, 257

Pope John XXIII 147

Pope Paul VI 198

Pope Pius XII 41

Prayer 23, 127, 155, 166, 174, 184- 185, 196, 198, 219, 226, 249- 250, 253, 255-259, 264, 268

Pre-biotic Soup/Cocktail 83-85, 92

Proteins 61, 66, 68-70, 72-79, 83, 85, 91, 266

Reason 24, 34, 38, 40-41, 47, 57, 86, 101, 138, 141, 144-150, 152-156, 164, 171, 173, 175, 238, 241, 254, 267

Relativism 137-138, 143

Religion 1-4, 31, 35, 38, 49, 129, 147, 152, 178- 179, 182, 190- 191, 205-206, 210, 215, 250-251, 255, 263, 266-268

Resurrection 24, 153, 160, 182, 186-188, 194-195, 204, 209, 211, 214, 218-220, 222-223, 231-233, 235, 245-246, 248, 252-253, 258-259

Revelation 3, 6, 11, 25, 27, 42, 56, 144, 147-148, 151-155, 170-171, 183, 191, 193, 208, 221, 238, 264

Ronald Nash 173

Sacred Scripture 42, 55-56, 117-118, 121- 122, 125, 128- 129, 139, 163, 174, 188, 190-191, 193, 199, 202, 205-207, 210- 211, 214, 233, 243, 249-250, 253, 256, 263

Sacred Scripture/canon was decided by the Church 222

Science 1-4, 6, 17, 20, 28, 33, 35-36, 38, 47, 49, 52, 84, 86, 94, 101, 114-115, 117, 128-129, 139, 152-153, 155, 178, 190, 246, 251, 263, 265-267

Sex 134, 143, 179, 254

Skepticism 138, 175

Son of Man 192, 196, 216-218, 231

Soul 23-25, 27, 34, 40, 136, 161-162, 182, 194-195, 199, 219, 232, 247, 253, 255-256, 260

    Animal (perishable) 25, 162, 179

    Human (imperishable) 24-28, 38, 41-42, 140, 196, 238, 244, 248, 252, 267

        Created out of nothing 41

Space, Time, Matter & Energy 10-12, 92, 132, 149, 240

Specified Complexity 50, 53-54, 66, 68, 71, 78, 86, 89, 105, 149, 265

St. Augustine of Hippo 256

St. Catherine of Genoa 254

St. Cyril of Jerusalem 190, 253

St. Ignatius of Antioch 184, 209, 256

St. Irenaeus 186-187, 195, 214

St. Thomas Aquinas 139, 142, 159-161, 163, 165-166, 169

Strobel, Lee 202, 203, 213, 214, 220, 221, 231

Suffering 25, 35, 159-161, 163, 224, 226, 230, 248-249, 259

Supernatural Revelation 152

Tacitus 205, 207, 210

Tilby, Angela 127, 244

Transitional Species 18-19, 94, 95, 96, 98, 99

Trent 186, 222

Truth 12, 20-21, 38, 86, 132-143, 145-151, 153, 155-156, 159-160, 165, 170, 180, 183, 191, 193, 203, 206, 211, 218, 237, 239-240, 251, 262, 268

    Moral Truth 135-136, 143

    Objective Truth 132-133, 136, 143, 165

    Subjective Truth 132, 137-138, 143, 152, 233

Universe 5-13, 27-28, 31-35, 38, 49, 52-58, 70, 76-77, 84, 87, 101-106, 108, 112-115, 135, 149, 152, 155, 166, 168, 172, 175, 179, 191, 237-240, 243, 252, 256, 259-260, 262, 265-267

Vatican I 149

Vatican II 147, 152, 154, 186, 187

Watchmaker Model 30, 178, 179

Yamauchi, Edwin 203, 205, 215

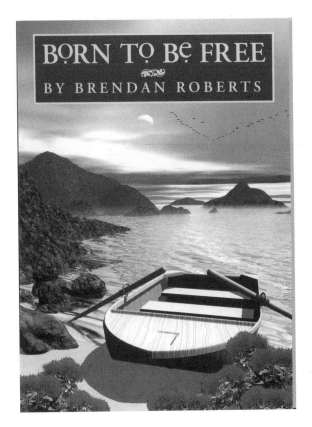

ORDER COPIES OF *SET FREE!* AND *BORN TO BE FREE* OR *GOD: FACT OR FICTION* TODAY

On-line orders via the Internet: www.kiwig.com or www.godfact.com
email: orders@kiwig.com orders@godfact.com (for additional copies
of *God: Fact or Fiction?*)

Postal orders: Kiwi Graphix, c/- 9 Elm Place, Tikipunga, Whangarei,
New Zealand

RRP US $15   NZ $25   for Set Free! or Born to be Free
RRP US $30   NZ $35   for God: Fact or Fiction

Contact the above for 10% discount off all books by Brendan Roberts,
and option for autographed copies if requested. Then I will let you know
how much p & p will cost in addition to the RRP.